D1452424

940.531   Out of the inferno : Poles remember the
O   Holocaust / Richard C. Lukas, editor. --
          Lexington, Ky. : University Press of
          Kentucky, c1989.

          201 p. : ill.

          ISBN 0-8131-1692-9: $23.00

7980

          1. World War, 1939-1945--Poland.   2. World
       War, 1939-1945--Personal narratives, Polish.
       3. Holocaust, Jewish (1939-1945)--Poland.   4.
       Jews--Poland--History.   5. Poland--Ethnic
       relations.   I. Lukas, Richard C., 1937-

19

                                           89-5646
                                           MARC

19

Out of the Inferno

Out of the
Inferno

Poles Remember
THE HOLOCAUST

RICHARD C. LUKAS, Editor

THE UNIVERSITY PRESS OF KENTUCKY

Copyright © 1989 by The University Press of Kentucky

Scholarly publisher for the Commonwealth,
serving Bellarmine College, Berea College, Centre
College of Kentucky, Eastern Kentucky University,
The Filson Club, Georgetown College, Kentucky
Historical Society, Kentucky State University,
Morehead State University, Murray State University,
Northern Kentucky University, Transylvania University,
University of Kentucky, University of Louisville,
and Western Kentucky University.

Editorial and Sales Offices: Lexington, Kentucky 40506-0336

Library of Congress Cataloging-in-Publication Data

Out of the inferno : Poles remember the Holocaust / Richard C. Lukas,
    editor.

    p. cm.
Bibliography: p.
Includes index.
ISBN 0-8131-1692-9 :
    1. World War, 1939-1945—Poland.   2. World War, 1939-1945—
Personal narratives, Polish.   3. Holocaust, Jewish (1939-1945)
—Poland.   4. Jews—Poland—History.   5. Poland—Ethnic relations.
I. Lukas, Richard C., 1937- .
D802.P6088   1989
940.53'15'039240438—dc19   89-5646

This book is printed on acid-free paper meeting
the requirements of the American National Standard
for Permanence of Paper for Printed Library Materials. ∞

Unrespited, unpitied, unreprieved

—Milton, *Paradise Lost*

CONTENTS

ACKNOWLEDGMENTS

I owe a debt of gratitude to many individuals for their assistance in helping me complete this book. I am most grateful to the men and women who graciously agreed to relate to me their wartime experiences in the form of depositions or interviews.

My thanks go also to Dr. Wojciech Kostecki, Ms. Elizabeth Barbarska, Ms. Jadwiga Dolżycki, Dr. William Schrader, Dr. T.W. Gruchacz, and K.T. Czelny.

Special acknowledgment must be made to the Kościuszko Foundation, which provided generous funding to collect, edit, and, in many cases, translate the depositions in this book. I also owe a debt to John J. Gmerek and the New York Metropolitan Chapter of the Kościuszko Foundation for their encouragement and support.

Without the encouragement of my wife, Marita, and my daughters, Jennifer and Renée, this project would not have become a reality.

INTRODUCTION

Fifty years after the outbreak of World War II, it is ironic that, among works published in the English language, there is no major collection of personal accounts by Poles of the savage occupation by the Germans under Hitler.

This book fills that void in the literature.

The Poles here who wrote their recollections of those years, or who spoke with me in interviews, live today in countries ranging from Poland and Great Britain to Canada and the United States. Of diverse socioeconomic backgrounds, they lived during the war in various parts of occupied Poland. Some of the men and women who recounted their experiences did so with great difficulty, as for them it was not merely a matter of remembering but of reliving the torments of the war years. One Polish woman was so pained by her memories that she recounted her family's aid to Jews in almost cryptic form. Though hers is an extremely brief account, it has a place in this anthology; it tells us far more than would seem could be conveyed by a few paragraphs on the printed page.

These vignettes of what life was like for the Pole in occupied Poland touch on a subject about which the world knows very little—and that little badly flawed by a kind of selective history, practiced by many historians and popular accounts of the Holocaust. One of the subjects about which there is much misunderstanding, confused even more by the film *Shoah*, is Polish-Jewish wartime relations. The following accounts will give the reader the chance to get acquainted with a number of Poles who risked their lives to shelter and save Jews.

With the exception of two accounts, these reminiscences are derived from interviews and written depositions that have never before been published. They are told simply and straightforwardly, sometimes eloquently. It is a privilege to have worked with these remarkable men and women, who, through the windows of their personal experiences, allow us to see what it was like to suffer the horrors of German-occupied Poland. Most of these Poles are elderly, many are ill as this manuscript goes to press, and some are no longer living.

But their memories prove to be sharp. I sensed in them a genuine respect for historical truth; when a specific detail escaped them, they admitted it and did not try to dissimulate. Most of them revealed a keen urgency to tell the world what it was like for the Poles to be among Hitler's major victims.

As the late Reverend Jan Januszewski, told me in an interview: "The world rightly knows about what happened to our Jewish brothers and sisters, but it knows so little about us. We should not be forgotten."[1] This saintly man constantly relived the nightmare of the Nazi years. On walks from the rectory to the church where he served as pastor in Florida before his death, Januszewski would glance from side to side almost as if anticipating the next blow from a concentration camp guard. A victim of Dachau, he never left a crumb of bread or a morsel of food on his plate.

As one would expect from a varied group of memoirs, these accounts vary in historical and literary merit, but together they create a vivid picture—a kind of microview—of a people under German occupation. The diverse memoirs all give a sense of immediacy to the conditions the Poles faced during that terrible time. Presenting the accounts in alphabetic rather than thematic order dramatically reveals the diversity of experiences that characterized the life of Poles during the war. These recollections make it clear that there is no room for glib generalizations about how Poles felt, thought, and acted during the German occupation of their country.

Since these are historical documents that have obvious value to the study of World War II, I have limited my editing to the requirements of space and to punctuation and the like. In many instances, the testimonies were submitted to me in the Polish language, and the translations are mine.

Hitler hated Poles only slightly less than Jews. When the Germans invaded Poland, the initial focus of Hitler's wrath was the Poles, not the Jews. After the Polish military defeat, Hitler ordered that Poland's Jews be confined to ghettos while his henchmen inaugurated a program of systematic terror, enslavement, and extermination of Polish Christians. The Nazi annihilation of the Poles in fact began when the Wehrmacht crossed the Polish frontier in September 1939. German soldiers had been directed by the Führer himself to kill "without pity or mercy all men, women, and children of Polish descent or language. Only in this way can we obtain the living space we need."[2]

The German theory of empire in Poland dehumanized the Poles. From the Nazi point of view, Poles were *untermenschen* (subhumans) who lived in an area coveted by the superior German race. Poland was not simply to be defeated and occupied, as the nations in Western Europe later were. "The aim is not the arrival at a certain line," declared Hitler, "but the annihilation of living forces."[3] The man responsible for implementing Hitler's hatred of the Poles, Heinrich Himmler, said outright that "all Poles will disappear from the world. . . . It is essential that the great German people should consider it as its major task to destroy all Poles."[4]

Even after Hitler and his executioners singled out the Jews as the primary victims of the Holocaust, the German policy of enslavement and extermination of other Poles continued. It focused largely but not exclusively on eliminating anyone with the least political and cultural prominence. The German definition of "elite" was so broad that it included not only teachers, physicians, priests, officers, landowners, government officials, and writers, but also anyone who had attended secondary school. The victims were shot in street executions or died in prisons and concentration camps like Pawiak and Auschwitz. The first victims of the gas chambers of Auschwitz, in fact, were Poles and Russian prisoners of war.

The Nazi determination to obliterate the Polish intelligentsia wiped out forty-five percent of Poland's physicians and dentists during the war, forty percent of the professors, fifty-seven percent of the attorneys, thirty percent of the technicians, almost twenty percent of the clergy, and a majority of the leading journalists.

The Germans realized that if their policy of enslaving the Polish nation was to be successful, they had to destroy the organization and leadership of the Roman Catholic Church, an institution that historically had fostered the spirit of Polish nationalism and acted as a unifying force during times of political and social turmoil. The German policy of annexing western Poland to the Third Reich and turning the remainder into a penal colony—the General Government—succeeded in destroying the structure of the Polish church. The clergy in the annexed lands suffered especially cruel treatment at the hands of the Germans; deportations to concentration camps and executions were commonplace. In 1941, five hundred priests from the Wartheland, part of the area annexed to the Third Reich, were in concentration camps. The losses among the clergy of the annexed lands were higher than among those in the General Government. In Wrocław, 49.2 percent of the Polish clergy died; in Chełmno, the death rate ran to 47.8 percent. The Nazis seemed to be particularly sadistic in tormenting the Polish clergy in the prisons and concentration camps where they were confined. The Germans sent a large number of Catholic priests to Dachau, where they suffered huge losses from hard labor and malnutrition.

In the process of destroying Poland's intelligentsia, the Nazis embarked on the process of de-Polonizing the Polish lands they had annexed. Hundreds of thousands of Poles and Jews were deported to the General Government, which Berlin intended to serve as a German colony. The victims of the deportations were packed into cattle cars without water, food or sanitary facilities, were inadequately clothed in winter, and were dumped like commodities at the destination. Many died. Even in the General Government, especially the area around Zamość near Lublin, the Germans evicted 110,000 Poles from their homes to accommodate German settlers. There were massive deportations of Poles to Germany too, where they furnished slave labor for factories and farms. Most were treated abominably, and many never saw their homes again.

Germanization efforts extended to blue-eyed, blond Polish children, thousands of whom were sent to Germany. Children selected for Germanization ended up in schools or institutions run by the Lebensborn or the SS. The Polish youngsters were forbidden to speak Polish or to see their parents if they were still living. Everything was done to destroy their Polish identity, including changing their names.

The ruthless German policy of destroying Polish society extended to the economy. Under a plethora of bureaucratic agencies, the Germans confiscated and administered Polish property they considered essential for the war effort. The consequence was to turn the Polish people into paupers. Without the black market for food, they would have starved to death.

After the Jews, the Poles had one of the lowest food rations of any people in German-occupied Europe. Despite food shortages in Poland, Governor General Hans Frank increased the shipments of grain from the General Government to Germany sixfold in 1942. The new levies, he declared, "will be fulfilled exclusively *at the expense of the foreign* [Polish] population. It must be done cold-bloodedly and without pity [italics added]."[5]

Diseases among malnourished and overworked Poles were rampant. One German medical official told Frank that "the number of diseased Poles amounted today already to 40 percent."[6]

The Germans regularly maintained fifty thousand to eighty thousand SS and police forces in Poland, infamous for the severity of their subjugation. Reprisals against Poles for real and imagined offenses were commonplace and bore no correspondence to the gravity of the alleged crimes. As Frank himself stated, "My relationship with the

Poles is like the relationship between ant and plant louse. In cases where in spite of all these measures the performance does not increase, or where the slightest act gives me occasion to step in, I would not even hesitate to take the most draconic action."[7]

The German principle of collective responsibility was drastic. For every German killed by a Pole, at least a hundred Poles were shot in retribution and in some cases as many as two hundred to four hundred. In Lublin, the Germans wiped out the entire village of Józefów for the death of one German family. In all, the Germans destroyed some three hundred Polish villages in reprisals and so-called pacification.

Poles, along with others, served as guinea pigs for the medical experiments of infamous German physicians. Polish children who ended up in a German camp were often murdered. Poles who escaped individual or mass executions were starved or worked to death by the Germans. In concentration camps, they died either at hard labor or in gas chambers. During the German occupation, three million Christian Poles perished, out of a total Polish population of some 27 million in 1935.

In response to the German occupation, the Poles organized one of the most effective underground movements in Europe, with both civilian and military sections. The first clandestine military unit, organized by General Michał Tokarzewski-Karaszewicz in September 1939, was Service for Poland's Victory (*Służba Zwycięstwu Polski*), soon eclipsed by the Union for Armed Struggle (*Związek Walki Zbrojnej*). The ZWZ, as it was commonly known, was most closely associated with the brilliant, charismatic General Stefan Grot-Rowecki. The final stage in the evolution of the military component of the underground came in February 1942, when the ZWZ became the Home Army (*Armia Krajowa*), the name it retained until the end of the war.

The Home Army, or AK as it was known, was a large umbrella organization of many military groups, representing all shades of political opinion except the extreme left and right, both of which had their own political and military units. The right-wing National Armed Forces (*Narodowe Siły Zbrojne*) fought mainly the Germans but sometimes attacked democratic Poles, Jews, and Communists. Often their attacks against Jews were erroneously blamed by their victims on the AK. On the other hand, there were cases of assistance to Jews by members of the National Armed Forces.

The Communists, regarded by most Poles as traitors, had their own small resistance army, the People's Guard (*Gwardia Ludowa*, or GL), which in 1944 became known as the People's Army (*Armia Ludowa*, or AL). That group, eager to impress the Polish people as being more militant than the AK, conducted partisan operations in eastern Poland. Within the Polish Communist ranks were a large number of Jews. The Polish Communists, who worked closely with the Kremlin, established the Polish Committee of National Liberation to challenge the authority of the legal Polish government-in-exile (located first in France, later in England). For some Poles who saw Jews collaborating with Poland's "other enemy"—the Soviet Union—long-standing Polish charges of Judeo-Communism were confirmed.

The Home Army and its predecessor were clearly the largest and most effective of the resistance groups that operated in Poland during the German occupation. Although the primary goal of the ZWZ/AK was not to conduct sabotage and diversionary operations but rather to prepare the country for an uprising against the Germans when they were at the point of military collapse, the Poles conducted an array of operations against the enemy. The ZWZ/AK was impressive in both size and degree of organization, but it was no match for the German occupiers, and its sabotage and diversionary actions usually invited savage German reprisals. The ZWZ/AK was thus in no position to squander its limited strength in rescue operations on behalf of Poles and Jews incarcerated in prisons and concentration camps. That was a role for the Allies. More than once the Polish government and Jewish groups had requested the British and the Americans to bomb Auschwitz, but the Allied powers believed that the way to defeat Nazi genocide was to hasten an end to the war.

When the Jews of Warsaw decided to challenge the Germans by launching an uprising in the ghetto in April 1943, the Home Army joined the Communists in conducting more than two dozen combat, rescue, and supply operations on behalf of the Jews, who fully recognized that their effort was suicidal and doomed to failure. However, the Home Army, husbanding its strength for a confrontation with the Germans when there was a chance of winning, was unwilling to take on the brave but obviously futile operation. When the Home Army finally launched its own uprising against the Germans in August 1944, in somewhat better circumstances than those surrounding the Jewish effort more than a year earlier, the Poles were defeated and the heart of the Polish underground destroyed.

But resistance in Poland was not confined to the organized activities of the Home Army and its predecessor. Virtually all Poles resisted their German oppressors, at least passively. Resistance took many forms. Boy Scouts painted over German slogans with patriotic Polish challenges. Men and women in factories brought machinery to a halt by cutting conveyor belts or putting sand in lubrication systems. Resistance involved thousands of people who worked at producing and distributing the underground press, one of the largest in Europe, and the millions who read the clandestine newspapers and pamphlets. The thousands of high school and university students who attended underground classes were part of the resistance, along with those who participated in and listened to forbidden plays, dramatic readings, and concerts. Thousands of Polish peasants, when commanded by the Germans to make confiscatory grain deliveries, resisted by operating on the basis of the slogan "As little, as late, and as bad as possible."[8]

The political arm of the Polish underground was the Government Delegacy (*Delegatura Rządu*), headed by the one who was responsible to the Polish government-in-exile in London. General Władysław Sikorski headed the government abroad until his death in a suspicious aircraft accident off the coast of Gibraltar in July 1943, when Stanisław Mikołajczyk succeeded him. Poland's major political parties—Peasant, Socialist, National Democrat, and Labor—were represented in underground political organizations that experienced considerable evolution. The Chief Political Committee (*Główny Komitet Polityczny*) transformed itself first into the National Political Representation (*Krajowa Reprezentacja Polityczna*), and in 1944 into the Council of National Unity (*Rada Jedności Narodowej*).

Although the Poles were deeply committed to defeating the Germans, their political divisions drained some energy from the immediate task of resisting the enemy. It is ironic that, during the time of the German occupation, the Poles enjoyed a high degree of freedom and individualism in the political life of their underground—a kind of state within a state—which proved that the Nazis had failed to subdue the Polish nation.

One of the most controversial aspects of the history of wartime Poland is Polish-Jewish relations. Scholars, popular writers and filmmakers usually stereotype the Poles as anti-Semites who, at a minimum, were indifferent to the Germans' treatment of the Jews and at worst collaborated with the Nazis in their systematic extermination. The Poles are the victims of an artificially constructed idea of collective responsibility.

As the following personal accounts make quite clear, the Poles themselves were direct targets of the Germans. They share in the tragedy that befell the nine or ten million Christian victims of Nazi terror and genocide. In no way does their story detract from the particularity of the Jewish tragedy; Jews were Hitler's primary victims.

As a consequence of persecutions elsewhere in Europe in late medieval times, Jews flocked to Poland, where the government's tolerant policy toward minorities allowed them to enjoy an autonomy unique in Europe. As a leading rabbi once observed: "As long as Poland was powerful, Polish Jewry enjoyed an inner autonomy and freedom equalled by no other contemporary Jewry. Furthermore, it cannot be too often repeated that to Poland belongs the priority among European peoples in religious and cultural toleration.[9]

Unlike Jews in Western Europe, Jews in Poland did not assimilate into Polish society. Despite some assimilation trends prior to World War II, most Jews were still Jewish in language and in religion. According to the census of 1931, almost 80 percent of the Jews declared Yiddish to be their mother tongue, and a similar percentage considered themselves to be Jewish by nationality. Their lack of fluency in the Polish language, along with their Semitic features, made them easy targets for the Germans who would herd them into ghettos and exterminate them.

Jews maintained their own lifestyle and values and preferred to have only limited contact with the Poles, usually confined to business dealings. Little wonder, then, that Poles and Jews did not really know each other very well, even though they had lived side by side for centuries. To be sure, some Poles and Jews cultivated cordial and even close relationships, especially true of the minority of Jews who chose to assimilate. On the other hand, individuals of both groups expressed suspicion, even contempt, toward one another. On the Polish side, anti-Semites endorsed official discriminatory practices against Jews, and the more extreme even participated in physical attacks on Jews. In the period 1935-37, 118 Jews lost their lives in such attacks, which were, however, put down by the police.

In the Polish countryside, peasants often regarded Jews suspiciously, if ambivalently, but not necessarily with hatred or hostility. This attitude, erroneously dubbed anti-Semitic by some was essentially no different from the peasants' attitude toward other strangers— Germans, Russians, Ukrainians, or even Polish peasants from another village.

To be sure, there were anti-Semitic Poles, but many of them had an abstract dislike of Jews. Once they got to know Jews, these Poles felt no personal animosity, and as demonstrated over and over again during the war years, even developed affection for those who were familiar to them. Perhaps the clearest evidence of the Polish response to the plight of the Jews during the war is the large number of anti-Semites who, grasping that they were facing a common enemy, turned to the Jews with support.

Jews exhibited the same range of attitudes towards Poles. Samuel Oliver, a Jewish scholar who was raised in Poland, stated: "The Jews regarded the Poles with contempt and caution, but we had still been on good terms."[10] Or, as Lucien Steinberg said: "The non-Jews were not wholly responsible for [the] inevitable barrier [between them], even though they might greet any friendly advance with reserve. The Jews themselves distrusted those of their own kind who tried to strike up a relationship with 'the others,' and there was always that underlying fear of losing substance."[11]

The more that is said about Polish anti-Semitism, the less understanding we have about the subject. Conversely, we hear or read virtually nothing about Jewish antipathies toward the Poles, a topic that needs to be explored to bring much-needed balance into the discussion of Polish-Jewish relations.

Anti-Semitism existed in both prewar and wartime Poland. In prewar Poland, however, Jews had to contend more with economic and bureaucratic discrimination than with physical assaults. Reports of widespread pogroms in Poland during the period 1919-1939 have been largely discredited. There were no Nuremberg-type laws in Poland because the philo-Semitic currents proved stronger than the anti-Semitic. What happened to the Jews in interwar Poland, in other words, had nothing to do with their annihilation by the Germans in World War II.

A connection between Polish anti-Semitism and the building of extermination camps on Polish soil by the Germans has often been cited, without offering any evidence to substantiate it. There are clear reasons, however, why the camps were located in Poland. First of all, more Jews lived in Poland than anywhere else in Europe. Obviously, establishing the camps where most of the Germans victims lived would reduce logistical and financial costs. The Germans furthermore hoped to keep the murder of the Jews a secret, especially from Western public opinion. It was easier to do this in Poland, which was isolated from the West. When Polish and Jewish reports reached the West about the "final solution", neither Western governments nor the public would believe what they heard. The Germans even tried to keep their grisly work a secret from the Poles themselves. The deportation of the Jews to the death camps took place on Polish soil, however, so the Poles soon found out. Even before the Jews arrived in Auschwitz, the Poles had discovered the fate of Polish and Soviet prisoners of war—the first victims there. Polish intelligence was swift to piece together what the deportations from Jewish ghettos meant and conveyed this information promptly to the West.

The commander of the Home Army, General Stefan Grot-Rowecki, admitted to the Polish government-in-exile on September 25, 1941, that the Poles were "anti-Semitically inclined,"[12] thus suggesting as fixed an attitude that could—and in fact did—change according to circumstances. One of the factors that had a negative impact on Polish public opinion prior to the deportation of the Jews to the death camps was the collaboration of many Jews with the Soviets when they occupied eastern Poland.[13]

Nevertheless, there is evidence in archival sources, buttressed by some of the accounts in this anthology, which suggests that when the full surge of German criminality against the Jews became clear by 1942, compassion became the prevailing Polish attitude toward the Jews. Grot-Rowecki's message, cited above, specifically referred to the fact that German persecution of the Jews, of which most Poles disapproved, created a backlash of Polish sympathy for the Jews.

Polish attitudes toward the Jews during the German occupation were complex, not lending themselves to generalizations. As I wrote in *The Forgotten Holocaust:*

> It is impossible to generalize about Polish attitudes toward the Jews during the German occupation, because there was no uniformity. Despite German persecution of the Polish people, a small minority of Poles openly approved of German policies toward the Jews, and some actively aided the Nazis in their grim mission. But even the anti-Semitic National Democrats in Poland altered some of their traditional views toward the Jews as the bizarre logic of German racial policy became apparent in the extermination campaign; and some National Democrats personally aided Jews. Other Poles showed no outward pleasure at the removal of Jews from Polish offices, professions, and businesses but were not opposed to the economic expropriation involved. These people had anti-Semitic views which were economic, not racial, in character; if we can hazard any generalization at all, it is that to the extent there was anti-Semitism among some Poles, it reflected this economic anti-Semitic attitude. Still others quietly felt compassion for the Jewish people; they might be described, in Philip Friedman's words, as "passive humani-

tarians." These people either feared becoming actively involved in aiding Jews because of the risk of the death penalty the Germans automatically imposed on Poles who helped Jews—Poland was the only occupied country where this was done—or were so pauperized by the war they simply could not afford to aid anyone without jeopardizing the survival of their own families. Then there was a very active group of Poles who were openly sympathetic toward the Jews, and many of these risked their lives to help Jews.[14]

One of the brightest chapters in the history of World War II, as many of the Poles in this anthology testify, was the efforts of the Polish people on behalf of the Jews. In view of the enormous terror that the Poles themselves endured, the wonder is not how few but how many Jews were saved by the heroes and heroines of Poland, the only German-occupied land where Christians *automatically* risked death for aiding Jews. So spontaneous and so extensive were the Polish efforts to aid the Jews that the Germans imposed the automatic death sentence. As is well known, of the Christians who have been cited for their uncommon courage in helping Jews during the war, approximately 25 to 30 percent were Poles.

The obstacles to aiding Jews in Poland were enormous. Not only the grave risk of death but the poverty in which Poles themselves lived, the fear of blackmailers and collaborators, even the Jews themselves—often helpless and confused, confined to ghettos surrounded by walls or wire—presented almost insurmountable problems. It was much easier for a Pole to be a part of the underground resistance than to help a Jew. Even Poles who had legal passes to enter a ghetto were often shot by the Germans.

More than one Polish Samaritan has commented that the unresisting attitude of the Jews themselves was a problem. "The greatest difficulty was the passivity of the Jews themselves," declared Władysława Chomsowa, a remarkable woman who played an active role in saving Jews in the Lwów area.[15] Her succinct but cogent observation recalls Bruno Bettelheim's controversial comment: "The Jews of Europe could have marched as free men against the SS, rather than to first grovel, then wait to be rounded up for their own extermination, and finally walk themselves to the gas chambers."[16] To be sure, there were some heroic efforts of Jewish resistance, but these incidents were rare.

Jewish leaders at the time of the German occupation of Poland had a more accurate understanding of Polish efforts on behalf of the Jews than many writers seem to have today. Leaders of the Jewish

Bund, which had close ties with Polish socialists, commented on how a majority of Poles—workers and peasants—resisted German anti-Semitic propaganda. Szmul Zygielbojm and Ignacy Schwarzbart, both distinguished Jewish members of the Polish National Council in London, commented at the time on how the Poles gave all possible help and sympathy to their kinsmen. Adolf Berman, a prominent Jewish leader who provided an important link between the Jewish and Polish underground, eloquently described Polish aid to the Jews:

> Accounts of the martyrdom of Poland's Jews tend to emphasize their suffering at the hands of blackmailers and informers, the "blue" police and other scum. Less is written, on the other hand, about the thousands of Poles who risked their lives to save the Jews. The flotsam and jetsam on the surface of a turbulent river is more visible than the pure stream running deep underneath, but that stream existed.[17]

The efforts of individual Poles to aid Jews should not obscure the organized efforts of *Żegota (Rada Pomocy Żydom)*, the Council for Aid to Jews, a unique organization in occupied Poland whose raison d'être was to help Jews. Organized in December 1942 and supported mostly by funds from the Polish government, *Żegota* was headquartered in Warsaw. Its products included forged documents, safe houses, medical assistance, and food to Jewish people. It also carried on an active campaign against blackmailers, informers, and the anti-Semitic propaganda that the Germans dumped daily on the Poles in the press and through loudspeakers in town squares.

We will never know the precise number of Poles who worked to help Jews during the German occupation of Poland. Some Poles sheltered Jews on occasion but could not or would not do so on a regular basis for fear of execution; other Poles took on the risk of housing Jews throughout the war. But shelter was only one form of aid. Some Poles who lacked accommodations volunteered to find food and clothing for Jews who were hidden by others. Other Poles served as guides, escorting Jews from one house to another, or securing forged documents for those Jews who could pass for Gentiles. Polish support for Jews took the form of a broad range of activities by Poles from varied political and socioeconomic backgrounds, as some of the memoirs in this anthology reveal. In some cases, the Poles had known the Jews they befriended before the war; in other cases, their Jewish charges were total strangers to them.

What is remarkable about Polish rescues of Jews is the quiet support that often came from many who were aware of a Polish family's aid, yet risked their own lives by keeping the secret. Poles accused of informing on Jews and on their Polish saviors often did so not because of anti-Semitism or the promise of bounty, but out of fear of being killed by the Germans for failing to report the "crime." To be sure, many unscrupulous Poles became informers and blackmailers for other motives. Yet the postwar statistics of the Israeli War Crimes Commission indicate that only seven thousand out of a population of over twenty million ethnic Poles collaborated with the Nazis.[18] Significantly, no major political figure emerged in Poland who was willing to collaborate with the Nazis as was the case in Western Europe.

According to Władysław Bartoszewski, who worked for *Żegota* during the war, "At least several hundred thousand Poles . . . participated in various ways and forms in the rescue action."[19] Recent research suggests that a million Poles were involved, but some estimates go as high as three million. My own research puts the figure much higher than is customarily accepted. The Polish record in helping Jews thus compares very favorably with that of Western Europeans, who were in far less threatening circumstances.

Estimates of the number of Poles who perished at the hands of the Germans for aiding Jews vary from a few thousand to fifty thousand. Most of the Poles who died trying to aid Jews will probably never be identified; like the Jews they died for, they are no more.

The estimates of Jewish survivors in Poland, ranging from 40,000 or 50,000 to 100,000 or 120,000, do not accurately reflect the extent of the Poles' enormous sacrifices on behalf of the Jews because, at various times during the occupation, there were more Jews in hiding than in the end survived. "If the truth were known," said one of my Polish respondents, who was researching the subject at the time of his death, "the number of Jews hiding in Poland—most of them helped in some way by Gentiles—ran into the hundreds of thousands."[20] Another informed estimate of the number of Jews sheltered by Poles at one point during the German occupation places the figure as high as 450,000.[21] In view of the decimation of the Polish capital during the Warsaw Uprising of August-September 1944, it is most probable that a large number of Jews perished along with their Polish protectors.

1. Jan Januszewski, interview with the author, August 1, 1982.
2. Janusz Gumkowski and Kazimierz Leszczyński, *Poland under Nazi Occupation* (Warsaw: Polonia Publishing House, 1961), p. 59.

3. Eugeniusz Duraczyński, *Wojna i Okupacja: Wrzesień 1939—Kwiecień 1943* (Warsaw: Wiedza Powszechna, 1974), p. 17.

4. Karol Pospieszalski, *Polska pod Niemieckim Prawem* (Poznan: Wydawnictwo Instytutu Zachodniego, 1946), p. 189.

5. U.S. Counsel, *Nazi Conspiracy and Aggression* (10 vols.; Washington, D.C.: Government Printing Office, 1946), 2: 637-38. On December 14, 1942, Frank bragged that the General Government had delivered 600,000 tons of grain to the Reich at a time when there were food shortages throughout Poland. See Central Commission for Investigation of German Crimes in Poland, *German Crimes in Poland* (2 vols.; New York: Howard Fertig, 1982), 2: 36.

6. U.S. Counsel, *Nazi Conspiracy and Aggression*, 2: 637.

7. Ibid., p. 643.

8. Stefan Korboński, *Fighting Warsaw: The Story of the Polish Underground State, 1939-1945* (N.p.: Minerva Press, 1968), p. 214.

9. Quoted in statement by Banaczyk at a meeting of the Council for Rescue of the Jews in Poland, May 25, 1941 (C11/7/3c/8), in files of the Board of Deputies of British Jews, London.

10. S. [Samuel] P. Oliner, *Restless Memories: Recollections of the Holocaust Years* (1979), p. 44.

11. Lucien Steinberg, *The Jews against Hitler: Not as a Lamb* (London: Gordon and Cremonesi, 1978), p. 168.

12. General Stefan Grot-Rowecki to Polish government, September 25, 1941, Central Archives, Central Committee of the Polish United Workers Party, Warsaw.

13. Karski Report, February 1940, Stanisław Mikołajczyk Papers, Box 12, Hoover Institution on War, Revolution and Peace, Stanford, Calf.

14. Richard C. Lukas, *The Forgotten Holocaust: The Poles under German Occupation, 1939-1944* (Lexington, Ky: Univ. Press of Kentucky, 1986), pp. 126-27.

15. Stanisław Wroński and Maria Zwolakowa, *Polacy Żydzi, 1939-1945* (Warsaw: Książka i Wiedza, 1971), p. 258.

16. Neal Ascherson, "The Death Doctors," *New York Review of Books*, May 28, 1987.

17. Lukas, *Forgotten Holocaust*, p. 141. Schwarzbart later became a critic of Polish aid to the Jews.

18. Ibid., p. 117.

19. Władysław Bartoszewski, *The Blood Shed Unites Us: Pages from the History of Help to the Jews in Occupied Poland* (Warsaw: Interpress Publishers, 1970), p. 222.

20. Jan Januszewski, interview with the author, August 1, 1982.

21. Władysław Żarski-Zajdler, *Martyrologia Ludności Żydowskiej i Pomóc Społeczeństwa Polskiego* (Warsaw, 1968), p. 16.

Out of the Inferno

JAN ARCISZEWSKI

The day before the outbreak of the Warsaw Uprising of 1944, our company of a hundred men met in a large empty building on Okopowa Street. We spent the night on the concrete floor. The older ones among us felt the effects of this night in our bones. We had so few weapons that it was laughable—a few pistols and one automatic. I went into action, like the majority of us, for that matter, armed with a wooden stick. About 5:00 p.m., we moved off in the direction of Stawki Street, where the Germans kept their supplies in a school building: uniforms, food, and such. Since we were not fully armed, my unit went into action in the second line.

After weak German resistance, we occupied the building. It was already dark, and we made ourselves comfortable for the night. Unfortunately, this did not last long. During the night the Germans counterattacked with the support of a "cow," a heavy mortar fired from an armored train. We retreated to the eastern side of Wola through the ruins of the ghetto.

Our next position was on Wolska Street, where few men armed with automatic weapons were sent up to the first floor [the second story]. However, one or two shells from a German tank quickly destroyed this position. An attempt to fire at an approaching tank on Młynarska Street ended in similar destruction [of our men on the higher floor]. If I had not gone down to the ground floor in search of a drink of water, there would be no one to write this account.

Our unit was then transferred to Old Town, where it was really hot. The Germans attacked several times a day, and our positions were bombed from the air regularly. We were now based on the large premises of Spiess and Son, which manufactured pharmaceutical products. One Sunday several bombs dropped on the gateway of the building while Mass was being celebrated in one of the side wings. There were many civilian casualties. One of those killed was my friend Danilewicz, who was sitting right next to me on a bench in the stairwell. Once again I was lucky. I got away with just a small wound in my right eyelid.

After a month of heavy fighting, it was decided to leave Old Town and get through to the City Center by way of the sewers. At the outset, there was great panic when someone at the front of the line of evacuees shouted "Gas!" All of us assumed that the Germans were gassing the sewers. But the smell in the sewers was actually coming from the fumes of chemicals and medicines from Spiess that we had thrown down the drains a short time earlier because they were highly flammable and likely to explode.

After about ten hours, we climbed out of the sewers in the City Center near the Prudential Building. After a bath—what bliss!—our unit was allowed to rest in comparative safety. We then took up positions on Bracka Street, on the first floor above the confectioners called Szwajcarska. Since I was only slightly wounded, I distributed barley from the brewers Haberbusch and Shieke, and carried water from the cellars beneath the "Swiatowid" cinema on Marszałkowska. In the end the tragic moment of the capitulation. Then I was deported to the camps of Ożarów, Sandbostel, and Murnau, all well known to prisoners of war.

Son of a former Polish premier, Arciszewski studied law at Warsaw University before the war. During the German occupation, he worked at the Warsaw Power Station. Today he lives in London.

IRENA BARBARSKA

I became involved in the resistance in 1941, when it was still known as the Union for Armed Struggle, while I was attending underground classes. I knew that many of my friends were members of the organization even before I joined, because they were not very careful about what they said.

About six months before the Warsaw Uprising, I was given ammunition and weapons to deliver to different addresses. I did this several times. On one of these occasions, I was on a streetcar carrying an ammunition case. As we approached Hala Mirowska near Grzybowski Square, I saw that the Germans were rounding up people. I could see soldiers and the waiting trucks. As the steetcar slowed down, I made my way to the rear and slipped out of the back exit. Fortunately, there were many people around so I quickly got away.

I still remember the awful sensation as I saw the German troops. I knew that if I was caught, I had no hope of bluffing my way out of carrying ammunition.

During the Warsaw Uprising, I was assigned to the Field Dressing Station at No. 37 Ujazdowski Avenue. Since we were on the premises of Cukiernia Gajewski, which was a pastry shop, we had access to a kitchen. The stores of the Red Cross were on the same premises, so at first we had freshly baked bread. We were mobilized the day before the uprising. That night we were invaded by bedbugs, which fortunately disappeared later. We were in a sort of no-man's-land between the German and Polish positions, so at first we were not involved, although we heard shooting. We just waited in an inside room without windows. I slept on a stretcher.

We had no contact with anyone. I was therefore delegated to go to our headquarters on Krucza Street to find out what was going on. Another woman volunteered to go with me, Wanda Przeworska, who was Jewish and the wife of a captain who served with the First Division in the West. She was a highly educated, very intelligent woman, and I was full of admiration for her. I felt I had no choice but to go, since she had volunteered. At one point during the first few days, there was a truce enabling the civilian population to get home, and that was when the two of us set out. We left through the main gate. Just as the gate was closed behind us, the Germans fired at it. We went past No. 39 Ujazdowski Avenue and around the corner into a small street leading to Krucza. I was petrified. I prayed that I would not be shot in the back. When we got to our headquarters, we were told just to go back to our station and wait . . . which we did.

When the Home Army broke through to Ujazdowski Avenue, the wounded started coming in to our field dressing station. One day they brought in four or five typical middle-aged, plump Warsaw townswomen, all civilians, who had been used by the Germans to shield their tanks. The Germans had forced the women to get on the Tiger tanks to stop the Poles from shooting. The legs of these women were like sieves, full of holes. They were soon moved to another hospital because we had no facilities to perform operations. What amazed me was the composure and cheerfulness of these women, who were so badly wounded.

When the uprising was over, the Germans told us to take the badly wounded to the corner of Marszałkowska and Jerozolimskie avenues. We carried the stretchers there. When we came back, we saw trucks standing outside the dressing stations. It turned out that one of our doctors had bribed some Germans to provide the trucks to take us to the hospital train. It had been converted from a goods train by the Germans for their own troops, and each car had a German medical orderly. Much to our surprise, we were given rations: vodka, chocolate, jam, and other luxuries we had not seen for a long time. The doors of the cars were then unlocked. Later we found out that there had been a Red Cross commission at the train, from Frankfurt on the Oder. After the Red Cross officials had seen the reception we received, the Germans locked the doors.

Born in Toruń, Poland, Barbarska was sixteen years old when the war broke out. She and her mother moved from the Soviet-occupied part of Poland to the General Government, where she became active in the Polish underground. After the war, she emigrated to England, where she lives today.

JAMES BOCHAN

I was about fifteen or sixteen years of age at the time of the Molotov-Ribbentrop Pact, which divided Poland between the Germans and the Soviets. At that time, I lived in eastern Poland in the town of Stryj, east of Lwów, which had been a great city of Polish culture for centuries. When the Soviets entered our area, they came in like a vast swarm of ants. They were barbarians. They robbed us. They raped the women and then cast them aside like rags. Many of the women were killed.

My father had died four years earlier. As the only man in the house, I had to assume responsibility for my mother and sister. There were shortages of everything, and like other Polish citizens I had to deal on the black market.

I remember one time when my uncle, my cousin, and I had slaughtered a pig. Half of the pig I carried slung over my shoulder. We were walking across town to trade the pig for soap, which was almost impossible to find at the time. When my cousin and uncle spotted some Soviet soldiers in the distance, they ran away without saying anything to me. There I stood by myself. When I saw the soldiers, I started to yell, "Uncle! Uncle!" The soldiers, who saw no one else around me, assumed that I was mentally deranged. If they had chosen to investigate the matter, there is no question that they would have imprisoned or even shot me for dealing on the black market.

When I was eighteen or nineteen, the Germans, who were then in occupation of the area, summoned me and several other young men of the village for forced labor to build fortifications against the advancing Soviet armies. I had been involved earlier in several round-ups by Germans who forced me to work. This time, I decided that I was through with working for the Germans, so when the summons came, I did not report for duty. I hid myself in the loft of a barn. Unfortunately, a German sergeant who remembered me from previous roundups found me in the loft. He yanked me by the ear and held it tightly as he dragged me to the commandant's headquarters. The pain was so excruciating that it felt as though he would rip off my ear.

When we got to the commandant's office, I fully expected to receive the death sentence. After all, thousands of Poles who refused to work for the Germans had been shot. But by a stroke of luck, the commandant was so preoccupied with other matters that he simply told the sergeant to put me in a column of men forming outside his office, on the way to work.

After a week of building fortifications for the Germans, they ordered me and the other young Poles to a railway station, where we boarded a train for France. Our job was to build antiaircraft fortifications in France. By that time we had heard of the allied invasion of Normandy. We realized that the war was finally coming to an end.

One morning our work battalion arrived at a construction area only to find that the German officers and enlisted men had run away in the face of the advancing Allies. When the Americans and British discovered us, needless to say we were all elated. It was the happiest day of my life to be liberated by the Allies.

The British sent me and other Poles to Great Britain. I underwent military training in Scotland. After that, we served with the Seventh Royal Engineers in France against the Germans. At long last, I was able to make a positive contribution in the war against the Germans. I was fortunate to have survived both the Soviet and the German occupations of Poland. There were so many Poles who perished at the hands of both these invaders.

Born in eastern Poland, Bochan endured many harrowing experiences at the hands of the Germans and Soviets prior to his service with the British Army in France. After the war, he entered the hotel and restaurant busines, and he now owns the Fisherman's Haunt in Winkton, England.

ANTONI BOHUN-DĄBROWSKI

As World War II drew to a close, I commanded the Świętokrzyska Brigade, which had made its way between the German and Soviet lines in Czechoslovakia. After months of hardship, my unit stopped in the small village of Vshekary, hoping to join the forces of General George Patton.

When we arrived in Vshekary, members of the Czech underground informed me and my adjutant that the Germans had constructed a concentration camp for women a few miles away. It housed a thousand prisoners. Among the inmates were 280 Jews, housed in heavily guarded barracks surrounded by high-voltage wire. There was no way for them to escape.

I decided that something had to be done to liberate the camp. On May 4, 1945, members of the brigade scouted German positions to determine the kind of opposition we could expect. The next day, I ordered the entire brigade on full alert, beginning at 6:00 a.m. We began our assault against the Germans at 11:30 a.m. It was not an easy matter to liberate the camp since my unit encountered heavy German machine-gun fire. But thanks to the element of surprise, many of the SS-men were taken off guard and were eating lunch at the time of our attack.

After my unit overran the bunkers and a munitions factory that was part of the camp, the Germans surrended. We took two hundred SS-men and fifteen women prison guards into captivity.

Needless to say, the inmates cried with joy that they were now free. The courtyard of the camp was filled with emaciated bodies, dressed in striped prison clothes. But the joy was tempered when my adjutant informed me that two nearby barracks housing the 280 Jewish prisoners, were cordoned off by two rows of high-voltage wire. I ordered the German commandant to turn off the voltage. When I asked him why these Jews were isolated from the other prisoners, he replied that he had orders from Hitler to set fire to their barracks before the Americans could liberate Holiszów. When I pursued the matter further and inquired whether he intended to execute Hitler's brutal orders, the German demurred, saying he was an officer of the Wehrmacht and did not intend to carry out the orders.

When the doors to the Jewish barracks were opened by members of my brigade, the scene that greeted us was one of absolute horror. The Jewish women were skeletons, barely able to stand. From the buildings themselves, the stench of human waste and decomposing bodies was indescribable. One Jewish woman hugged me and handed me a bundle, wrapped in newspaper. She said, "I was fortunate to hide a few dollars from the Nazis. Please take them for saving my life." Of course, I did not take the money. I told the woman that our reward was the satisfaction of knowing that so many people had been saved from virtually certain death at the hands of the Germans.

The number of freed inmates from Holiszów was approximately a thousand women of various origins, including Jews, Poles, French, Czechs, Romanians, and Yugoslavs.

Born in Vilna, Colonel Bohun-Dąbrowski commanded the Świętokrzyska Brigade, composed of former members of the National Armed Forces, some of whom had an anti-Semitic reputation. Today Bohun-Dąbrowski lives in retirement in California.

ZBIGNIEW BOKIEWICZ

During the summer of 1939, I was away from Warsaw. Since I was a Boy Scout, I was mobilized into the *Pomocnicza Służba Wojskowa* (Auxiliary Military Service) on my return to the capital. As a telephonist for the antiaircraft troop located on Barska Street, I took a call from headquarters announcing that thirty Polish bombers had attacked Berlin and returned without any losses. The news was read out to the assembled company. Since there were constant German air raids on Warsaw, this was obviously a Polish propaganda exercise.

As the Germans approached Warsaw, Colonel Umiastowski ordered that all young people were to leave the city to continue the fight against the Germans elsewhere. Since I was only sixteen years old, my mother refused to let me go on my own, and we set out together. We got as far as a village near Garwolin. While we were there, the Germans came and took away all the men between the ages of eighteen and forty. When we heard that Warsaw had capitulated, we decided to return home. There were rumors that Warsaw was starving, so my mother and I bought various foodstuffs, such as potatoes, to take back with us.

After the capitulation of Warsaw, Polish authorities tried to restore a semblance of normality to our lives. Before the war, I had attended the Stefan Batory gymnasium, on Myśliwecka Street. This was a very exclusive school. The building had been damaged by machine-gun fire; the roof especially needed repair. But by the end of October, the school reopened. As far as possible, normal lessons resumed. The Germans soon abolished secondary schools for the Poles. There were to be only primary and technical schools. One day during class, the Germans arrived and told us all to get out because they were taking over the building for their own use. It became a German school. We took the precaution of removing the gymnasium records and some of the paintings. A portrait of Stefan Batory, and a copy of Jan Matejko's painting of the Battle of Grunwald went to the apartment of one of our teachers. A week later our studies resumed as a technical school in a building on Chałubinski Street. After about a year, the Germans realized what was going on and closed that school too. My education then continued in secret. Groups of six or seven students met in private apartments and the teachers went to the various apartments to give their lessons.

Along with other Scouts, I distributed the *Komunikat Radiowy* (*Radio Communication*), which was copied on a duplicating machine, as well as the news sheet of the Home Army's Bureau of Information and Propaganda, which was published in German. Entitled *Der Hammer*, it purported to be anti-Nazi German propaganda and was intended to demoralize the Germans in occupied Poland. We dropped copies through the open windows of parked German cars or tucked them into motorcycles. Scouts also engaged in what was known as small sabotage—painting anti-German slogans and passing out anti-German leaflets.

Since the Germans showed mainly propaganda films or newsreels, there was a Polish campaign aimed at stopping people from going to the cinema. A slogan to the effect that "only pigs sit in cinemas" was very popular. We even extended the campaign into the theaters themselves by exploding stink-bombs during performances. We worked in pairs. While one dropped a bomb from the balcony into the stalls, the other sat downstairs and tried to create as much panic as possible when the bomb went off, hoping to clear the cinema.

On one such escapade I had a most annoying experience. I had just bought myself a new hat, of which I was very proud. I went into the stalls downstairs while my partner was upstairs. Unfortunately he threw the stink-bomb straight into my hat. I was furious. I gave such full vent to my feelings that the cinema emptied in three minutes. My hat, of course, was ruined.

I was a very keen athlete, but most sports facilities were closed to the Poles. In 1940, the only athletic track available to the Poles belonged to the Sports Club for jockeys' which was attached to the racecourse on the *Pole Mokotówskie* (Mokotów Fields). In August or September 1940, I took part in an unofficial athletics competition organized on this track. Many competitors and spectators were there. The Germans arrived during the event and started rounding up people, but since the Germans did not surround the field, we were able to run in the opposite direction. I fled in my sports shorts and vest. Fortunately, I had all my clothes with me in a bag, so I left nothing behind. Others were not so fortunate; they had left clothes and documents behind which the Germans then used to trace them.

Beaches on the Vistula were open, but as they were frequently raided by the Germans, we tended to avoid them. At Sadyba Czerniakowska, between Warsaw and Wilanów, there was a fair-sized lake that was relatively safe, so we often went swimming there. There were a few villas around the lake, one of them belonging to my friend's father. One day, Klemens Szaniawski, another friend, and I went to the lake to swim. We left our clothes at the villa and went into the water. The lake was divided into two unequal parts by a bridge. We went into the smaller of the two parts, which was overgrown with reeds and other greenery. Suddenly we heard sirens; the Germans arrived and completely surrounded the lake. My friends and I managed to take cover under the bridge. We hid motionless in the water between the posts of the bridge for two hours. Many young people were seized by the Germans in the raid. Three or four of those who refused to get out of the water were shot. Most had to go and collect their clothes so they had no chance of escaping undetected. It was just luck that we had left our clothes at the villa. Nevertheless, we were terrified while the sentry paced up and down over our heads. Our lips turned quite white. When we finally got to the villa, my friend's father made us drink some spirits, and that helped.

During the occupation, it was impossible to support yourself solely from earnings unless you were a physician or lawyer. To make ends meet, everyone traded. I had a friend whose fiancée worked at Warsaw's railway freight yards. She told us that it was possible to buy German goods there by the truckload. Both German and Polish railwaymen opened wagons of goods at the freight yards, loaded the contents onto trucks, and sold the entire contents as they stood, without letting their purchasers know what they contained. We were told to stand somewhere near the sentry's hut at the entrance to the goods yard. Eventually someone approached us and asked what we wanted. We told him, and he quoted a price. (We had borrowed twenty-five thousand zlotys for this purpose.) After we paid, a German driver got into the truck and asked us for directions to our prepared storage place. It was only after the driver had gone that we could take a look and see what we had purchased. It turned out to be injections for treating varicose veins, not the coffee we had hoped for—obviously not a successful transaction. It took us six months to get rid of the merchandise profitably, but we managed to do it. Through my mother, who worked for a Polish pharmaceutical wholesaler, the injections went as "special offers."

At the end of October 1942, I joined the Home Army and took an officer cadets' course, which I completed in 1943. Exercises and drills were carried out in private apartments using broom handles in place of rifles. One of our instructors was in the Polish Blue Police, which allowed him to carry his Wis pistol legally. Field exercises took place in the suburbs of Warsaw. Eventually I was assigned to the Batory Company of the *Wojskowa Służba Ochrony Powstania* (Defense Units of the Uprising). First I was a section commander, then a squad leader, and just before the uprising, deputy commander of the platoon.

Four to five days before the uprising, we had a trial mobilization. The rumble of Soviet guns could already be heard. There were Soviet air raids over Warsaw. The Germans fled in panic in anything they could lay their hands on—cars, carts, motorcycles, even on bicycles. The east-west route through Warsaw was jammed. On the streets of Warsaw one could see many young people wearing items of [Polish and German] military dress. I thought we might yet revenge ourselves on the Germans for all the suffering they had caused.

I lived in an apartment at No. 16 Hoza Street. In an apartment building across the road was a primary school that served as a temporary camp for German troops on their way to and from the eastern front. There were always many Germans milling around the place. When the trial mobilization was announced, I was walking along my side of the street toward Marszałkowska, some distance behind a German soldier with a pistol in his holster. A young man walked up to the solider from behind, pressed the top of an empty beer bottle into his back, and told him to put his hands up in the air without turning around. The German pleaded that he would be sent to a penal company but to no avail. The young Pole removed the pistol. When I saw this, I fled, since there was an armed German sentry only thirty meters away.

At the concentration point for my unit in Czerniaków, the entire platoon gathered in an apartment, a somewhat dangerous enterprise in view of the many *Volksdeutsche* who lived in the building. The company commander came to the apartment accompanied by a pre-war officer cadet, and the commander put him in charge of my platoon. Since I was only the acting platoon commander and all prewar ranks automatically outranked wartime ones, there was nothing I could do. The weapons were distrubuted, and we stayed in the apartment, waiting for the signal that was to herald the start of the uprising. During the night there was a Soviet air raid. The air raid warden insisted that all the occupants of the apartment building leave and take shelter under the former garrison church. Not surprisingly, as the thirty or so of us trooped out of the apartment and down to the shelter, we were given some very suspicious glances.

In the morning we received news that the uprising had been called off. Since it was Sunday, I decided to spend the day at the house that my friends and I rented in Leśna Podkowa. On Monday I returned straight to the philatelic shop on Przeskok Street that I ran with some friends. It was there that I found out at about 3:15 p.m. that there was to be an uprising after all. I had not been notified earlier because our new platoon commander had changed the system for informing the members of our unit when the uprising was to start. My system had been based on each man notifying those who lived nearest to him. The new system had not even been tested, and as a result I did not find out about the uprising until very late.

Since all my things were at home, I started out in that direction, but never reached my destination because shooting on Jerozolimskie Avenue started around 3:30 p.m. In the circumstances, I had no alternative but to return to the philatelic shop.

One of the men who ran the shop with me belonged to the air base section of the Home Army. From the autumn of 1943 to the beginning of 1944, the Germans had taken many Poles from Silesia and Poznań into the air force. The people from the air base section of the Home Army had made contact with these Poles and offered to help them if they chose to desert from the German forces. Since the philatelic shop had two entrances, one leading into the street and the other into the courtyard in the back, these "German" deserters were encouraged to come to our shop. Anyone could enter from the street without arousing the slightest suspicion about a visit to a philatelic shop. When the coast was clear, the deserters would go to the office at the rear, where their identities would be changed—new clothes, documents, hairstyles—and then go out the back door. One of the problems was how to dispose of the German uniforms we were left with. We were reluctant to put them in the cellar, where they might easily be discovered. In the end the problem was solved by stuffing the uniforms into sacks and hanging these sacks in an unused toilet in the courtyard.

When I returned to the shop on the day of the uprising, I decided to get the uniforms out of their hiding place because I thought they might come in handy one way or another. I went to the caretaker for the key. Together we went to open the door, and when he saw for himself what had been hidden on his premises, he fainted. I later found out that the *Rada Jedności Narodowej* (Council of National Unity) had held their meetings in the same building where the shop was located, so we had put Polish officials at considerable risk as well.

Since I was unable to get to my unit, I joined a unit in the seventh sector under Colonel Topor-Kojszewski. We had so few weapons that those we had stayed in position; only the people manning the positions changed. I had been trained in the use of a Spandau light machine gun.

Our emplacement was in the Metropol Hotel between Chmielna and Marszałkowska, overlooking the Polonia Hotel and the Café Wiktor. We could also see a tower where we knew there was a sniper. We had tried but could not kill him. He was a superb shot. From where he was concealed, he had the whole of Marszałkowska and all the barricades there in his sights. We attached small mirrors—twenty-five centimeters in diameter—to poles that we hung out of the windows, and he hit all of the mirrors from a distance of about fifteen hundred meters.

I came to relieve a friend who was trying to put this sniper out of action. We had filled in the windows on either side of a narrow opening with bricks. The friend I had come to relieve was wearing a steel helmet. Suddenly as I stood there, he collapsed without a sound, and I saw that there was a bullet hole in the front of his helmet. I took the helmet off and to my astonishment there was no corresponding hole in his head! The bullet had gone around the inside of the helmet, leaving a red band around my friend's head, and then quite literally disappeared. We looked for the bullet everywhere, but without success.

I myself had a lucky escape as I was entering the house on Wspólna Street at the beginning of September. At this time the Germans used very large caliber shells fired from guns mounted on armored trains. While I stood in the gateway of the house, there was a tremendous crash; everything went dark and there were clouds of dust everywhere. When visibility returned, I looked around and saw that an unexploded shell had fallen through the top of the building. It now lay in a heap of rubble beside a body, which must have fallen from one of the upper floors.

At the end of the uprising, the situation was so hopeless that I stopped taking any precautions for my safety. I decided that we were all going to be killed anyway, so there was no point in hiding. Indeed, the sooner death came, the better it would be for me.

Born and raised in Warsaw, where the incidents in his account occurred, Bokiewicz left Poland after the war and now lives in London.

MARYLA BONIŃSKA

On April 23, 1943, a quarter of an hour before I was arrested, I had been given a message, written on Japanese tissue, from General Grot-Rowecki, head of the Home Army. He signed the message with just the capital *T* within a circle, which stood for Tur, one of his pseudonyms within Home Army headquarters. The message stated that he forbade the Polish Blue Police to shoot Jews, or else he would deal with them. (The Ghetto Uprising had commenced on April 19, 1943.) I passed this message on to my deputy to pass to the relevant authorities for action.

Meanwhile, I left to meet a fellow conspirator on Nowogrodzka Street, but unfortunately I also took the manuscript of an article I had written for Żołnierz Polski (*Polish Soldier*), a clandestine publication, to be typed. I left all other incriminating materials in a safe place, except for a list of ways to reach the *Komenda Główna* (High Command) in case of emergency during the Easter holidays. It was coded in my own special way. I needed this because General Rowecki and the other generals had changed their usual addresses and telephone numbers for the four days of the holiday.

The article I had written was to be published on May 12, the anniversary of Piłsudski's death. It alluded to the lessons he had taught us, especially the need for a final struggle with the Germans, an obvious reference to the future uprising. The article was well hidden in a secret compartment of my handbag, though it would have been discovered if the bag had been ripped apart. Having been warned that the premises on Nowogrodzka where I was going were unsafe, I walked along Krucza Street. The Gestapo stopped me, bundled me into a car, and took me to Gestapo headquarters on Szucha Avenue. On the way, they took my handbag. If they found the article, I knew it would be the end. I was not afraid that the emergency access list would incriminate anyone else, because it was written in such a way as to be meaningful only to me. But discovery of the access list would entail torture for me, or at the very least a severe beating, because they would try to extract the meaning of the coded message from me. Fortunately, though the list was in the breast pocket of my suit, the Germans did not find it because it was very tightly rolled up at the very base of my pocket. However, they did take the headache powder I kept in the same pocket and tore out a chiffon handkerchief I had pinned there.

While I waited for questioning, guarded by SS-men, I managed to get the access list out of my pocket, rolled it into a ball, put it into my mouth, chewed it with great difficulty, and swallowed it. My handbag was still in the possession of the Gestapo. During the questioning, the Gestapo repeatedly hit me on the right side of my face, using their hands, fists, and even that handbag. The blows knocked me off the chair.

After the first questioning, I was taken to Pawiak prison. Six days later, I was back again at Gestapo headquarters, where they returned my handbag, emptied of its contents except for a comb. Sitting once again in the waiting room, I checked whether the article was still in its compartment. It was, but I decided that if they looked at the bag again, I might not be so lucky. I had to get rid of it. There was no way of doing anything under the gaze of the German guard, so I pretended to be in great pain.

Under the threat of death, people do amazing things. My acting ability surpassed my own expectations. I cringed with pain, calling to the guard that I wanted to go to the lavatory. The guard called someone to take his place while he took me outside. He stood all the time by the slightly open door. Under cover of wails and groans, I tore up the article and flushed in down the toilet.

During the second questioning, I was asked whether I belonged to any organizations. I replied that I did—to the Red Cross, the co-operative society, and so on. "Do you read the underground press? And who passed it to you?" they asked me. I told them I did read it but said I had no idea who was responsible because the newsletter was left under the doormat in my home. "What did you do with them after you read them?" the Gestapo persisted. "I threw them away," I replied. The Gestapo had also found a note in which was written: "NKW Cpt. Chołowiecki among the bodies uncovered in Katyn forest." They wanted to know what this message meant. I felt a surge of relief that at long last I was able to answer truthfully: NKW stood for *Nowy Kurier Warszawski*, an official paper censored by the German authorities that had carried news of the discovery of the mass graves at Katyn. Chołowiecki was my friend's brother.

Finally, the Gestapo made me sign a declaration that everything I had told them was untrue. But I signed to the effect that "they made me sign that everything I said was untrue." Back in Pawiak I received a message from General Tadeusz Pełczyński, my chief in the conspiracy and Chief of Staff of the Home Army, that my apartment had been "spring-cleaned" by my sister. That meant that all incriminating evidence had been removed. My children were safe because they had gone to Rogow for Easter on the day of my arrest. Another message from Pełczyński assured me that he had unbounded faith in me. This gave me a great deal of pleasure. In the same message was a code name for me that proved the authenticity of the sender—"Pekasia," a pet name that only someone who had known me very well in my youth would have called me.

These messages were smuggled by a trusted old prisoner who performed the duties of a medical orderly. Despite my protests, she made me take a spoonful of some medicine, passing the message to me under the cover of the cloth with which she wiped my mouth. I wrote to my family and to my superiors by the same route. Another prisoner helped me write a letter to my family in German, which I was entitled to send. She told me who was in the other cells and passed other information to me, much to the annoyance of the guard, who was probably a Latvian. My main worry was whether there would be a problem with my colleague, Wanda, who had been walking with me until just before I was arrested. While I had continued along Krucza Street, she had turned into Hoza Street. The Gestapo told me that they had arrested her too and that she was telling them a different story. But I received a smuggled message, "The rascals are lying. Wanda is free," so I knew there would be no confrontation.

All this time I had been kept in solitary confinement. On the night of May 11-12, I was transferred to a general cell in time to watch the Soviet bombardment of Warsaw that night. At 2:00 a.m., along with another 118 women and 337 men, I was taken out to the transport headed for Auschwitz.

From August 6, 1941, until my arrest, I was chief of the communications center of the Home Army General Headquarters. At that time it was common practice for couriers to meet at streetcar stops and similar locations. I decided that it was much too dangerous because such meetings could be observed far too easily. As part of my contribution to the security of resistance communications, I devised a system of courier meetings for my section that I called *na kwadratach* (in quarters). The couriers who were to meet would be assigned to walk around a block of streets starting from opposite directions, so that they were bound to meet sooner or later, but each meeting would appear purely accidental to any outsider.

Bonińska was the wartime pseudonym of one of the most active women in the Polish resistance movement. She prefers to use her pseudonym in matters that concern the war years. Today she is involved in Polish affairs in England.

ZOFIA RYSŻEWSKA BRUSIKIEWICZ

In 1939 when World War II broke out, I lived with my parents and two younger brothers in Warsaw at No. 7, Nowy Zjazd Street. I was twelve years old at the time and attended commercial school on Kiliński Street in Old Town.

The most important thing for this account is to describe the place where we lived. The flat my parents occupied consisted of three rooms—two adjoining and one with a separate entrance. The bathroom was large enough to make into a separate small room. This room, after my grandfather did some work on it, was a very good hiding place in case of danger to the thirteen Jewish people who lived in our home.

An additional advantage of our building was that it had more than one way out. People living on the first floor used one entrance to enter and exit from the house, which was connected with Rynek Mariensztacki. Other tenants living in the building, which had three floors and six flats, used the major entrance from Nowy Zjazd Street. It was possible, therefore, to enter the building by one entrance and leave by the other, to avoid being noticed.

In 1942 I learned from my parents that in a short time we were going to have a Jewish person living with us, a bookseller by the name of Artemowicz. My father's friend, a journalist, had asked my father to hide Mr. Artemowicz. And that is the beginning of the whole story.

What I am going to describe may not be quite precise because I was very young at the time. I do not know all of the details because I was not informed about all of them, especially contacts with the Polish underground. Probably because I was so young at the time, I saw the war in a different way than the adults did. Yet I participated in all of their activities.

A few days after my father informed us about Mr. Artemowicz living with us, he arrived and was accepted as part of the family. After some time, my father had a very serious talk with me to explain the whole situation. Since I was the oldest child, he asked my opinion: What did I think about Mr. Artemowicz staying with us permanently? In spite of my young age, I was able to understand how the Germans treated Jews and the tragic destiny for our new tenant if he did not find shelter with us.

In a few weeks we accepted additional members of Artemowicz's family. They included a couple by the name of Funt, who had a four-year old daughter. A little later, Marian Kasman and his brother-in-law, along with Lipa Szymkiewicz, joined us. In this way, seven people of Jewish origin found their way into our home. Our flat was priceless. I would like to add that we had double doors, which gave us the protection of sound-proofing.

It was a big problem to buy food for so many people without attracting the attention of the neighbors. My mother and I took care of grocery shopping, and we tried to bring home the groceries in such a way that no one would pay attention to the amount of food that we carried in. It is very hard for me to say where we got the money to buy the food. Probably part of the money came from the Jewish people we sheltered. But some of the Jews had no money at all, like, for example, Mr. Pinelis and his wife who, along with Mr. Arsymowicz, came to our home later. I was not informed about all these details. But one thing is certain: My father was unable to cover the cost of maintaining so many people because his salary as a singer in a choir was insufficient to maintain even the meager existence of our family.

In 1943, as the Warsaw Ghetto Uprising approached, we allowed six more Jewish people to join us: Mr. Pinelis and his wife, two sisters by the name of Anna and Róża Lewin, and Mr. and Mrs. Ludwik Opal.

Increasing the number of Jewish people in our home to thirteen was like dancing on the edge, a provocation of fate. Yet even in the new circumstances, we were able somehow to maintain our life. My mother and I took care of the food. In dangerous situations, when we thought the Germans were about to enter the house, our tenants were able to hide in the hiding place in the bathroom.

Even though I lived in this place, it is so difficult for me to recreate the situation and to imagine how it was possible for thirteen people to live together in a three-room apartment. We used to sleep wherever it was possible—on the bed, on the floor, and one person even slept in the bathtub. We all used to have meals at about the same time. Usually we had soup, very rarely with a piece of meat, with plenty of bread and potatoes.

In the evening we played cards or read the official publications and the underground press. We conversed about various subjects— what was going on in the city and on the fighting front. On one occasion, Mr. Kasman's cousin came to visit us. He didn't have to stay in hiding because he did not look Semitic and had false documents, which allowed him to move around the city. These visits provided for an exchange of information between the people who were hiding and those who lived on the outside. The Jews we were sheltering were able to learn something about their family and friends; in addition, Kasman's cousin was able to run some errands for them. He also brought us the underground press. An additional source of information was the German propaganda program, broadcast so loudly outdoors from the Rynek Mariensztacki that we were able to hear it quite well inside our apartment. The Jews who hid with us were not able to leave the apartment at all; they realized that they were in great danger. We shared and risked our lives together.

The way we lived completely excluded us from any social life. We were not allowed to visit anyone or to have visitors. This concerned us children too. For our own safety and the safety of the thirteen people we sheltered, we were alert all of the time. We did not want to give away our secret. We had to be very careful with our neighbors, with people we met casually, even with our friends at school.

At that time, most young Poles participated in the resistance movement, but for me this kind of activity was not allowed. Because of possible danger to the thirteen people, I was not allowed to participate in any kind of outside activity, and as a consequence, I often had to face the disapproval of my peers because of my passive attitude.

The circumstances forced us quite often to make sudden decisions. For example, we had to have morphine for one of our Jewish charges, Anna Lewin, because she suffered from cancer.

Only today do I realize how dangerous it was for me and my family to hide thirteen people for two years. The fact that our secret was not revealed seems a miracle to me today.

At the time when only Mr. Artemowicz lived with us, we had to deal with a visit from my father's classmate, who spent a few days with us. Later on, we learned that he had been a German informer. Permanent danger threatened us from the German police who were stationed in the house next door.

From the perspective of time, as an adult and a mother, I am able to appreciate how exceptional was the behavior of my parents, who endangered their lives and the lives of their children to save strangers who found themselves in mortal danger.

In August 1944 the Warsaw Uprising broke out. A few days later, everyone had to evacuate the burning building on Nowy Zjazd Street. My mother was on the Praga side of Warsaw at the time. After a month, my father, siblings, and I were sent by the Germans to the Pruszków camp, from where my father went to the concentration camp at Oranienburg, while I was sent to Ravensbruck. My siblings were sent to the farms of Polish peasants. We remained at these locations until May 1945.

Leon Funt died in September 1944, identified and shot as a Jew by the Germans at the Pruszków camp. The rest of the thirteen Jews survived the war. Ludwik Opal and his wife today live in Belgium. Alexander Artemowicz married Róża Lewin and emigrated to Canada. Anna Lewin died. Izaak Pinelis and his wife emigrated to the United States. Lipa Szymkiewicz went to Israel, and Marian Kasman went to England. Lea Funt emigrated with her daughter to France where she remarried.

After the war, Brusikiewicz married a Polish actor of Jewish origin. She lives in Warsaw.

EWA BUKOWSKA

My contacts with the Jewish community were very limited. One year I was not feeling very well. The doctor recommended rest and good food, so I went to stay with my aunt in Otwock. Before the war Otwock had a large Jewish community, so there was a large ghetto. My aunt lived in an area of small, individual houses. While I was there, I saw ragged Jewish children six or seven years old who were small enough to slip through the barbed wire surrounding the ghetto to beg for food. They always approached very carefully, and my aunt gave them what she had. Then they would disappear as quickly and quietly as they had come.

My family and I lived in Warsaw. The apartment next to ours belonged to a Jewish family who had lived there for years and with whom we had always been on very good terms. When they had to move to the ghetto, they left some of their belongings with us. As long as they were able to leave the ghetto, they returned from time to time and took whatever they wanted from their bundles, until everything was gone.

At one point, on the recommendation of one of our relatives, we rented one of the rooms of our apartment to a frail, very old man who must have been an academician. We always suspected that he was Jewish because all the members of his family lived in different places. Since he always telephoned them, we could not help but be aware of this. Occasionally he typed late into the night. This created many problems, as the noise of the typewriter was very noticeable at night, especially since the curfew made the street very quiet. We did our best to keep it quiet. We gave him pads to put under his typewriter. We even tried to soundproof his door. But it was very risky because the Germans regarded typing itself as a suspect activity, regardless of who was doing it. Then one day I noticed some suspicious characters hanging around the staircase of the house. We warned the old man about them, and soon afterward he moved away.

On the other side of the apartment house lived a German family, although they had a Polish surname. My sister, who did not go out to work, was liable for deportation to Germany if she was ever caught in a *łapanka* (roundup). The German lady told my mother that if ever the need arose, my sister should leave our apartment by the back stairs and go to hide in their apartment until the danger had passed.

I was a teacher. In 1939 I had completed my training at the Higher Commercial College in Warsaw, where I studied economics and took a teachers' training course. I taught commercial subjects at a former grammar school there, but some of the "lessons" were in fact a cover for classes in subjects forbidden by the Germans. I continued to sit in the class and there would be an exercise in bookkeeping, for example, on the blackboard, but another teacher taught the forbidden subject. I only took over in case of emergency. Although the Germans never made an appearance while I was on the premises, I do know that the alarm system worked. The classrooms were very well situated on the first, second, and eighth floors of a large building on Bagatela Street with an internal lift. Different schools used the same premises at various times. If the Germans arrived for whatever reason, they were directed to some other part of the building or held up in some way while warnings were sent out to all those in danger.

During the Warsaw Uprising of 1944, I was a member of an organization that helped the soldiers. Initially I had been assigned to organize front-line canteens, but nothing came of this scheme. Instead I was reassigned to visiting the sick in hospitals to help them keep in touch with their relatives and friends. I also collected food and medicines for the civilian casualties of Warsaw.

One hospital on Hoza Street had been a private clinic that treated many German patients. When the hospital was taken over by the Polish insurgents, the Germans were moved from the beds to mattresses on the floor. Once when I was there, an older German complained loudly about the lack of cigarettes. He was told in no uncertain terms to stop his complaints, but he was not harmed in any way.

On August 1, 1944, I was sent from our base in the school on Bagatela to Leszno Street to notify other members of my organization that the Warsaw uprising was to begin. The return journey proved to be fraught with difficulties, and I was forced to spend the night on the stairs of an apartment house. After a couple of days, I got as far as Polna Street. The whole street was in flames, so I went into one of the courtyards. Then the Germans arrived and made us all go to Union Square, where by this time they had herded a large crowd of civilians, whom they forced into the cellars of the large Fire Brigade building. The next morning we were ordered to go to Szucha Avenue, to be sent back to our own people. Szucha was in German hands, and here we joined up with yet more people, among whom I met some of my friends from the school on Bagatela, including one of the caretakers.

We had no idea what the Germans would do with us as we sat on the ground and waited. After some time, the Germans started to line up the women from the crowd into ranks of six or so. My friends and I kept together, and as each new rank was formed we dropped further back to the rear of the group. We then saw that the Germans were taking headscarves and the more brightly colored dresses from some of the women and putting the clothing on over their uniforms. Dressed like this, they mingled with the crowd of women. All of this must have taken well over an hour.

It then transpired that the Germans were preparing an attack on the telephone exchange, known as Pasta. Armed troops were to be followed by the crowd of women, interspersed with the disguised Germans and flanked on both sides by tanks. Then we were told that the attack had been unsuccessful and would have to be repeated. (After the war, I found out that there had been remarkably few casualties, as the women had gone to the sides, out of the main line of fire.)

Again we sat down on the ground and waited. By now dusk had fallen, and the Germans started going around, ostensibly looking for women to help in their kitchens. We noticed that they were choosing the younger women. Since we were all young then, we huddled together and hoped that they would pass us by.

When it was quite dark, we were crowded into the courtyard of an apartment house on Szucha. There were so many of us that it was difficult even to sit down. At the far end of the courtyard was a fence, and an earthbank had been prepared that we were told not to approach. The building itself was occupied by the Germans. We could see the barrels of machine guns in the windows, and at intervals through the night they fired guns at Polish positions on Marszałkowska Street. We spent the whole night in that courtyard, speculating on how we were likely to die. If we were not killed by the Germans, we were very likely to catch some disease from the extremely unsanitary conditions in the courtyard.

The next day was the Feast of Christ's Transfiguration, and the caretaker kept our spirits up by assuring us that something was bound to change for the better on this feast day. In the morning the Germans again started to line us up. Again the whole process took a very long time. The worst thing was not knowing what they intended to do with us. Finally, when the Germans were satisfied with the way we were lined up, we were led across Marszałkowska to Zbawiciel Square and to the beginning of Mokotówska Street. The streets were empty except for a few corpses. Some distance away from a barricade, the Germans stopped us and told us to go to City Center and tell "our bandits" what we had gone through.

At first we did not realize that it was a Polish barricade because the Poles manning it wore German camouflage jackets. But then we noticed they were also wearing red and white armbands. When the Poles saw us, they called out to us to cross the barricade as quickly as possible and then hurried us through the underground passages away from the barricade. This naturally took some time because the crowd was so large. The Germans fired no shots until after the last person had gone through the barricade. Obviously, by this exercise the Germans hoped to demoralize the Polish civilian population.

I remained in City Center for the rest of the Warsaw Uprising.

After the Warsaw Uprising, Bukowska was held in various German prison camps. At the end of the war, she emigrated to England, where she taught school. Bukowska holds a teaching diploma from the Central College of Commerce in Warsaw.

K.T. CZELNY

When Germany attacked Poland, my father, who was a major in the reserve of the medical corps of the Polish Army, was asked to report to a field hospital near Lwów. He prudently took the rest of the family with him. In the face of a total lack of help from Poland's allies, Britain and France, and the hopelessness of fighting armored Nazis, supported by the whole might of the Luftwaffe, my father decided to take me and my cousin and escape to Romania.

After several days of traveling by all feasible means toward the Romanian frontier, under incessant vicious attacks by low-flying Nazi planes, news reached us on September 17, 1939, that the Soviet forces had crossed the border and were racing toward the Romanian frontier to cut off that escape route. A rapid confirmation of this shattering news came soon from the skies, when a small flight of Soviet planes bombed the Polish columns. Faced with this, we had to turn back and flee in the direction from which we had come—toward Lwów. For a while we traveled by train, but after the Ukrainians blew up the tracks, the remaining two-thirds of the journey had to be on foot.

As we approached every Ukrainian village, we were fired upon. In towns, we were also shot at by the Jewish militia, armed with stolen Polish army rifles and wearing red arm bands. As we approached the outskirts of Lwów, we came upon a tragicomic spectacle: In a meadow beside the main road, about ten of the Jewish militiamen were guarding a sizable squadron of one of the elite Polish cavalry regiments. Soviet tank forces had disarmed the Polish regiment and had assigned their new "allies," the Jews, to guard the Poles. I recall a feeling of pain and disgust that those who were Polish citizens should behave so treacherously. Lwów, the once proud city, was in the firm grip of the Soviets. People moved about as though they were in a trance, humiliated and stunned by this double-sided aggression and the new partition by Poland's ancient enemies.

The so-called free and democratic elections followed, and of course the inhabitants of what was now called the Western Ukraine "unanimously" voted for incorporation into the Soviet Union. In view of the circumstances and after the ubiquitous NKVD began house-to-house visits to register Poles, my entire family opted to cross the demarcation line into German-occupied Poland at the town of Prze-myśl.

The German troops on the border were Wehrmacht, and I vividly remember a young officer saluting my exhausted mother and taking from her my baby sister, whom he carried to the waiting train. I recall thinking, Thank God we are back in European civilization. However, the illusion was shortlived.

As soon as we arrived at our new home in Rabka-Zdrój, we noticed huge posters announcing the executions of hostages or listing new hostages, a hundred at a time, to be shot in case of "crimes committed by Poles against Nazi Germany." Walking in the street, we had to step off the sidewalk if only one or two uniformed Germans approached from the opposite direction. What is more, as a sign of respect for the "super race," we had to take off any headgear we wore.

As the months passed, the Gestapo terror intensified, and every night members of this sadistic, bestial force arrested leaders of Polish society, as well as former Polish officers and any young people. At that time, when many Poles were taken away and subjected to brutal tortures, beatings, and interrogations in the cellars of the central Gestapo headquarters, in the former Sanatorium Palace in Zakopane, Jewish citizens had to wear the Star of David arm bands but were not molested as yet by the Germans.

Already in 1940 and then throughout 1941, the Germans embarked on draconian measures. On the outskirts of town on the excursion track to Lubon Mountain (Rabka was a summer and winter resort), the Germans requisitioned whole suburbs to create a Jewish ghetto. Into it they forcibly herded not only Jewish families from the town but also those evicted from nearby provinces incorporated into the Reich. Having prepared lists of those interned in that Jewish quarter, the Germans executed them on a daily basis in the nearby hills and mountains that surrounded Rabka. We heard machine-gun, rifle, and pistol shots from early morning until dusk. Rabka had many large sanatoriums in which there were two SS Gestapo centers— namely, a training center for the SS and one for Ukrainian Auxiliary SS. These two "brotherly" forces were responsible for the daily mass shooting of the unfortunate Jewish families.

At that time, I remember, I was officially registered as a male nurse in my late father's medical dispensary. My father, despite the orders of German authorities that no Aryan doctor treat Jewish patients under any circumstances, clandestinely received pleas for treatment of sick Jews from the Jewish council. He risked not only his life but also the life of every member of his family by treating Jews in his dispensary. I assisted him in his surgery, first as a receptionist and later as a male nurse. Naturally I heard heart-rending stories of what went on in the Jewish ghetto and of the progress of the Nazi annihilation.

We passed on all these horrible accounts to the local delegates of the Union for Armed Struggle. In fact, this was one of the main reasons why my father and I were treated so brutally in 1942, when we were both arrested by a team of SD [security service of the SS] and Gestapo. Some members of the underground organization who had been arrested before us knew about our medical assistance to the Jews, and they gave our secret away under unspeakable torture.

Two incidents before we were arrested are firmly embedded in my memory. One day my father was out on a visit to a patient, and my mother went out to buy bread in a nearby bakery. She took my oldest sister to help her. From my second-floor room, where I was reading a paper, I could hear in the street below a Jewish column being force-marched by the SS and their Ukrainian stooges to a distant execution spot. I stepped to the front window and, standing to one side, saw about seventy or eighty Jews of all ages being driven along by blows dealt out indiscriminately by the crazed SS. The Jews were not all able to keep up the fast pace demanded by the SS-men, and one old man, after being hit on the head with a rifle butt, fell to the ground. A senior noncommissioned officer kicked him several times and then coldbloodedly shot him in the head three times in rapid succession. They left him where he fell and marched on. At that moment, my oldest sister screamed to me from the lower floor for help. Apparently my mother, returning from the bakery, had seen the incident and fainted from horror. We both carried her up the stairs. It was some weeks before she recovered from the shock she suffered.

As the intensity of the terror increased, such atrocities were repeated several times a day. What puzzled us was why the Jews, among whom were many able-bodied men and women, never, not even on one occasion, offered any resistance to their executioners, whose intentions were clear to everyone at that time.

One day I escorted a young Jewish woman by a devious route that led through rye fields to the back of our house. She had a medical appointment with my father. I found out that she had graduated in English from the University of London, obtaining a bachelor's degree a year before the outbreak of the war. My heart jumped for joy. I asked her if she could teach me English. She hesitated. If we were caught, it would have meant death for both of us. However, in the end she agreed, providing I came to get her and escort her each time.

One day she came out of the ghetto sobbing bitterly, near total nervous collapse. She had learned that she and her husband and their two young sons were on the list to be shot in three days. I remember her last words before we parted, after I led her back to the ghetto: "You are young and now are able to communicate in English. I feel happy that I was of help in this, but if you can ever tell the world, which has abandonded the Poles and Jews in Poland to these Nazi beasts, about what has been done to us, you must do so. It is your sacred duty to tell them about it!" I promised and we parted.

One night in mid-August 1942, I woke up to wild shouting from behind the locked door to our apartment. The voices were German. Kicking the door in a fury, the Germans demanded immediate entry. I jumped out of bed and without putting the light on, looked down from the second floor. There were black uniformed men outside. The house was obviously surrounded, so it would be madness to try to jump out to escape. By then the shouting was a veritable pandemonium. While my youngest sister in her cot in my parents' bedroom screamed in sheer terror, my father went to open the front door. I was horrified to hear him being beaten. In the previous two arrests of my father, the Gestapo had been scrupulously polite and even called him *"Herr Doktor."* I realized that this time they must have known of our assistance to the Jews and of our contacts with the Polish underground.

And so the Gestapo entered our house, taking turns at beating up my father. My mother became hysterical with grief and anger. My sisters cried. An officer of the SD, wearing a black leather coat, entered my room with a Luger pointed in my direction. He put the light on and barked in German: "Get up, dress immediately, and no funny business or you are dead!" We were immediately led out. The night was very dark. Outside the house stood a cabriolet-type Mercedes car with three men in it. One was the driver, and the other two were armed escorts sitting on the rear seats with their pistols drawn. After my father and I were both handcuffed, I was told to sit by the driver. My father sat in the back with the arresting officer, Franz Victorini.

We drove to the former public school for girls, a huge modern edifice at the foot of a hill, which was now the Gestapo training center. The Germans led us to the courtyard, covered with fine pebbles. We saw motionless figures lying side by side, face down, on the pebbles, and the Gestapo ordered us to do the same. We thought we were going to be summarily shot, like the Jews. After what seemed like an eternity, they led my father and me along with two others to a tiny lavatory, where they crammed us in. Early in the morning, they let us out. Outside stood a small truck that the local butcher used to transport calves to the slaughterhouse. We lay face down on the excrement-covered floor, as ordered, and one of the Gestapo, using a long piece of thick rope, tied our legs together. When we were ordered to turn face up, the rope tightened to the point that we felt a severe, constant pain. The Germans also handcuffed us. As we traveled through the town of Rabka, we saw people we knew recoiling in horror.

After approximately a two-hour journey, the truck drew up in front of a former sanatorium, now the Gestapo center. It seemed that all the Gestapo came out like a reception committee, with Obersturmführer Weissman at the head. They untied our legs which, because of the restricted blood flow, were totally numb. When we jumped off the truck, we could not stand but fell on our faces. This provoked all the Gestapo, including Weissman, into a frenzy of kicking.

Weissman, having unloaded his pent-up rage on my father, who lay unconscious in the courtyard of the sanatorium, ordered us to march inside. Those who could not walk were unceremoniously dragged into the building by their legs, while their heads banged on the stone steps. Inside the vestibule we stood up against the walls on both sides of the entrance doors, with our hands over our heads. Under a heavily armed guard, we were kept like that for most of the early hours of the morning without any food or water. Now and again, passing Gestapo men chose to abuse us verbally or physically, leaving several of us slumped against the wall. Eventually they transferred us to two large rooms on the ground floor, where we were left lying on the floor in a row, each man handcuffed to the one on either side.

It was obvious that the prison cells in the basement were filled to the limit, and that room had to be made for us. It soon became obvious to us how this was being done. Throughout the night, we heard from the back of the building the hoarse shouting of the executioners, screams in Polish of "Long live Poland!" and the loud bangs of small arms fire. The young Gestapo who guarded us wasted no time in reminding us that our turn would come soon.

The Gestapo were no more than twenty years old. Some were baby-faced, seventeen or eighteen years old at the most. I observed their behavior and reflected on how the Nazi ideology of persecuting the enemies of National Socialism had warped their minds. The were willing automatons in a wholly institutionalized and meticulously planned extermination of whole nations and peoples. Nazism had imbued them with a fanatical mania of infinite hate and murderous impatience to extinguish all who opposed their evil.

At dawn we were freed of our handcuffs and led in groups into the basement, where ten to fourteen men were to sleep in one cell on the damp earth. It was only because of help from other prisoners that I ended up in the same cell as my father. At the time, I thought that the Gestapo had allowed it to happen through an oversight. Later I realized that it all fitted into their master plan to facilitate their interrogation.

My father and I had the same pair of interrogators. The man in charge was Victorini, the SD officer who had arrested us. He was a native of Vienna and at one time had been a heavyweight boxer. The other interrogator had a Polish name—Mazurkiewicz, from Polish Upper Silesia. He had been a blacksmith and with his enormous biceps could knock people unconscious with one blow. Those two men interrogated us for thirty-nine days and nights.

It was an orgy of sadism and unspeakable cruelty, cynically planned and executed. Their methods ranged from attempts at mild persuasion to brutal beatings and ingenious torture, such as handcuffing the prisoner's hands behind his back and hanging him, by means of a hefty rope threaded through the handcuffs, on the inner door of the interrogation room. After a short while, the excruciating pain in the joints brought unconsciousness. The method used to bring us back was to push a lighted cigarette against either the belly or the genitals. My father, who was a stout man, suffered agony at this treatment. They dropped him from the door where he was hanging onto the floor, poured cold water over him, and tried to force me to beat him with a heavy rubber truncheon. When I refused, I had to pull down my trousers and, with the same truncheon, they took turns beating me in the small of my back and in the area of the kidneys. My urine was the color of blood for weeks.

Both of us were convinced that if we refused to reveal the names of secret contacts and activities, we would eventually convince the Gestapo that we were innocent. However, we did not realize that the Germans had already been working on two underground organizers, Captain Ziemba and a priest, Canon S. Dunikowski, whom they had arrested before us. The two had been beaten so badly that in place of their buttocks, they had two gangrenous and festering wounds, which the Germans continued to beat daily. It appeared that weeks of withstanding German torture were all in vain for my father and me because these two colleagues of ours had revealed everything about us to the Germans.

The final Gestapo investigation report was drawn up and typed for my father and me. They called us in separately to read and sign it. At this final meeting, I had an incomprehensible discussion with Victorini.

When I was led into his office, he hit me in the face very hard several times: "This is for being a stubborn liar!" He then pushed the bulky investigation report, opened to the last page, in front of me and told me to sign it. I said I could not sign it without reading it. He replied that I had been given the death sentence and would be sent to Auschwitz in any case, so it really made no difference. Finally, I signed.

It was one of the amazing idiosyncrasies of the Gestapo that, having done their duty by literally beating confessions out of their victims, they then occasionally became almost civilized and humane. During the interrogations, the Germans had succeeded in knocking out all of my teeth, yet I felt that my hard and uncompromising refusal to denounce any of my compatriots had made a positive impression on these otherwise cynical and brutal men. Victorini invited me to sit down, and Benewitz, the second in command of the Gestapo at Zakopane, came in as an observer and sat next to Victorini. (We spoke all along in German, in which I was fluent.) Victorini, after commenting that I wasted my "typically Polish unwise bravery," asked me who I thought was more efficient in their detection of "the crimes of Poles" in the regions of partitioned Poland which they occupied—the NKVD [Soviet security police] or the Gestapo.

I thought rapidly, sure that whatever I said would only result in more abuse and further blows. I did not answer his question. Be-newitz, adopting a paternal posture, admonished me that I, in common with most of my countrymen, suffered from ignorance. He said that the Gestapo and the NKVD had been exchanging their experiences in suppressing Polish dreams of regaining independence for a long time. In fact, he said, the personnel of both security services had exchanged visits to each other's centers of training. He added that German methods were infallible. However, the Soviets had enriched German knowledge of Polish tactics and organization. Thus the Gestapo had the best of both worlds and, thanks to the help of the NKVD, were the most skillful in dealing with the Poles.

After seven weeks of savage interrogation in the torture dungeons of the Gestapo at Zakopane, my father and I traveled by truck to the Tarnów prison, a transit point en route to Auschwitz. Exactly six months after our arrival at Tarnów, where twelve of us were held in a tiny cell like mice in a laboratory box, without being allowed out for the daily walk around the inner prison yard, the Germans took my father to the prison's bunker. They took me out of the cell and deported me with some two hundred other prisoners to Auschwitz, where we arrived on an extremely cold winter's day, January 21, 1943. My father arrived several weeks later, a shadow of his former self. The Germans placed him in the medical block, where he was given the task of cleaning the primitive lavatories.

On October 28, 1943, the Germans transferred us to the camp hospital of Sector E in Birkenau, the Gypsy camp. The sector, which eventually housed twenty-eight thousand Gypsies from all over Europe, was in the corner of the huge rectangle of the Auschwitz II camp complex. This was very near the special railway siding where the Nazis unloaded the cattle car trains that arrived regularly with Jews destined for gassing and burning in the three huge crematoriums that adjoined the gas chambers. We were there until September 1944. The whole death factory of the Nazis was so near to us that we could see the agony and martyrdom of all the Jewish arrivals in that period of time, the highest intensity of the destruction of the European Jews.

Upon our arrival in Sector E of the main center of Birkenau, it became apparent to us that we were on the doorstep of a veritable death factory, confirmed by the three chimneys of the crematoriums, which emitted a thick, greasy, heavy black smoke every day.

The railway siding, where thousands of people arrived and the SS doctors made their selections, could be seen from a distance of less than a hundred meters. The brutality with which the SS drove the new arrivals toward the crematorium and gas chamber complex brought immediate stark reflections that the camp Gestapo must have received orders from Zakopane to liquidate us too.

The SS-men got a sadistic pleasure in screaming at us, "Jews and Poles will be exterminated here." We learned from our compatriots, already long housed in the camp, of Poles and Russians who had been gassed and burned in the ovens. We learned how desperately these unfortunates had tried to attack the SS guards. We learned how people from the region of Lublin in Poland, young boys and older men—whose hands were tied with barbed wire behind their backs so as to make every movement an agony—threw themselves at their executioners, kicking and biting wildly, when they realized they were being driven to the gas chambers. They died fighting.

Then came the mass Jewish transports. The SS had orders to speed up the *Sonderbehandlung,* as they called the racial mass murders. They wasted no time in reminding us Christians daily that we were destined to follow the Jews "to heaven." It was not long before we were to witness the highest intensity of the "final solution," when the Germans brought the Hungarian Jews in huge numbers to the railway siding. Whole families, including babies in arms and senile aged people, were terrorized by SS troopers from the moment they left the cattle trucks. The Germans forced them to leave all their belongings on the ramp. By rifle butt blows and kicks, as well as bites from Alsatian dogs, the Germans formed columns that were force-marched to the "showers and a hot meal," which, the SS shouted, "will be cold" unless they hurried.

We were at a loss to comprehend: Why did none of these unfortunate Jews—among whom there were able-bodied men and women—realize that they were being driven to their death? After all, the brutality of the SS and the omnipresent stench of burnt flesh should have made them realize that here human beings were being incinerated. We reached the conclusion that probably because these people originating from a country that was once part of the Austro-Hungarian Empire, they simply could not accept that Germans, from a "cultured nation," would kill whole families not guilty of any transgression against them.

In any event, a few of us, motivated by hatred of the SS and their savage and cruel treatment, and by the idealistic belief that their murder of innocent families should not be made so easy by the passivity and credulity of their naive victims, decided to make these victims aware of the real purpose of their arrival at Birkenau. On the side of the camp nearest to the unloading ramp was a deep ditch, which served as an obstacle in case camp prisoners thought of rushing into the electrified wires to escape. The ditch was several meters in front of the first row of wires and deep enough for an average man to stand at the bottom of it with just his head protruding above ground level. Our plan was easier to implement because the two SS machine-gun watchtowers were some distance away, and the SS were unlikely to hear anyone shouting from the ditch.

We chose the time after the evening roll call, when for a half-hour the Germans allowed us to walk between the barracks. Two of us who spoke German unobtrusively slid into the ditch and waited for the new arrivals to be formed into a column. When the column began to move toward the death factory, we shouted loudly: "You are going to your death! Resist or you will be gassed!" I shall never forget what followed. Although heads turned in our direction, obviously the Jews thought we were joking. There was no reaction to indicate that they took us seriously. After several attempts, we decided there was no point continuing this extremely hazardous task if no one took our warning seriously.

The end came quite unexpectedly. The Germans ordered us to form a small marching column and to stand inside the walls of the yard, awaiting further orders. After the rest of the prisoners had left with the SS escort, a big truck arrived, followed by a small open truck for the SS guard. When we started on our journey, it soon became obvious that we were being driven in the direction of the main Auschwitz I camp. A sudden fear gripped our throats that this was the end, that we were destined for Block 11, the execution block. Instead, we arrived at two other blocks, already jammed full of other prisoners, from whom we learned that the Germans had assembled us for an evacuation to another camp. Opinions varied widely as to which camp it was going to be. But one thing was certain: We were being transferred to the Reich's German territory.

We stood outside for some time, awaiting the arrival of the SS camp doctor, who had to satisfy himself that we were fit and did not have any infectious diseases. After that, the SS spent a long time counting and recounting us by calling out our camp numbers.

Finally, we marched to the main gate, divided into small units, and were ordered to climb into tarpaulin-covered transports. Throughout this process, we were under heavy guard by SS troopers with dogs. Our entrainment into a cattle train waiting for us on a siding at the main station in the town of Auschwitz followed a routine pattern with one difference—namely, in the tightly packed wagon there was a hole in one corner in lieu of a "closet." Before entrainment, the Germans issued us half a loaf of dry, hard bread. We received nothing to quench our thirst. The train started almost immediately. From the shouting we heard, we concluded that we would travel the rest of the afternoon and all night. The doors to the wagon were secured with a heavy steel bar. There were no windows or vents. Our journey into the unknown continued, with one stop on the way for the SS to satisfy their natural needs. The excitement of the day and the heat inside the packed wagons resulted in short tempers. However, when night came, prisoners tried to arrange themselves into clusters and groups, leaning against each other to get some rest. But sleep was possible only for a few sturdy individuals who had learned to doze off in any position.

I detected near the locked wagon doors a narrow, perpendicular slit or crack in a board, through which light showed when we passed stations. It took a sustained effort to force myself into a position against the side of the wagon with the crack right above me. My purpose was to see at dawn what sort of landscape we were passing, to identify where we were being taken.

Just after dawn, the train was only creeping along. Through the slit I saw that the train was passing a big urban area. Then an amusement park came into sight. To my amazement, I could see a huge wheel in the midst of the amusement booths. I had seen its picture so many times in books and photograph albums that I could not be wrong. We were passing the Prater with its Riesenrad, the giant wheel. I would never have believed that fate would bring me to Vienna in such deplorable circumstances.

A very sobering thought instantly entered my mind: We must be going to Mauthausen. Nothing could be more chilling. We all knew of the huge granite quarries and how the SS literally worked thousands of people to death there. A mood of resignation and gloom descended over us. The train stopped soon after, and we stood waiting. The sound of several other passing trains told us that we were probably waiting for military transports to pass on the main track beside us. We endured these hours in hunger and excruciating thirst. We discovered that some people who seemed to be sleeping in utter exhaustion were in fact dead.

We began to have fainting fits. My poor father appeared to be at the end of his strength, and yet there was absolutely nothing I could do. When the train finally stopped late in the afternoon and the bars on the heavy doors were lifted, the SS were in a nasty, bloodthirsty mood. When we fell off the wagons to the ground, the SS put on a show of brutality such as was seldom seen even in Auschwitz. On the other side of the railway track, our escort, a whole company of SS with several Alsatians, waited to take us. A sign at the side read: Mauthausen. As we were led through this small town, the inhabitants—men, women, and young teenage children—shouted insults and obscenities at us.

I shall never forget our march up a steep mountain path. The SS, in a fury, beat us incessantly with their rifle butts, hit us with their fists, and kicked us from all directions. Several prisoners bled from the bites of the savage Alsatian hounds. It was like running a gauntlet of savage henchmen, drunk with the sight of our suffering. Later we were to learn that the company that escorted us was the same infamous gang of bloodthirsty thugs who daily performed the same ritual inside the main quarry. It was a welcome release when we reached the top of the hill, where the sight of a fortress of enormous granite blocks met our eyes.

The Germans herded us into a large rectangular concrete yard. Above us, several heavy machine guns were mounted on swivel stands with SS-men standing behind them. At the corners were big watchtowers with panoramic glazed windows. Inside each one were several SS-men. As evening approached, the SS ordered us to disrobe totally and to pile all our camp clothes and wooden clogs by the locked gate through which we entered. After that, a special commando of local prisoners arrived with a primitive wagon and took it all away. Any hope we might have had that soon we would go to the warmth of the showers, followed by registration and sorting out to blocks, was shattered when the SS announced we would spend the whole night naked where we were.

What can one do against such deliberate and calculated barbarity, especially when looking straight into the muzzles of four heavy machine guns? All we could do to counteract the freezing mountain winds was to huddle together in one big mass of suffering humanity and pray to God that at dawn we would still be alive. What was most important was to be strong enough to withstand whatever the SS had in store for us.

When dawn came, we had lost all feeling in our bodies, which were stiff and numb. Our psyche was so numbed that we ceased to care any longer what awaited us. Several of my friends in the transport had been released from that living hell. They were dead.

After the war, Czelny settled in England, where he completed his higher education at the Polish University in London and at the University of London. A distinguished engineer, he was made a member of the Order of the British Empire in 1973 for his services to the automobile industry and to textile technology.

MARIAN DĄBROWSKI

After the death of our parents, my two younger brothers and I lived in the Henryk Dietz Orphanage in Bydgoszcz, which was run by the Sisters of Charity. Many of the boys in the orphanage belonged to the Boy Scouts. When the war broke out, we took part in intelligence and observation work, helping the Polish forces in Bydgoszcz. We wore our Scout uniforms and our troop leader even had a small pistol. We were very excited and thrilled to be involved with the Polish Army.

On one occasion, we were on duty at night on Kościelecki Square near Bernardyńska Street when we heard a rustling sound. We saw some armed civilians hiding in the churchyard of the German Evangelical Church. Since we knew that there were German fifth column units preparing something in the town, we immediately informed the nearest unit of the Polish Army. By the time a Polish patrol arrived, the Germans had disappeared, but during the subsequent search, the patrol discovered traces of broken boxes inside the church, which led them to the church tower. Upon climbing the tower, they found a mounted machine gun covered by a rag.

On September 5, we looked out of the windows of the orphanage and saw soldiers slowly approaching. We knew at once that they were not Polish. At first we thought that they might be the French or English army and our spirits rose. Then with horror we realized from the markings on their helmets that they were Germans. We tried to escape through the windows on the opposite side of the building, but the Germans had us surrounded so we went back inside. The Germans threw us all out into the street. Nuns and boys stood huddled together surrounded by German troops, with several machine guns pointed at us. All the civilians who were in the building were taken away; many were shot. The Germans threatened to shoot us all if the mother superior did not give them the information they demanded. One of the nuns spoke excellent German. She assured them that there was nothing hidden in the orphanage, and eventually they let us back into the building. We still wore our Scout uniforms. Now we took them off quickly and hid them in the huge attic of the orphanage.

One day the mother superior received orders that boys between fourteen and sixteen years of age were to report to the SA [Brown Shirts] office in Bydgoszcz. Mother Superior complied with the order but sent the gardener with the four of us. I was sixteen and the oldest; Mieczysław Cichosz was fifteen, and the other two, Czesław Jelka and Teofil Pilarczyk, were fifteen and fourteen, respectively. We still wore short trousers. The SA told the gardener that they could use more boys like us, hoping no doubt that he would leave us there. But the gardener insisted that he had been given instructions that on no account was he to return without us. The Germans insisted that they would look after us and that in any case we would have to undergo a medical examination. We were taken to a room that looked like a doctor's consulting room and kept there for a very long time, but no one came to examine us. We decided we were being kept there deliberately because the SA wanted to overhear what we were saying. Eventually, we were allowed to return to the orphanage on the condition that we reported to the railway station the following day, February 27, 1940.

Little realizing what was in store for us, the nuns had gotten us ready as well as they could, but we were very inadequately dressed. The winter of 1939-40 was a very hard one, yet under our jackets we wore only sweaters and our orphanage suits with short trousers. We had no coats, gloves, or heavy boots. When we arrived at the station, we saw a large crowd of adults. We were the only boys. We had no idea what was in store for us until the Germans told us that because we had no parents we would be sent to school in Germany. Then we realized that we were being taken as forced laborers. Mieczek Cichosz had already anticipated the situation and had hidden a map in preparation for escape.

We arrived in Elbing in East Prussia and were led under escort of SA men to the local labor exchange, where each worker was to be sold for fifteen marks. Among the Poles in that labor office there were some prisoners of war from the September Campaign. One was doubled up with pain; he had had his appendix removed the previous day. When we saw the state he was in, we collected together the few pfennigs we had among the four of us, wrapped them up in a scrap of paper, and tried to slide it across the floor to him. Unfortunately, one of the SA men noticed and demanded to know who was responsible. Mieczek confessed at once, and the German kicked him and threw our few pfennigs in the waste bin.

Strong men or those who had a useful trade were quickly taken, but the four of us were obviously too young and weak to be of much use to anyone. In the end, we alone remained in the labor office. At long last the son of one of the local farmers stopped in. When he saw us, he said he would have preferred one strong worker, but since there was no one else left, he would take the four of us. He paid for us and we climbed into the sleigh, still dressed in our totally inadequate garments. We finally arrived at the farm of Erich Salwey at Oberkerbswalde, six miles from Elbing. Salwey took one look at us and asked his son why he had bought us, since we were quite unsuitable for any work. By then it was very late, and we were taken to a small cubbyhole off the stable and given supper, which consisted of watery soup and a slice of bread.

The next morning Salwey found us some old trousers and put us to work. We still had no suitable shoes; it was only later that I got some wooden clogs. Our first job was digging up beetroots, which were stored in deep trenches in the ground. The work was very hard because we had to use pickaxes and hammers to break up the frozen soil, and none of us had ever done any manual work before. We worked in temperatures of twenty degrees below zero without gloves. Soon our hands were frostbitten. We used to pull down our sweater sleeves over our hands, but this was hopeless. Eventually we made crude mittens out of rags to protect our already very sore hands.

After a few days, Salwey decided we were not paying our way. He told us that he could afford to keep only one of us. We ourselves would decide which one it was to be. Mieczek said that since I had younger brothers, I ought to stay. The others returned to the labor office. Before he left, Mieczek and I arranged that as soon as he was ready to escape, he would let me know so that I could join him. The signal was to be a cross above his signature. The other boys were not included in the plans because we did not think them mature enough to cope with such an enterprise.

Salwey had instructions to keep all contacts with me to the absolute minimum. When my mother's German friend came to the farm to ask Salwey to treat me humanely, he would not even talk to her. I ate all my meals alone in that small cubbyhole in the stable. Polish laborers were subject to numerous regulations. The use of bicycles was forbidden. Travel by bus or train required special permission. We even had to have a pass to go to the next village. We always had to wear the letter *P* sewn on our clothes. Our attempts to fasten the letter in a temporary manner were strictly forbidden. Salwey was very reluctant to give me permission to go anywhere; I would have to wait for the right moment to ask him. He also punished me from time to time. The usual punishment was not to give me any supper, but like all the local farmers, he also threatened to send me to Stutthof concentration camp. The longer the war lasted, the more likely this seemed. All of us had heard of people who had been sent there, and nothing more was ever heard of them. We consoled ourselves with the thought that the Germans were so short of labor that they would not carry out their threats, but the fear was there all the time. It became such an obsession that every time I saw a group of people being led along the road, I automatically imagined that they were being taken to Stutthof.

Salwey had a very condescending attitude toward Poles. One day when clearing out the attic, he threw out some sketches his son had done at school. I found them and drew a portrait of his daughter on the back of one. When he saw this drawing, Salwey told his wife that I must have German blood in me if I could draw as well as that. When I heard that, I was so annoyed that I also sketched his wife to prove that I did have ability and that I had not achieved a good likeness of the daughter by accident. Similarly, they were surprised when they noticed that I corresponded with my friends and relatives. They were convinced that all Poles were barely literate.

The food I was given was of very poor quality. After I had been at the farm for some time, they took on a fifteen-year-old Polish peasant girl named Reginka. The poor girl wept for her mother day and night for many weeks. When she had settled down somewhat, she used to bring me food from the kitchen. I also augmented my diet by stealing cream from the milk churns. I used my only cup for this purpose. I had no hot water to wash it out, so it developed a ring of cheese on the inside. It was unpleasant but did not deter me. Later Reginka used to take the cup to wash it in hot water in Salwey's kitchen when she was certain she would not be caught.

All the Poles on forced labor in the area used to meet as often as possible. If any of the farmers was known to be away on a Sunday, we would meet on his farm. These meetings were very important in keeping up our morale. We exchanged not only news but also items of a more tangible nature. One of the boys, Kazik, had access to a radio and used to listen to the broadcasts from London, thus keeping us informed about the situation on the war fronts. We anxiously waited for this news. Another member of our group knew some English, and he would write the latest news from London on scraps of paper, which were then left along the path taken by English prisoners of war from Stalag XX B on their way to work. They in turn left us cigarettes. We all helped each other as much as we could. Clothing was obtained in various ways and then exchanged. Once I took a pair of boots belonging to Salwey's son, who had gone into the army. They were hanging up in the attic and I knew they would not be needed for a long time. I exchanged them with a Pole from another farm, on the condition that he in turn pass them on to someone even farther away.

Since we were not supposed to be out after 9:00 p.m., we did not use the roads to reach our meeting places but went across the fields. Once in November 1941, I was returning from one of our gatherings and I had to cross a very narrow bridge over a canal. As I approached the area, I saw SA men on sentry duty. Since they were bound to see me if I tried to cross the bridge, I decided to go over the ice. The ice held until I reached the far side of the canal, but there it was very thin and cracked under my weight. I barely managed to keep from falling into the water by grabbing some overhanging branches. The noise alerted the sentries, who ran toward me. Fortunately, they were on the other side of the canal and I managed to avoid capture. But for days I was petrified that they would trace me across the fields to Salwey's farm. Since the farms were scattered, it was at least theoretically possible for my route to be followed.

The younger Poles adapted themselves to their new lives fairly well. The older ones had more problems. I was once sent to another farm to translate for a Polish woman, about forty years of age, who was said to have gone insane. The day I saw her, she was still coherent, though clearly upset. She kept repeating, "What have they done to us?" When I went to see her a week or so later, she no longer recognized me. She was taken away and I never heard of her again. It later transpired that she came from the Bydgoszcz area. Her own farm had been taken by the Germans, and her husband had been sent to a concentration camp.

Dąbrowski managed to reach England in 1944 and later served with the Polish First Armored Division. He completed his studies after the war and worked as an engineering technician. Now retired, he pursues an interest in the postal history of Poland.

BOGNA DOMAŃSKA

One morning I heard a banging on my apartment door. I had allowed my apartment to be used by the *Rada Pomocy Żydom* (Council for Aid to Jews), so many Jews showed up there. The address was No. 5 Mławska Street. It was very close to the ghetto and therefore was very dangerous. My older son opened the door that morning, and Dr. Alfred Borenstein entered. He was almost unconscious, propping himself up with a stave of wood. We knew him to be a charming, cultured man who spoke Polish well; he did not have Semitic features. He and his wife, along with several other Jews, were living on Leszno Street with a Polish family.

Dr. Borenstein told us that the previous evening two Poles had stopped him and demanded twenty thousand złotys. If these men did not receive the money, they threatened to denounce him to the Germans. He told them he did not have that much money, but he would try to get what they wanted by the following evening. Last night he and his wife had been so terrified that they had taken a large dose of sleeping tablets. This morning he had been unable to awaken his wife, and indeed he himself was barely conscious. He had come to ask for help. I urged Dr. Borenstein to sit down and told my sixteen-year old son to get him some tea while I tried to get the money from Władyslaw Bartoszewski [a prominent member of *Żegota*, the Council for Aid to Jews]. I could not find Bartoszewski or any of my other superiors. I returned, after about an hour, with nothing.

Dr. Borenstein decided that he had to get back to his wife. Personally, I thought it very likely that she was no longer alive. However, my son and I took him to the nearest streetcar to Leszno, which left from Teatralny Square. It was still early and there was an empty streetcar waiting. The young conductor must have realized what was going on, because when I asked him to take Dr. Borenstein to Leszno, he assured me that he would not let the older man get off if it was unsafe. Since Dr. Borenstein was not himself, my son volunteered to accompany him. Some time later my son rushed back home in a state of shock. As the streetcar neared Leszno, the conductor stopped the vehicle because a crowd of civilians and Germans had gathered there. But that did not prevent Dr. Borenstein from rushing off to look for his wife. The crowd had gathered because all the occupants of the apartment building where Dr. Borenstein lived had been taken out and executed, including a Polish family and their children and all the Jews. Dr. Borenstein was one of the casualties.

In the Council for Aid to Jews, I was involved, among other things, in the transfer of money to Jews. I often dealt with Fajner, who looked like an old Polish *szlachcic* (aristocrat). There was relatively little problem in transferring sterling or American dollars, since the bundles of money were not very bulky. However, złotys were a different matter. Tens of thousands of notes were involved. The money was brought to me in large bundles of wood that had been hollowed out. The courier who delivered them always carried some spare wood for sale in case he was stopped by the Germans along the way. The caretaker of my apartment building asked why I needed so much wood. I told her a story about my preference for wood over coal, and she was apparently satisfied because there was no trouble.

The most terrifying day of my life was the day I went into the ghetto. A letter had come to the Council for Aid to Jews from a Polish officer who was a German prisoner of war. The letter was for his wife, who was of Jewish extraction. At that time she was looked after in the ghetto by Father Marceli Godlewski who, despite his rather right-wing views, had insisted on remaining in the ghetto looking after his parishioners—converts from Judaism—in the parish of All Saints at Grzybowski Square. Both the Polish officer and his wife were very worried about each other; the wife was quite distraught. I was asked to go to the ghetto and give her the letter. Carrying false documents and wearing the requisite arm band, I went into the ghetto. On the way to the church, I visited a friend of my father's from his days at the Polytechnic, a Jew from Łódź, to whom I took a student photograph. I also saw Dorota Zylberbaum, a primary school teacher, who was a friend of my mother's. I brought her a small memento.

In the ghetto, corpses were lying in the street. Small children sat on the curbstones. I remember a small girl with a tiny baby in her arms. I gave what food I had to the children, but there were Germans wandering about so I had to be very careful.

At the church, Father Godlewski asked me whether I wanted to meet the woman for whom I had brought the letter. I declined on the grounds that the less one knew, the better. But I asked for a letter to forward to her husband because he was so worried. Meanwhile, I sat in the sacristy, thinking about how—or even whether—I would get back home. Again the priest asked me to meet the woman; again I declined. In the end we met, but without seeing each other's faces. Then I left.

The ghetto was divided into two parts, connected by a narrow road that led to the entrance of the Pawiak prison. The road was packed with people. I was so frightened by the crush that I went into the foyer of an apartment building. All I could see was a sea of heads; there was no question of anyone being able to move on an individual basis. Everyone was just carried along. Suddenly the characteristic sirens of German vehicles could be heard. There was a slight panic. The German vehicles came into sight. First a horse-drawn cart appeared, carrying two Gestapo agents armed with whips, which they used on the crowd. Cars loaded with officials followed. Finally, I saw a trailer with prisoners being taken to Pawiak. There was an incredible silence. Only the voices of the Germans could be heard. After they had passed, about a third of the people were lying on the ground. Suddenly there was a great surge of voices as the Germans insisted that the dead and wounded be cleared away.

I intended to leave the same way that I had come—namely, by climbing the wall of a mansion from a road in the ghetto. Friends were waiting for me at the top of the wall; the mansion in the non-Jewish part of Warsaw. It was winter and the wall was very slippery. Opposite this wall there had previously been a shop; now there was only a kind of alcove where an old Jew stood behind a counter, on which stood a soda-water syphon. As I stood in this alcove, waiting for the right moment to climb the wall, I heard German voices and saw three Gestapo agents coming toward me in the dark. The old Jew gave no sign of seeing me, though he could have given me away, and fortunately the Germans walked by without seeing me. But a Jewish policeman had seen me. Once the Gestapo had passed, he jumped out to see what I was up to. He told me that whether I was Polish or Jewish, I had no right to be there. I told him that my friends would see to him if I was harmed in any way. At that moment, the voices of my friends could be heard at the top of the wall. That is when he said he would ignore me. I then told him it would be better if he were kinder to the Jews. He retorted that I must be Jewish, after all. I replied that it was none of his business who I was.

It was the most terrible day of my life. Seeing the hell of the ghetto, my own fear was so great that there were moments when I did not know whether I would have the strength or the courage to go back there. I came out full of admiration for Father Godlewski, who voluntarily remained in the ghetto. Hungry as I was, it was a long time before I could eat anything.

The courthouse on Leszno Street was a meeting place for Poles and Jews. A Polish couple had arranged to help a Jewish family, but only the little boy stayed with the Polish couple; his parents decided to go back to the ghetto to nurse a sick grandmother. I supplied the Polish couple with money to look after the boy from the Council for Aid to Jews, since the husband earned very little as an artist. The boy was a beautiful child but very suspicious; he refused to come anywhere near me. On another occasion I brought him a toy, but I got the same reaction. I was very shaken when the woman told me that the child had refused to have anything to do with me because he had been forced to show a German that he had been circumcised. Eventually, the Polish couple went to the country for safety, though I still met them from time to time to give them money. The wife later worried about which religion to raise the boy in. She knew nothing about the Jewish religion; besides, it was dangerous to teach Judaism. I told her not to worry, advising her to do the best she could in the circumstances because, after all, it was the same God.

After the Warsaw Uprising, Domańska was imprisoned in Zeitheim and later Molsdorf. She then joined the Polish Second Corps in Italy. She later went to England, where she taught school and then worked for a jewelry manufacturer. She was prominently featured in the recent television series "The Struggles for Poland."

WANDA DRACZYŃSKA

During the German occupation, there never was a moment when we did not feel threatened. Every time we left home, we never knew whether we would ever see it again.

In Warsaw, most people had some affiliation with an underground organization, even if they did not formally take an oath. I always seemed to be running errands for the Home Army without formally being a member. In the end, I got rather annoyed with this state of affairs and decided to do something about it. I told a friend whom I suspected of being involved in the Home Army that I wanted to join. She told me where to go. When I arrived at the appointed place, I found that they knew all about me, and I was allowed to take the oath.

I was assigned to the decoding department and received instructions by telephone to go to a certain apartment at 6:00 p.m. On the way I felt very conspicuous. I thought that everyone was looking at me and everyone knew where I was going. When I got to the apartment, my contact told me we would have to leave immediately, so we left, taking her suitcases with us, and went to a safe apartment that belonged to a lieutenant in the Home Army. I was disappointed that while everyone around me seemed to be in danger from the Nazis, I alone seemed to have no exciting experiences.

In 1939 my brother had been wounded during the defense of Lwów. A dum-dum bullet had shattered his hand, and though the wound had subsequently healed, he had lost the use of it. His early attempts to leave Poland failed, and he returned to Warsaw, where he joined the underground. Our apartment became a safe house for various illegal papers and documents and sometimes weapons. I lived in constant fear of arrest.

One day my brother's friend arrived at our apartment with his wife and child because their apartment had been compromised. At about 7:00 a.m. we received a telephone call from this man's place of work to report that he was being pursued by the Gestapo. We all left the apartment immediately. I took the child in its carriage; the others went to a relative of mine. Eventually, my brother's friend and his wife went to the country to hide, and the child was taken to their relatives in Piotrków Trybunalski. After hiding for some time, we returned to our homes. But as so often happened, that is precisely what the Germans were waiting for.

My brother lived in his own apartment because he had gotten married after returning to Warsaw. At 6:00 a.m. on May 31, 1944, my mother and I got a phone call to say that my brother had been arrested. He had made arrangements with my mother that in case anything happened to him, she was to go to his apartment and clear out the hiding places where he kept incriminating materials. Three of us went to the apartment. I stayed outside while my mother went into the apartment and removed whatever my brother had hidden. Some days later we heard that the Gestapo had gone to my brother's apartment and torn the place apart. But they found nothing. Initially my sister-in-law was not arrested, but in a short time she was told that the Germans were also looking for her, and she remained in hiding.

Some weeks later my mother received a note telling her to come to Gestapo headquarters at 8:00 a.m. for questioning. We were advised to go into hiding, but my mother refused to do so, saying that if she did not show up, she would automatically condemn her son. We arranged that she would telephone if and when she was released. She took a spare pair of stockings in her handbag and went to Gestapo headquarters. As she told me later, she was surrounded by Germans, armed with machine guns, and taken to a room with a large table on which there were many copies of various underground press publications. There a German official addressed her in Polish. He asked her why had she not gone down on her knees and begged him to release her son. My mother answered that her son was innocent, to which the German replied that in that case her son should have held on to her apron strings. Then she was shown photographs of people who had been in our apartment and asked what she thought of the underground press. She told him she did not think the publications were worth the sacrifice involved. After that, they let her go. She telephoned me as we had arranged, and we met in town and went home together. Her greatest fear had been that they would confront her with her son as a prisoner, but that had not happened.

Some time later, I heard a car stop at the gateway to our apartment house. I rushed to the window and saw the Gestapo hammering on the gate. I immediately woke my mother and told her to get dressed because it appeared that the Gestapo had come for us. We lived on the fourth floor, and we listened for the sound of heavy footsteps coming up the stairs. But they stopped halfway up the steps, and then there was silence. After an interval, we heard them leave the building, and from the window, we saw the Gestapo examining what looked like photograph albums. We learned later that the owner of the lower apartment had been away at the time, and the German search had revealed nothing. Little did the Gestapo know that the owner of the apartment looked after parachutists who were dropped clandestinely over Poland by planes from England.

We received a message from my brother from Pawiak prison, asking us to arrange a transfer. We were given the name of a German in the SA who seemed to be quite human and who had been instrumental in securing the release of our neighbor's husband. We went to see him. He told us there was absolutely no question of my brother being released, as there was too much evidence against him, and the only alternative was for him to be transferred to a concentration camp. Because of my brother's useless hand, we worried he would be unable to work in the concentration camp and was likely to be executed.

The matter was soon taken out of our hands when the Warsaw Uprising broke out. We hoped he might have been freed during the uprising. But we heard nothing of my brother until many years later. My father was on vacation in Bournemouth, England, and met someone who told him that my brother's execution was described in a book entitled *Za Murami Pawiaka (Behind the Walls of Pawiak)*.

During the war, we had very little money. My mother managed to get a license to sell alcohol and cigarettes. I worked in the office of a trading company under nominal German control, though two of the directors were Polish. Both of them used the premises unofficially. One had business interests in a dried vegetable packing concern; the other did work for the Government Delegate's office and the Home Army, and I used to type his correspondence. The offices were near Napoleon Square and were often raided by the Gestapo. Every time the Germans showed up, all compromising materials were hidden.

My cousin Krysia, who was later tortured and finally executed by the Gestapo for her activity in the Home Army, once asked me to help her find work for Wanda (I do not remember the surname), the daughter of my cousin's Jewish doctor. Both of Wanda's parents were in the ghetto, but Wanda had managed to stay on the Aryan side. She was married to a Roman Catholic Pole. I managed to get her a job packing dried vegetables, and I alone knew that she was Jewish.

Traveling with false papers, Draczyńska managed to leave Poland with her mother in October 1945. They went first to Italy and from there emigrated to England in 1946. Draczyńska married in 1947 and found work with an insurance company. She now lives in London and works as a volunteer for the Polish Institute and Sikorski Museum.

WŁADYSŁAW AND WŁADYSŁAWA DUBIK

Between the wars, in the community of Grodzisko Dolne there lived approximately fifty Jewish families. They were engaged primarily in trade; they also worked as shoemakers, tailors, and wagon drivers.

After the occupation of the area by the Germans, the Jews received instructions to gather at assembly points, and from there they were carried off in wagons to camps in Pelkinie near Jarosław.

Those who did not present themselves voluntarily to die were later captured by a Gestapo agent sent from Jarosław, a man by the name of Jeske or Joske. He apparently was a German who had llved in Poland, because he knew Polish. He took the Jews he had caught to a cemetery where he personally shot them. The community was obligated to appoint someone to dig the graves. This function was performed by Jan Chmura and Stanisław Kuras, who live in the town of Grodzisko to this day.

Not all the Jews allowed themselves to be caught, especially those who before the war had enjoyed good relations with the Poles. These Jews were hidden by Poles. In the home of Stanisław Baj, who at that time was mayor of the village, a married couple by the name of Fingerhut, who called themselves Konicz, was hidden. The couple survived to the liberation, when the commandant of the local Polish militia personally escorted them to the railway station in Lancut, where they departed for Kraków. Later they left Poland for the United States, where they still live.

In Chałupka, now Nowe Grodzisko, Stanisław Faust-Styczyński, hid himself and lives there to this day. His sister-in-law, Hanna Faust-Hajcer, also survived. She worked during the occupation as a nurse in Lublin.

The daughter of Liby Winegarten also survived among Poles. After the liberation she lived in Leżajsk, then moved to the West.

Antoni Majkut, called Chaptys, from Grodzisko Górne, was sent to a concentration camp for hiding a Jew. He died there.

Szul Kestenbaum survived the occupation; he was hidden by Poles. He even carried a revolver.

Stanislaw Dec in Grodzisko Dolne hid Jews, and during the time of a general search of homes, he was shot.

In 1941, Mrs. Verderbeer came to Grodzisko from Kraków with her children and hid herself there. Later she decided to return to Kraków, and in 1942 a Polish woman, Maria Markocka-Lichorowiec, helped the entire family to return there.

In Grodzisko Dolne, near Orenda, a Jewish woman married a Pole by the name of Rydzik. She survived the occupation. After the liberation, she left her husband and fled the country.

Before the war, Chaim (or Illex) Beller lived in Grodzisko. He left the town before the war and now lives in France. In 1981, he published a book in French about Grodzisko. He wrote about the Jews living there and concluded by saying that the Germans burned his town. This is not true because some Jewish homes stand there to this day; there never was any fire in the town of Grodzisko. The community council took charge of the Jewish cemetery and appointed a Pole, Mieczysław Piasecki, to take care of it.

Before the war, the Jews dominated all commerce. They derived profit from the Poles, and for this reason they were not liked by the residents. After the war, they dominated all of the highest offices, including the police establishment. They were responsible for the death of many innocent Poles.

After the war, Władysław Dubik was employed by the local government of Grodzisko. His wife, Władysława, worked in the local library. Both are now retired.

MARIA DUSZKIEWICZ

My husband was a major in the Polish army. I received one letter from him from Starobielsk,* but after that all trace of him vanished. We lived on an estate at Rembertów. When the Germans came, I went to Brześć (Brest-Litovsk), where I met a Russian who told me to return home. Fortunately, my apartment had not been requisitioned, so I lived there with my son until his death of diphtheria in 1941. I lived by selling my possessions; the first to go was the dining room suite, which I sold to a trader who came to the apartment. With the proceeds I bought flour, potatoes, and sugar. In the winter of 1939-40, the Germans allowed wives of Polish officers to go to the army forest to buy wood.

After my son died, I went to Warsaw to look for work. I had never worked before, but I eventually found employment in the Wilbra factory, which produced paints and other chemicals on Ceglana Street in the ghetto. I remember seeing how the Jews were taken away while the children called for their mothers.

One morning I arrived at work only to be told to go back home because the Warsaw Uprising was due to start at 4:00 p.m. At that time I lived on Narbut Street in Mokotów. For several days the Home

Army fought with Molotov cocktails, but then had nothing left to fight with. The Germans came and took all the men to the barracks on Rakowiecka Street. My friend's son was taken away and she asked me to go and visit him in her place because she could not bear to go herself. The Germans let us go to visit the men at midday. We made a white flag out of some material and went. There were many corpses on Narbut Square. When we got to the barracks, I saw Zbyszek (I do not remember his surname) and talked to him. What struck me most was how annoyed he was that his mother had not come to see him herself.

Tiger tanks were everywhere. A woman who leaned out of a gateway was shot. She lay there for some time, but no one could get to her. Eventually someone tried to pull her into the entrance, but he too was shot, and the two bodies lay there for several days.

Then one day the Kalmucks came. They were drunk. They stole only what they wanted, then poured petrol over everything else and set it on fire. I went to stay with a friend in a house on the same street that was still standing. A few days later the Germans took us all away. First we went through the ruins to the railway station. Then we went to Pruszków, where we were herded into cattle trucks. Seventy people were crowded into a truck with no water or anything else for two days. The only toilet facilities were in full view of the guards on the few occasions when the trucks were opened.

Finally, we arrived at Mauthausen. All the inmates there were very upset when they learned that women and children had been brought to Mauthausen. All the women were made to strip their clothes off and take a bath while a ring of German guards stood around us and watched. I felt so depressed and humiliated that I cried, but Mrs. Grabik told me not to be stupid and not to look at the men who ogled us.

While at Mauthausen I worked for a farm near the camp. There I had to perform drudgery such as cleaning the floor of a pigsty that had obviously never been cleaned before. The farmer's wife always taunted me for doing such humiliating work, reminding me that I was a Polish major's wife. Later I was forced to work in an underground aircraft factory near Graz.

When I was moved from Mauthausen, one of the Polish physicians with whom I worked gave me some bread. He also asked me to write to him from wherever we were being taken. He thought we were going to be exterminated, and he wanted to find out if his suspicions were correct.

The Soviet camps at Starobielsk, Kozielsk, and Ostashkov were initially used to imprison Polish officers and enlisted men who found themselves on the Soviet side of the Molotov-Ribbentrop Line, which had been decided by the Soviet-German Non-Aggression Pact. Fifteen thousand of these prisoners disappeared. Then in April 1943, the Germans announced the discovery of the corpses of more than four thousand Polish soldiers, most of whom were officers, in the forest of Katyn, and they charged the Soviets with the atrocity. The German allegations were correct; the Soviets were responsible for the mass murders. See J.K. Zawodny, *Death in the Forest: The Story of the Katyn Forest Massacre* (Notre Dame: University of Notre Dame Press, 1962).

After the war, Duszkiewicz was liberated by the Americans and joined the Polish Second Corps in Italy. From there she went to England, where she has lived since 1947.

EUGENIUSZ M. FOLTA

In June 1942, I started to work in an ammunition factory in Hasag in Częstochowa. In the concentration camp near the factory, there were several thousand Jewish inmates. I estimated eight thousand to ten thousand people.

I had completed commercial school at the head of my class, and I worked in the factory's bookkeeping department, calculating costs. By virtue of my job, I had access to various offices and positions in the factory. At the beginning, I survived the selection of prisoners whom the Germans deported for execution.

I tried to help the unfortunates in the concentration camp within the limits of the possibilities open to me. The inmates begged for bread and onions. Furnishing bread to the inmates was not easy because of the presence of guards. For giving bread, my brother was arrested and my father paid with his life in Gross-Rosen concentration camp.

I received a special allocation of bread and vodka for working in the munitions factory. The vodka I exchanged for more bread, and often I gave away my own portion. I began to experience more and more difficulty in furnishing bread and onions to the inmates, but I found a way out of the problem: I became acquainted with two Ukrainian guards of the *Werkschutz* (Work Security). Today I cannot really explain how that happened. Perhaps it was my attitude in not admitting my advantage over them. Knowing the Ukrainian language allowed me little by little to change their attitude and to warn them that, in the end, after Germany's defeat in the war, they would be hanged. At any rate, they began to help me in providing bread. Moreover, the two of them deserted at the beginning of 1944. I remember the name of only one of them: Jan Sabat, from the vicinity of Borysław.

One day, on my way to the kitchen, I met my friend from the gymnasium, Henryk Wodzisławski. Since he was a Jew, he ended up in the concentration camp. With his help, I established contact with the Jewish Fighting Organization, which was active in the camp. I arranged a contact between my friend Wodzisławski and the guard Sabat. He made possible Wodzisławski's flight to the partisans in Kielce in October or November 1943. An entire group [of Jews] also fled. I do not remember the circumstances; besides, it was better at the time not to know.

Toward the end of November 1943, a messenger came to me carrying a letter from Wodzisławski, who wanted to establish contact with the Jewish Fighting Organization in the concentration camp. The messenger was a young girl who came once or twice a month with an infant in her arms. In the baby's clothes and shoes were letters written in code, newspapers, and money. (The underground press was printed on very thin paper.) I did not know then and do not know now the messenger's name. Nor do I know where she came from. Under the circumstances, it was better not to know.

I remember the sums of money she brought. Each time we received an amount between ten thousand and fifteen thousand dollars. I remember because it was my obligation to give all of the money to the Jewish organization in the concentration camp.

My first contact with that group is well fixed in my mind. The girl messenger told me to go to a watchmaker in the concentration camp and ask for someone who used the code name "Black One." It was necessary for him to transmit the first letter establishing contact between the partisan group of the Jewish Fighting Organization and the group that operated in the concentration camp.

It was difficult for me to get to the watchmaker. I did not have a special reason for going there. Using the pretext that I needed my watch repaired, I received permission from a German official to see the watchmaker. In keeping with my instructions I asked for the "Black One." A man made himself known and assured me that he was that person.

After the war, I found out that there were two men from different organizations in the concentration camp who used the same code name. A quarrel developed about the contact with me. It could have ended badly, but finally the matter was resolved.

Further contacts were not easy. I established a pattern of having a Jew repair a calculator in my office and making contact with him at the time of the break for dinner. While extending my hand in greeting, I handed over a consignment of the underground press and the money. Handing things over in the factory or the camp was dangerous because of searches and street roundups. Sometimes the surveillance was so intense that handing over a consignment took several days. I organized and conducted the entire operation to deliver the underground press and the money from the High Command of the Jewish Fighting Organization until the liberation in 1945.

Folta, who lives in retirement in Bytom, Poland, says he now seldom thinks of his wartime experiences.

The following letter, provided by Dr. Teresa Prekerowa, a Polish professor of history, cites Folta's contributions:

Częstochowa, 23 April 1945
District Jewish Committee in Częstochowa
To [Eugeniusz] Marian Folta in Częstochowa:

The Jewish Committee in Częstochowa expresses its sincere and warm thanks to citizen Folta for his many heroic deeds, discharged on behalf of Jews interned in the concentration camp of Hasag in Częstochowa.

By furnishing the underground press, correspondence, and money from the High Command of the Jewish Fighting Organization, he contributed remarkably to the maintenance of the spirit of underground work in Jewish organizations in the above-mentioned concentration camp.

(Signed) S. Markowicz, Chairman
Jewish Committee

For the former conspiratorial committee in Hasag:
A. Czarny [Czara]
L. Brener

BRONISŁAWA GNIEWASZEWSKA

Did I help Jews during the occupation? It was entirely normal for me to help someone whom the Germans intended to kill. But I do not like to talk about it.

In 1943, I lived in the village of Woźnik, a short distance from the prewar German frontier, together with my mother, sister, and two brothers. I was the youngest child. We lived in the third house from the main road. Often Jews came to us from the town of Żelów, a distance of twenty-five kilometers. They hid in our barn for two or three days. Then I would escort them to Piotrków Trybunalski. At night, they secretly crossed the "green frontier"—a dangerous field, an open space. Then there were two villages—Mzurki and Budków— where Germans lived. In Mzurki there was a police station. At that point I escorted them to Piotrków Trybunalski.

At the very least, I was afraid. I walked several hundred meters in front of them. We had an understanding that in the event of some danger or if I saw something suspicious, I would stop and they would flee to the side. If there was a German patrol, I would try to talk to them to stop them. Some Jews returned to Żelów, and they too stopped with us. Then I would escort them across the green frontier. I did not interest myself in their names, but I do remember two— Laski and Manel. They were Jews in Piotrków whom I helped and contacted later. I also remember two brothers, twenty or thirty years old. Their name was Bicz. Several times I escorted them in both directions. I know that in 1946 they left for Israel.

In 1944, the Germans began to deport Poles from Woźnik and to settle German people there to put an end to the crossing of the frontier. From February to April of that year, I lived in Warsaw in the home of Mr. and Mrs. Frackiewicz at 120 Grochowska St. The apartment was on the second floor. The Frackiewiczs helped Jews. A Jewish family with a little boy of three years was sheltered there for about two months. Later the Frackiewiczs arranged other lodgings for them in Saska Kępa, where they stayed until someone informed on them and they were caught by the Germans. En route to the concentration camp, the Jewish couple tore out a board in the railroad car and let the child down through the hole. Later they themselves jumped out.

Something happened that they were unable to find the child. They searched for three days in the woods, but they did not find him. When they returned to Grochowska Street in Warsaw, they were in shock. They stayed in the apartment for two weeks. Mr. Frackiewicz then found them another place to stay—I don't know where—because it had become too dangerous on Grochowska Street. They walked barefoot in the apartment to muffle any sound. If anyone rang the doorbell, they hid themselves in a secret receptacle in a wardrobe behind the tile stove. I remember how the mother despaired after the loss of her child. The worst thing I remember were the moans I heard from the secret hiding place.

The Frackiewiczs often helped Jews. In May 1944, Mr. Frackie-wiczs's daughter, Hanka, brought to us in Woźnik a Jewish woman and a child, Adasia, who was four years old. The mother and son lived with us for about six weeks. When the Germans prepared the village for deportation, the two had to leave for Warsaw. I do not know what happened to the child.

Gniewaszewska completed her secondary education in Poland after the war. She is now a retired postal worker.

ZOFIA GRUSZCZYŃSKA

Beginning in the fall of 1941 and continuing through the winter and spring of 1942, the Germans brought Jews to the camp in Szebniach. Poles, Gypsies, and even Soviet prisoners were also brought there.

One day, old man Kiwa came to our house and said to my father: "Wasik, I came to say farewell because pretty soon we will all be together. The Germans say that Jews should go to the Promised Land. They are making camps and deporting large groups of Jews there." In the fall of 1942, the head of the village received an order to supply horse transport for the Kiwas, who were to report with their packed suitcases at the registration depot in Brzostka. Our Kiwa left with his family, and we never heard from them again.

In Brzostka, Jews were loaded into heavy trucks, vulgarly known as *budy* (doghouses), with their belongings. All types of baggage were sent on different heavy trucks. The Germans told the Jews that they were going to a registration depot in Szebniach where they would receive their luggage and then wait for a transport to the "Promised Land." The trucks with the people never reached Szebniach. Four kilometers outside Szebniach, they turned left to the Warzycki Woods and there they were put into trenches, killed, and covered with quick-lime. After this massacre, the Germans had a drinking bout in a villa at the end of the woods, in the village of Berówka.

From the Kiwa family, only one son was saved. His name was Herszek. When the Germans surrounded his house in Kaczoroway, he jumped out a window. He found shelter at the home of a friend from childhood days, Rozalia Kurc, a widow living with her two children near the Smarzowski Woods. There Herszek lived in the barn, coming out only to get fresh air at night. He also at night made contact with a few other people who lived on the edge of the Sobczyków Woods. Rozalia had a hard enough time feeding her own hungry family, so Herszek risked his life by wandering at night in search of food. If Herszek is still alive, I believe he is in New York.

Fisiek and Mechcio, the sons of Moskowa from Grudny, ran away before the raids. They too lived through the war with Polish friends. When their mother came to collect the family, she hid with neighbors. There she lived, for several months, but during the raid for Jews early in the spring of 1943, she tried to escape from her hiding place and was shot. Her two youngest children, Sianda and Nusiek, were sent, like Kiwa, to the registration depot in Brzostka.

One day at the end of summer in 1942, I was returning from my sisters in Jaso . . . . On my way to the railroad station, . . . as I neared a place where the street led up a hill, I heard a sharp "Halt!" A German with a helmet on his head pointed his rifle at me and threatened my way. In my childish simplicity, I did not realize the danger. I was only thirteen years old. I turned and followed a path leading to Glinik.

I got to a hill where old one-story houses with gardens were separated from the market place of the city by a wall. As I came to the houses, I heard women screaming and children shrieking, and over them the yelling and cursing of Germans. I walked along a narrow path between two homes, where the wooden gate from the street was closed. I saw blood under the gate. My veins froze.

In the marketplace were several heavy trucks into which Germans herded the Jews—women, children, and old people. Jewish men who were able to work had been arrested and sent away earlier. Feathers were flying from ripped pillows and feather beds. Bundles of clothes were kicked around. Women hugged their children to their breasts, trying to protect them with their bodies from being beaten by the German whips. One woman who stooped to pick up a small bundle or suitcase was hit on the head with a whip and dropped her baby. The German picked up the infant by the feet and, with all his strength, smashed its head against the brick wall of the church. Other Germans tore babies from the arms of their mothers and threw them like stones inside the heavy trucks. They kicked old people helpless on the ground and women who had dropped to their knees. I put my fist in my mouth, and leaning with my other hand against the wall, I hurried to the garden among the sunflowers. My instinct to save myself helped me to hurry down the road, and I ran farther and farther away.

My brother-in-law, Antek, as the owner of a horse, had to haul logs from the forest to the sawmill in Kolacice. At home, we were often hungry and cold. At the beginning of 1943, we had to deliver grain quotas to the Germans. Not giving up the required quota meant being sent to Auschwitz. One day early in the morning, Antek went to the forest, taking with him a potato pancake for breakfast. Around noon he carried the wood to the sawmill, and while he waited in line for the wood to be unloaded, he was eating his first meal of the day— the cold potato pancake. A German came up to him, hit him in the face, and yelled, "You Polish swine! You, eating?" He knocked the pancake out of Antek's hand and ordered him to pick it up and feed it to the horse. In the evening, Antek returned home, drenched, muddied, hungry, and with a black eye.

One cold evening, someone knocked at our door. Mother opened it and let in two ragged people, a man and a woman. The red-headed man had a Semitic face. The woman held a child in a worn blanket, a little boy about two years old. The man introduced himself as Thomas Terlecki, a barber from Lwów. He said they were on their way to Tarnów, looking for employment.

My parents asked no questions. Mama stoked up the stove, heating water for bathing. Since we had only a one-room house, the barn served as the bathroom. Mother gave the newcomers her own linen, fed them potato soup, and prepared a makeshift bed for them by spreading out bundles of straw on the floor. After eating supper, our three guests knelt down and conspicuously said Catholic prayers aloud. After a few minutes, they fell into a sound sleep. The woman was restless, several times muttering words in her sleep we did not understand, cuddling her sleeping child close to her.

Our guests stayed with us through the week. Often when someone knocked on our door, we had to hide them in the barn. People often came to our home, bringing shoes for my father to repair. After a week, my father escorted our guests at night to my uncle, Leonard. There they stayed approximately two weeks, after which they headed in the direction of Tarnów. I do not know whether they survived the war and the annihilation of their race. On the other hand, I do know that the residents of Baczaka, Brzezin, Grudny and other villages, especially those who resided near the woods and streams, often took in Jews. In Grudny Górny, a resident by the name of Kaczka sheltered a Jewish family during the entire war, just as Rozalia Kurc had sheltered Herszek.

In the fall of 1943, a large detachment of SS-men, dressed in black uniforms with the insignia of skulls and crossbones on their hats, came to Jasło. Officers were quartered in private homes. Mr. Matera, for whom my sister Maria had worked in 1943, had been arrested. After he spent several days in the prison in Jasło, the Germans sent him to the concentration camp in Szebniach. The SS requisitioned one of the two rooms in Matera's home. With the help of one of the SS-men, my sister had received permission to take a change of clothing to Matera. The clothing that my sister brought back from Szebniach was soiled with dried blood and pus. Later the Germans sent Matera to Auschwitz.

The Germans used the room in the house with an entrance from the hall. The other room had an entrance from the kitchen. The windows of both rooms faced west. After the arrest of Mr. Matera, quite often I visited my sister, staying with her a few days. I remember one visit during the Christmas holidays. After a warm, sunny day, a light frost covered the ground in the evening. My sister and I were getting ready for sleep when we heard a scratching at the window in our room. My sister thought it was a cat. She opened the window. At once a completely naked man jumped through the window. He was about twenty-eight years old. His body was streaming with blood. Words cannot describe our fright. Behind the wall, in the next room were the SS officers. The three of us stood like stone. Then we heard the door open into the kitchen and the footsteps of one of the Germans coming toward our room. My sister pointed to the couch, and the man jumped like lightning under the covers.

Into our room came the taller officer. He looked at us, then at the floor, which was covered with blood. He went to the couch, raised the covers, and said: "Wash and dress." Pointing to the open window, he told the man: "That way." Then he left the room. We could not believe the generosity of the German.

My sister brought a pan of water. While he washed, our guest told us where he came from. He said that at about five o'clock, the Germans had loaded three heavy trucks with Jews at Szebniach concentration camp and hauled them to the Warzycki Woods. Two other trucks were loaded with Germans. In the woods the Germans surrounded the Jews and commanded them to undress and stand on the edge of the trenches that had been dug. Our guest, already naked, ran like a tiger, not thinking of the German machine guns. Thanks to his swift running, he reached the thick brush. Luckily, not one bullet hit him. With whatever strength he had, he ran through the woods and into the fields. He dragged himself to the vicinity of Jasło, where the Matera orchard looked like a heaven. By then, it was very late. He could not go any farther naked, so he knocked at our window.

After a few minutes, which felt like an eternity, again the German officer entered the room, carrying army boots in his hand. Hanging across his shoulder were underwear and socks. I remember that they were white woollen socks. He opened the closet door and saw Mr. Matera's suit. He pointed to it and left the room. In less than a minute, our guest had dressed in the German's underwear and the short pants, sweater, and coat that he had taken from the closet. He left by the window, without saying a word. With a heavy beat in our hearts, we waited to hear shots from the other window in our house. But there were none. How much time elapsed, I don't know. We thought it was an eternity.

Again the German entered the room. He showed the blood stains on the floor to my sister and said: in broken Polish, "Wash and clean it as though no one had been here. Nothing has happened. Laugh and talk as usual. Any minute my roomate will return. He is a rascal. . . . Forget this incident. My name is Willi Dikiel. I am Bavarian. I became a member of the SS so I could help people as much as possible. Sometimes that is possible, but not always. This time I was able to do it because I was alone. I have an old mother at home and would like to return to her. Remember, no one was here." He left.

After some time, the SS division left Jasło for the eastern front. Did Willi Dikiel rescue anyone else? Did he return to his old mother in Bavaria? I don't know.

A resident of Rzeszów, Poland, Gruszczyńska occasionally visits the United States, where she has many friends. She is retired.

URSZULA HOLFELD

My sister-in-law, Jadwiga Rydygier, was Jewish and was therefore confined to the Warsaw ghetto. I remember we received a telephone call one day asking us to bring her some sugar and if possible some alcohol. My husband, an army doctor killed at Katyń, had been part owner of a drug store on Żelazna Street, so I received an allowance of two kilos of sugar and one liter of alcohol every month. My sister and I went to the ghetto to take my sister-in-law the sugar and alcohol she had asked for. We entered the ghetto from the side guarded by Latvians because it was easier there. My sister-in-law met us, gave us arm bands with the Star of David to wear, and took us to where she lived. It was a tiny room filled with bedding but without any bed linen. When we returned home, the relative with whom we were living was furious because the Germans had announced that disease was rampant in the ghetto, and she was afraid that we might have caught some infection.

Some time later, in the winter of 1943-44, there was a knock on the door. By this time, my sister and I were living on our own. I opened the door to see a woman dressed in mourning. It was Jadwiga Rydygier. She had false papers. Though I was afraid, she stayed with us until the Warsaw Uprising of 1944. I taught her some Catholic prayers in case we were caught. One day her son, Wiesław, came to our apartment. He had no idea that she was there. We had been in the dining-room, and Jadwiga had hidden herself under the desk. Wiesław went into the bedroom to comb his hair in front of the mirror. Suddenly I saw him stop and look in the direction of the desk. He then continued combing his hair as if nothing had happened. It was only later, when we met again in Italy at the end of the war, that he told me he had seen his mother but had decided not to tell anyone, even me, in case something happened and we blamed him. He was fourteen or fifteen years old at the time.

On another occasion, Jadwiga was seen by Karol Zipser, the director of the firm where I worked. Normally, if anyone came, Jadwiga hid on a suitcase rack in the bathroom. For some reason, Zipser went into the bathroom and climbed up a ladder we kept there, but he said nothing. We all knew what was in store for us if the Germans found out. In the same apartment building there had lived a Polish policeman married to a Jewish woman; they were both shot by the Germans.

On August 1, 1944, I went to the Praga district of Warsaw to look for Zipser's brother, who had apparently been arrested on suspicion of sabotage. We had received information that he was in the custody of the German police in Praga. He was indeed there, bent over double in a low shed of some sort. While I was in the office asking the officer in charge, Lieutenant All, to release Zipser, a German soldier rushed in exclaiming that the uprising had started and that the post office and other buildings had been taken over by the Poles. Lieutenant All retorted that it was not the uprising, just sporadic shooting. But he did release Zipser.

We went to the Kierbedz Bridge to return to the other side of the Vistula, but the bridge had been closed by the Germans. Since we had nowhere else to go, we found shelter in the cellars of the Church of Our Lord's Resurrection, where we stayed for eleven days. One night Zipser and some others went to look for food. They found the stores of some charitable institution and took some meal which we mixed with water out of flowerpots and ate. I never went back to my apartment because I was deported to Bavaria. I only learned later that my sister-in-law had survived the war.

Early in the war, I remember coming home from work unexpectedly one day, to be met at the door by a complete stranger. For all I knew, he could have been a member of the Gestapo. However, when he said my sister had asked him to tell me that my meal was in the oven, I guessed he had nothing to do with the Germans. In the dining room were several other men sitting around the table. It was only then that I realized that my sister was involved with the Home Army. Until then, I had absolutely no idea. I had not allowed my sister to go out to work because I was always afraid that being a tall, blue-eyed blond, she would be taken by the Germans and end up in the *Rassenamt* [race office].

Holfeld was in Bavaria when the war ended. She then went to Italy and with the help of the Polish Second Corps, found her way to England. She later remarried.

STASZEK JACKOWSKI

I lived in Stanisławów in eastern Poland, where there were fewer Poles than Jews and Ukrainians. I think there was far less anti-Semitism in central Poland than in eastern Poland. One big reason for this was the fact that thousands of Jews willingly cooperated with the Soviets after their occupation of eastern Poland in 1939.

I have been called a hero because I saved the lives of thirty-two

Jewish men, women, and children in Stanisławów. I don't consider myself a hero; many other Poles also helped Jews. I did what I had to do. After all, Jews were human beings. But I never dreamed that my home would become a haven for so many of them.

It all started with my attempt to find and rescue an old school friend, Max Saginur. We had been friends for years, a friendship that both his parents and mine tried to discourage. Unless Jews were thoroughly assimilated, few of them wanted to have close personal relationships with Polish Gentiles.

The situation for the Jews in Stanisławów was horrible. They were forced by the Germans to build their own ghetto. Probably as many as eighty thousand of them were herded into it. Thousands were shot in the city; others were sent to the death camps.

Fortunately, I found my friend Max and his wife, Gitya, who, along with Gitya's brother and sister-in-law, made their way to my home from the ghetto early in 1943. At first I hid them in a partitioned area behind the kitchen, but that didn't work out because they almost suffocated from lack of air. Besides, it was possible to hear every move they made behind the partition. That's when I decided to build a bunker in the cellar.

Before it was all over, I ended up building three bunkers. Little by little, more and more Jews came to me for help. One group of Jews came from another "basket"—the name given to a place where Jews were hidden—that was maintained by another Polish rescuer. This Pole, Bogdanowicz, was afraid to keep his Jews any longer for fear of getting caught by the Gestapo. After all, any Pole caught helping a Jew was automatically executed. I even took in some Jews who had threatened to denounce me and their kinsmen whom I was hiding if I didn't help them.

I had made preparations to receive six Jewish physicians, but shortly before they were supposed to come to my home, the Gestapo arrested them. The unfortunate doctors took poison rather than wait to be shot by the Germans.

It wasn't easy looking after thirty-two people in a place that was a stone's throw from Gestapo headquarters, yet keep a secret of it. The bunkers were well equipped with water, electricity, beds, and stoves for cooking. I managed to provide electricity without it being metered. I brought in water by digging a twenty-five–foot well. The Jews in the bunker had water downstairs but I had no plumbing at all upstairs! I bartered and bought food from the peasants in the neighborhood.

I visited my charges every day, usually in the evening when I finished baking bread for them. I talked, joked, and played cards with them, trying to keep up their spirits and mine.

One of my worst experiences occurred when I was caught by the Gestapo in a dragnet for forced labor in Germany. Many Poles died in the terrible circumstances there. I managed to escape before my transfer. After all, thirty-two people depended on me. Their lives were at stake. If I left, they were doomed. I would not allow that to happen. A few days after my return home, the Gestapo came looking for me. I jumped into the bunker with my Jewish friends. I had guns and ammunition there. Everyone was armed, ready to kill the Germans if they opened the trapdoor, but, thank God, they didn't find it.

Toward the end of July 1944, when I was certain that the Germans had left due to the arrival of Soviet troops in eastern Poland, I told the Jews that they were now free men and women. It was an emotional moment. They cried. I cried. But these, of course, were tears of joy.

Out of the thirty-two Jews who once made their home with me, many are dead now. But others live today in the United States, Australia, and Israel.

After the war, Jackowski emigrated to the United States with his family. Jews he had saved helped him go into business. Today he is retired and is a respected member of the Polish–American community in south Florida.

THE REVEREND JAN JANUSZEWSKI

The Germans came to my village on September 16, 1939. They ordered us to meet with them, including the new mayor. They told us that since the German people had suffered so much during the war, the Poles would have to pay restitution. My parishioners had to give money, and some even gave grain. A week later there was another meeting. A priest friend of mine, always an optimist, suggested that the purpose of the meeting was to praise us for the restitution.

When we got to the meeting, we were not allowed to sit, only to stand. The Germans blamed us for the suffering their people had to endure during the war. I said that I did not do anything to hurt Germans, and if the German officer who interrogated us wanted to know how I had acted before and during the war, he could ask the

German people in my village how I behaved. At that point, a German policemen leaped toward me with a gun and told me to shut up or he would blow my brains out. On November 11, 1939, I was arrested and sent to jail along with about a hundred other hostages—priests, farmers, businessmen. Twelve of them were shot. The remainder were released and returned home.

In February 1940, the chief of police and district governor told me and other clergy that Polish church authority had been eliminated and that we would have to cooperate with them. I told them that I had taken an oath, just as they had, to fulfill my duties as a priest. The chief of police warned, "You will be sent to a concentration camp." A short time later, the German police told me I would be transferred to Germany and another priest would be sent to take my place. One of the boys, who had always been in some kind of trouble, said to me, "Father, Christ suffered; now you will suffer too." That remark really boosted me up. If the remark had come from someone else who had been particularly religious, it would not have had the impact that it did coming from this young man.

In my village, a Pole named Gronek had bought a farm from a German several years before. The German did not want to leave the farm to his son, who drank too much. When the Nazis occupied the area, a local German told the new authorities that the farm owned by Gronek had once belonged to this German's father. The Germans gave Gronek two days to get out.

I remember an incident when young Germans who had gotten farms expropriated from Polish farmers went to a local parish and demanded wine from the local pastor, an elderly man. The priest refused, and the young Germans beat him up badly and left him outside. Fortunately, he was later taken to a hospital and recuperated.

There was no anti-Semitism in my region of Poland before the war as far as I know, although there was an anti-Semitic movement before the war among some students at the University of Poznań. What they did was to go to a Jewish restaurant and order just a cup of coffee and sit there until noon; then the first group would leave and another group of students would come and take their places, preventing the proprietor from doing business. I think that talk about Polish anti-Semitism before the war has been greatly exaggerated. I never grew up in that spirit. If there were some outbursts and demonstrations, it was because of some specific contacts these Poles had with Jews. It was not part of the general spirit of the Polish people.

During the war, I heard of many Poles helping Jews who lived nearby. In my village, there were few Jews. On the other hand, when

I lived in western Poland, I knew many German families and got along well with them. I was even warned by the mayor's mother, a German, about my impending arrest. I did not leave as I was urged to, because the bishop had sent me there and I wanted to stay.

When I was in Dachau, I worked with Jews. I remember one Jewish man telling me while we shoveled snow together: "It wasn't like this in our dear Poland." He was only filling the wheelbarrow half full. I warned him that he had better fill it up before the authorities found out. "Here," he said, "you have to have callouses not on your hands but on your eyes."

I was able to cope with concentration camp life because I had no sense of guilt for anything. I was arrested and sent to Dachau because I was a Polish priest. The Germans didn't even accuse me of anything; I was just lined up with other priests, arrested, and sent away.

In 1951, Januszewski came to the United States and settled in Florida, where he served as a priest in several Roman Catholic parishes. He died in March 1987, at the age of seventy-five.

WANDA JORDAN

The year 1943 was one of terror. Faced with a more active and better organized Polish resistance, the Germans increased their terrorization of the Polish people in Warsaw and other towns. The rule of collective reprisal for any act of sabotage, sign of enmity, disobedience, or violence against German authority was now applied on a grand scale by introducing public executions of innocent victims.

People were hunted down in the streets, trapped, put into vans, and driven to a prison. They formed a pool from which at random a hundred or more victims were taken at any one time to their death. Before being delivered to the place of execution, their clothes were changed for paper sacks, their mouths were taped shut to prevent them from shouting "Long live Poland!" as had happened in the past, and they were injected with a drug to deprive them of any physical strength.

I lived in Warsaw in a block of flats, in a corner room overlooking

Rakowiecka Street, across from barracks housing the Luftwaffe airmen. One day we heard shooting in the neighborhood, and we expected a new tragedy to follow. Indeed, the next day about 10:00 in the morning, the Germans cleared the street of traffic and pedestrians. Armed police with guns at the ready were posted along the street. An open truck with several armed police on board slowly passed by while a woman in uniform shouted through a megaphone in bad Polish: "Don't approach the windows or you will be killed."

I remained standing by the window, partly hidden behind the curtain. I knew that the truck with prisoners would soon pass and I knew that I must see it and be witness to the horror. Soon the truck approached. The top of the truck bed was covered but the back was open. I saw figures lying on top of each other, forming a mass of indistinguishable bodies in bizarre attire of the same light color. I caught only a glimpse of the truck when I heard a terrific bang. I fell on the floor, deafened and stunned for a while before I realized that I had been fired at by one of the policemen posted opposite our house. The bullet had made a small hole in the window pane, close to the spot where my head was, and had then exploded against the opposite wall. Sitting on the floor, I was waiting for the final act. I did not wait long before I heard rapid bursts of machine-gun fire, while at the same time dance music blared from German loudspeakers provided for the occasion.

One hundred seventy people were murdered that day. The next morning, huge posters listed the victims.

Joe was no more than nine years old. He was one of the youngest volunteers eager to take an active part in the Warsaw Uprising, which to these youngsters was a great adventure. They formed an army of messengers, mailmen, and newspaper distributors. Many of them were Boy Scouts. Their task was to organize a mail delivery service, a very useful venture with so many Polish families scattered, lost, or killed during the tragic days of August and September 1944.

Joe preferred to perform his duties alone. He delivered newspapers and important messages to the outpost barricades that marked the lines of the battle frontier. His route was a net of underground passages, but sometimes he had to run or crawl through open spaces.

At 6:00 a.m., Joe and his colleagues presented themselves at our press distribution office in the western part of City Center, which was still held by Polish forces. When Joe came the first time, I was struck by his determination, humor, and sense of fun. I did not know much about him except that he lived in a poor district of the city now under heavy bombardment. One day Joe appeared with a German helmet on his head, which would have covered his whole face had it not been supported by his ears. However, his most dramatic appearance was the day he came with a big bull terrier at his heels. From then on, the boy and his dog shared the dangers of his daily expeditions. There were very few dogs left in Warsaw; they quickly disappeared as starvation gripped the population of the city. One day Joe came to the office without his dog. "What happened? Where is your dog?" I asked. "They ate him," Joe said, sobbing.

Nineteen forty-five was the year of migration in Poland. Thousands of Warsaw inhabitants were returning to their deserted, ruined city, looking for traces of their previous life. From the east a wave of emigrants moved westward after being forced to abandon their native towns and lands. From the opposite direction came Poles liberated from German bondage. Among those who returned home were prisoners of war and survivors of concentration camps, now looking for a place to live.

With these crowds, the transport system was at a breaking point. The trains were submerged under the weight of desperate people struggling to occupy all possible vacant places on the roof and steps of the carriages, clutching fast to any prop at hand.

At this time, in the middle of the winter, I had to travel from Warsaw to Kraków. By a miracle I found myself inside the carriage, suspended above the floor by the sheer pressure of people around me. The journey lasted all night, and at the end I had to change trains, this time to open cars used for transporting coal. It was bitterly cold and snowing. From a dark-gray mass of shivering people, we were becoming more like damned white ghosts traveling to unknown destinations.

Within the crowd, I noticed a rather unusual-looking group. A young girl stood between an old man and a young boy, covering both of them and herself with a big shawl, in a gesture that implied care and protection. This I found strange in the prevailing atmosphere of the day, which could be summed up in the phrase "each for himself." From the talk I later had with the girl, I learned that she and her companions were returning from Germany after three years of forced labor.

The girl, Maryna, was a peasant from a small village near Bielsko, a town in the southern part of Poland. In Germany, she had been sent to a farm as a slave laborer. She was reluctant to talk about her life there, but from some of her remarks it was not difficult to guess how hard the work was and how harsh the treatment. She told me: "The farmer, his family, and workers were cruel people. They tried to humiliate me by calling me names and never addressed me other than 'You Polish swine.' " I could see in her face how the memory of those years hounded her. Then a faint smile appeared in her eyes, and with a gesture of dismissal, she said: "It doesn't matter." And, as if following her innermost thoughts, she added in a low voice: "It was for Poland."

Jordan, who had earned a degree in physics before the war, remained in Poland during the early postwar years. But in 1947, to avoid arrest by the Communists because of her Home Army affiliation and democratic loyalties during the war, she left Poland to do research at the Marie Curie Laboratory in Paris. She later moved to England, where she is now retired.

A.M. KALINKA

When the war broke out, Polish authorities evacuated my family from Toruń, but at the beginning of October, we returned. In mid-October, the Germans started to arrest Polish men. They arrested my father along with all the other Polish men in our apartment house and took them to the Toruń fortress. My mother decided that it would probably be safer if we left the city for Kutno, where her mother lived. We packed all of our possessions into large baskets, and my mother started to take some of our things to Kutno.

One morning when she was away, there was a knock on the door at 6:00 o'clock. I opened the door to see two German soldiers and a servant girl from a neighboring apartment, who acted as their interpreter. They had come to expel us from our apartment and from Toruń. I was terrified. They asked where my parents were. I answered that my father had been arrested, but on the spur of the moment it occurred to me that it might be better not to tell them the real reason my mother was gone. I told them that she had gone to Kutno because my grandmother was ill. They entered the apartment and started to look around. They saw all our things packed in the baskets. My sisters were crying. I sent one of them to warn the caretaker not to let my mother enter to the apartment if she should happen to return before the Germans left. The Germans told us to stay in one room, and they locked all the others. The soldiers said they would return in an hour. When they had gone, my mother came into the apartment, and using other keys we opened the locked doors and took what belongings we could to the caretaker's apartment. When the Germans returned, they saw that we had taken some of our things and threatened to arrest my mother.

My mother had a considerable amount of money in her possession from the sale of a small farm my parents had bought for my father's retirement. As she stood at the door to the room in the caretaker's flat where we were sitting, she tearfully said, "Oh, my poor children." I suddenly realized that she was carrying the money and that if the Germans arrested her, we would lose everything. I went up to her, and she managed to pass the money to me to hide. The Germans then told us that if we did not leave Toruń, my mother would definitely be arrested.

We went to Kutno. My father was released in January 1940 and joined us there. Since there was another spate of arrests at that time, he decided to go to Warsaw, where he got a job as a teacher. We joined him in June. He had been so badly beaten by the Germans that he never quite recovered from the experience. He died in 1943 and was buried in Powązki Cemetery.

I wanted to visit his grave, but my mother did her best to dissuade me. Despite my mother's warnings, one day I set off with my sister by streetcar to the cemetery. We had just passed the Jewish cemetery when the streetcar stopped. I shall never forget the sight that met our eyes. There had been a street execution just moments before. The corpses lay on the ground. Their brains had spilled out, and there was blood everywhere. There must have been at least twenty bodies. Then the Germans started throwing the bodies into a waiting truck, swinging them by the arms and legs. If was frightful. My sister and I were so shocked that we fled on foot. We heard shots ring out behind us, but we did not stop to see if they were shooting at us. We were too scared to go home, so we went to a friend's home, where we were given aspirins and put to bed until we had calmed down sufficiently to go home. It was two weeks before I told my mother what had happened.

Born in Nowy Sącz, Poland, Kalinka spent the war years in Toruń, Kutno, and Warsaw. She emigrated to England after the war. She is now retired.

BOGUSŁAW ADAM KALINKA

At the end of 1943, the incidence of street executions increased greatly. Prisoners interned in Pawiak or people caught up in street roundups or taken from their homes were executed, ten to twenty at a time.

I was arrested by the Gestapo together with my father on October 6, 1943. They came to our apartment at about 3:00 a.m. We were taken to Pawiak prison and kept there for six weeks, during which time we were interrogated three to four times a week. Both of us were beaten, and I lost several teeth. My father was told that if he did not divulge the names of his associates in the underground movement, they would arrest my mother and beat her until he told them what they wanted to know. I was accused of recruiting my fellow students at Wawelberg's Technical School for the Home Army. This was, of course, true, but I refused to admit it. My father and I were kept in separate cells all the time. I was in a cell with a young man whose surname was Kalicki, the son of a jeweler from Lublin, who had been arrested with relatives of his. With us in the cell were Dr. Zaorski, who was in charge of medical courses taught in the underground (the Germans had closed all Polish medical schools), and his son. Both Dr. Zaorski and his son were later released, but Kalicki remained.

Early in the morning of November 25, 1943, Kalicki, my father and I were taken from our cells to a large room. There were about eighty-five prisoners there. Sixty or so were criminals; the rest were political prisoners. As evening approached, the Germans tied black blindfolds over our eyes and tied us up by the hands and feet to the man on either side, in groups of five. My father was on one side of me, Kalicki on the other.

Then the Germans led us out to waiting trucks, lined with sheets of metal on the inside just like meat trucks. We were all aware of the increase in street executions at this time. My father said to me that this was the end. All of us were convinced that we were being taken to a street corner for execution. When the trucks arrived at their destination, we discovered with something akin to joy that we had stopped at a railway terminal. The Germans removed our blindfolds and led us, still tied up in fives, to a goods train. They crammed us into a car like sardines, standing so close together we could hardly move, let alone sit or lie down.

We traveled all night. There was no air. People shouted for help, for air, for water. Some became hysterical. Occasionally a German guard peered in through the inspection hatch, but the Germans ignored all requests to open the doors to let in more air. Conditions defied description. On the morning of November 26, we arrived in Auschwitz. When the doors were opened, the Gestapo met us with attack dogs. Of the original eighty-five prisoners in the car, ten or fifteen had died. They had suffocated during the night. Kalicki was one of them.

In 1944, huge transports of Jews from Hungary arrived in Auschwitz. I worked in a labor detail that shored up embankments. There were large areas around the camp that the Germans ordered to be sprinkled with lime. Jews were delegated for this task and made to throw the lime up into the air, so that after a few hours they would be half-blinded by the lime that got into their eyes. The rest of us saw what was happening, but there was absolutely nothing any of us could do when armed Gestapo guards, who did not hesitate to use their guns, stood all around us. After a day's work, the Germans led these Jews back to the main camp. The Jews were almost blind, and in a few days the Germans sent them to the gas chambers.

In 1944, as the Soviet army approached Auschwitz, we were evacuated to Leitmeritz, a branch of Flossenburg concentration camp, on the border of Austria and Czechoslovakia. Conditions there were even worse than at Auschwitz. During my stay in Auschwitz, the Germans had had less time for us because they were preoccupied with the Jews. We had also been able to supplement our meager rations of food with parcels received from home. At Leitmeritz, we no longer received food parcels and our food rations were even smaller than at Auschwitz. Every day new prisoners arrived—one, two, or three hundred. The existing accommodations became increasingly overcrowded. Bunks were arranged in five tiers. About three thousand prisoners died of typhus while we were there.

On the morning of May 7, 1945, we opened our eyes to find that all the Germans had gone. We knew that the Soviet army was approaching the vicinity of Leitmeritz. The Soviet prisoners in Leitmeritz decided to flee to the West, and we decided to follow their example. After a short time, we got to Prague and reported to the British Mission there, headed by Colonel Perkins. He advised us to go to Pilsen, the part of Czechoslovakia occupied by the Americans. Perkins was unable to help us in Prague, which was occupied by the Soviets, so we did as he suggested. When we arrived in Pilsen, the British flew my father, who was very seriously ill, to London. We arrived on June 30, 1945. My father had weighed ninety-six kilos before his arrest. On his arrival in England, he weighed only forty-five kilos. He had contracted tuberculosis, and never left the hospital until his death in 1949.

During the war, Kalinka's parents had a general store in Warsaw at 11 Świętojerska Street, where they also had an apartment. This shop was used by the Home Army as a *skrzynka* (mailbox). When the son of General Tadeusz Bór-Komorowski, who succeeded Grot-Rowecki as head of the Home Army, was born, Kalinka remembers taking milk from the shop to Bór's wife, as his parents knew the general very well. Some time after his arrival in England, Kalinka became superintendent of the Civil Engineering Department at the Thames Polytechnic. He is now retired.

EDWARD MARCIN KEMNITZ

As a reserve officer of the Polish army, I fought in the September 1939 campaign against the Nazi invaders. In December 1939, I joined the Polish underground movement and was active mainly in the Home Army's special unit, code-named Import. The unit dealt with drops by the Allied air forces of parachutists and containers with arms and ammunition destined for the Polish underground. My pseudonym was Marcin.

Being a director of my father's Warsaw manufacturing business, I was on good terms with many of our Jewish customers: Jakub Milard, Chaim Grun, Abraham Gepner, and others. Even if some of our Jewish friends had already been put behind the walls of the Warsaw ghetto, it still was possible for some time to contact them through the building of the Warsaw Law Courts that bordered upon the ghetto on Leszno Street. We processed their raw materials, stored them in our factory, and then transferred the proceeds from the sale, along with food, to our friends in the ghetto. Because of the ever-increasing plundering of Jewish homes, we stored their belongings in our factory warehouse, for shorter or longer periods.

Since Nazi atrocities against Jews and Poles alike intensified in 1942, the Government Delegate of the Polish government in Warsaw formed in December 1942 a council to aid the Jews, known as Żegota. Chairing the council was Julian Grobelny. Prominent members were the lawyer Tadeusz Rek, Dr. Leon Fajner, the writer Zofia Kossak, the historian Władysław Bartoszewski, and Dr. Adolph Berman. This group started intensive action to aid the Jews in the ghettos and those hiding outside the walls.

Through one of my friends in the Home Army, known as Wicher, I joined the Żegota organization in January 1943, and was deeply involved, until the outbreak of the Warsaw Uprising in August 1944, in activities to help the persecuted Jews. Leon Hercberg and his wife were among those we gave forged birth and baptismal certificates, as well as German identification cards. Hercberg—his assumed Polish name was Koszycki—was given shelter in the apartment of one of my friends. My father, Wojciech, and I provided this couple with money, food, and clothing. We stored their belongings until the end of the war. Both Hercbergs survived the war.

A friend of my wife's, Anula Rosenthal, whose father and brother were already in the ghetto, was provided with Aryan papers so she could live in Warsaw. Her pseudonym was Frackiewicz. Later Anula was taken to my wife's estate near Warsaw. We also gave her mother Polish identification papers. Both women survived. Thanks to my contact with the legalization bureau of the Home Army, I was able to supply all sorts of documents not only to those I have mentioned but also to many other Jews, many of them unknown to me.

In February or March 1943, I transported, in our two-horse factory cart, several boxes loaded with guns and ammunition to Elektoralna Street. Their destination was the ghetto. The load was disguised as aluminum sheets and lead bands for one of our customers, the Philips factory on Karolkowa Street. During the same period, I also helped in several purchases of small arms and ammunition for the Żydowska Organizacja Bojowa (Jewish Fighting Organization), known as ŻOB.

Our Żegota council, with branches in several other Polish cities, watched over the fate of four thousand Jewish people in Warsaw, including six hundred children. Financial means were provided by the Government Delegate. Essential help was given by the parish priest of All Saints Church on Grzybowski Square, the Reverend Marceli Godlewski, who provided documents and also gave shelter to many Jewish children, later transferred to monasteries in and near Warsaw.

In no other occupied country was there an organization such as

Żegota, and in no other country was the death penalty imposed for giving even a glass of water to a Jew.

Both Edward Kemnitz and his late father, Wojciech, were honored for saving Jews by Yad Vashem on December 14, 1983, at the Consulate General of Israel in Montreal, Canada, where Kemnitz lives today.

ROMAN KIERSZNIEWSKI

I lived with my wife, Irena, in Warsaw until the outbreak of the war in 1939, when I took part as a soldier in the September Campaign. After my return, Irena and I found other quarters in a one-story home in Zielonka, near Warsaw.

Toward the end of 1939, we found out from acquaintances about the troubles of Hania Rubin, who was of Jewish origin. Before the war she had been a chambermaid for a well-known wealthy Polish family. The death sentence imposed by the Germans on those who helped or concealed Jews caused Hania to lose her job. For several days she lingered on in one of the abandoned Warsaw villas.

Concerned about her fate, my wife and I went to the street where the villa was. We immediately saw that she lived with her aunt in deplorable conditions. There was no glass in the windows. In place of a couch they used a bag of straw. There was neither electricity nor heat. My wife and I decided to take the two women to our home in Zielonka.

After some time, I took Hania's aunt to live with acquaintances in Marki, near Warsaw, while Hania stayed with us. She lived with us until 1944, assisting our common budget with meager funds earned by sewing. One of her clients was even a German, by the name of Szulc.

From 1939 to 1944, there was a succession of inspections by the Germans in Zielonka. Two of these inspections involved my family— myself, my wife, and our four-year-old son, Andrzej. The first of these inspections, in March 1944, was a broad plan of action "to cleanse the land" of Zielonka of Jews. The organizers were the German police from Radzymin.

Early in the morning, a Jew whom we knew ran into our house

and informed us of the beginning of the German action. Hania, wearing a nightgown and slippers, fled through the window and later into the woods. In the evening, after the conclusion of the liquidation by the Germans, I took her clothes and a blanket.

Anticipating another action of the same type, we intended to lodge Hania with either our acquaintances or relatives in Warsaw. I arranged to get the necessary documents for her under the Polish name Halina Kwiatkowska. From April to August 1944, Hania lived with our relatives or acquaintances, often changing her place of residence.

In April 1944 there was another inspection at our home in Zielonka. This time Kripo, the criminal police, was directed to our address by reports that we had concealed Jews. By a stroke of luck, Hania was not living with us at that time; moreover, earlier that day my wife, anticipating danger, had burned in the stove underground newspapers and bulletins that we had brought home from work.

Close to the time of the outbreak of the Warsaw Uprising, the owner of the house where we lived discovered an old identification card of Hania Rubin's and told us to leave his place immediately. The owner was afraid that we were continuing to hide her and would bring misfortune on him. The consequence was that we moved to Warsaw. I was living in an apartment at 25 Iwicki Street at the time of the Warsaw Uprising. My wife stayed several streets away, in a stone apartment building on Widok Street. After two weeks she used the sewers to get through to Sadyba. After many adventures, during which time I took care of our five-year-old son, my wife and I were reunited in the village of Władysławów, not far from Warsaw.

During the occupation, I helped a Jewish man, Mieczysław Prożański, who concealed himself in a mechanic's workshop on Leszno Street in Wola, next to the Warsaw ghetto. He hid in the garret, where he did the bookkeeping for the shop. Working in the same shop as a watchman, I often gave Prożański food or clothes. Once I even participated in an action to ransom him from the Jewish militia, which had seized him after he was denounced by another Jew in the ghetto. Prożański was seized and shot by the Germans on the second day of the Warsaw Uprising.

After the liberation, Hania Rubin appeared at our home with her sister one day. Not long after, her sister went to India, where Hania joined her several years later. Today Hania lives in England and her sister in Israel.

Kierszniewski lives in retirement in Poland.

ZYGMUNT KOC

In November 1939 I left Milanowek, where I had been staying with my mother since I escaped from the hospital at Żyrardów. The principal doctor, a woman, had discharged me when she noticed that the Germans were trying to get all the Polish army officers who were there. (By this time, the male doctors had all fled to Warsaw.)

I decided to go to my family estate, Koce Basie, in the Podlasie region of Poland. I walked most of the way, a distance of some one hundred kilometers, though occasionally I got a lift on a wagon. On the way, I stopped at the estate of Sabnie, which belonged to the Moniuszko family. I still wanted to get to Koce Basie, but the Moniuszkos insisted that I stay with them rather than cross the Bug River.

At Sabnie I made contact with some underground organizations. One of these groups was organized by Bolesław Piasecki, who recruited me when he found out that I was an officer. He had a unit of some five hundred young men from Warsaw, with whom he wanted to cross the Bug. He instructed me to arrange a safe place. The Germans must have noticed that something was going on. They tried to encircle the unit near Sokołow Podlaski but failed to catch anyone. They then moved north and repeated the procedure, again with no success. I went to warn the commanders of Piasecki's unit that the Germans were trying to encircle the unit, but they chose to ignore my advice. I was told that it was none of my business, that the leadership of the unit had been taken over by regular officers and my role was at an end.

In the morning, I left quite calmly, went to the nearest village, and eventually got back to Sabnie. Meanwhile, the Germans had successfully encircled the greater part of Piasecki's unit. Of the original five hundred, only fifty men, who had been equipped with some sort of weapon, had crossed the Bug and thus evaded capture. The rest had disappeared. No word was heard of them again. After this episode, I left Piasecki's organization because I thought that Piasecki was irresponsible. The losses he was prepared to sustain were far too great. . . .

In 1944, after the Germans had smashed the Home Army in the Kampinos Forest, Adolph Pilch took over the command of the two hundred fifty cavalrymen who remained. I was his second-in-command. We crossed by night to a new area, and at dawn we went through a village where, unknown to us, Germans were stationed. Although we did not notice them, they saw us. At Biały Lug we stopped to rest and feed our horses. For once I was allocated a clean room and had every hope of spending a peaceful night, not bothered by bugs. At dawn, the Germans attacked us with a force of about 300. We had 125 men in the village. When the attack came, most of our men rushed out and escaped, but Pilch and I managed to gather seven of them. I was ordered to attack the Germans from the rear while Pilch took the other three men to fire at the Germans in front. When we attacked the Germans from behind the cover of some wagons, they must have thought they were being attacked by far greater numbers because they retreated.

On the night of September 2, 1944, Lieutenant Adolf Pilch's group took revenge on the Kamiński Brigade, an SS unit that had committed many atrocities against the Poles during the Warsaw Uprising of 1944. It was in the Kampinos Forest that Pilch's men virtually annihilated the enemy unit. See Pilch's account, pp. 137-39.—Ed.

In 1946, Koc made his way to Italy via Germany. As a civilian, he was evacuated with the Polish Second Corps to England, where he married and fathered two daughters. He died early in 1988, after a long illness.

STANISŁAW KOCYAN

Before the war, I was a regular officer in the Polish armed forces. After the September Campaign, I returned to my home town of Tarnów with the intention of crossing the border to Hungary. But in November 1940, a meeting with a friend who was to have been my companion on this venture failed to materialize. During my stay in Tarnów, I was a driver for the fire brigade.

In February 1941, I was arrested by the Gestapo. I was accused of several crimes, among them listening to the radio, training young people in the use of firearms and grenades, and distributing underground publications. The charges were largely fabricated. It was most unlikely that I would have trained anyone in an area where there was a sanitorium for Wehrmacht troops, which is what the Gestapo claimed. I learned I had been denounced, along with several of my friends from the grammar school in Tarnów, by another classmate. At that time, the Gestapo had been given orders to clear the area of all potential troublemakers in preparation for the invasion of Russia, and they arrested everyone on the slightest pretext.

We all knew that the informer had been arrested and released. What we did not know was that he had been released in order to denounce us. On the day of my arrest, the Gestapo triumphantly led him into the room where I was being questioned, and he urged me to confess. He reminded me that on a particular day I had given him some underground literature from the briefcase strapped to my bicycle. Naturally, I denied all his accusations on the grounds that on that day I had been on duty at the fire station. As it happened, on the day in question the chief fire officer had asked me to write Polish translations of the German safety regulations that were posted in the fire station. I was registered as being on duty, but because one of the fire trucks was being repaired, I was told to go and do the work at home. Actually, the informer was telling the truth about the underground publications, but when the Gestapo sent someone to inspect the records at the fire station, they discovered that I had indeed been on duty that day.

Unfortunately, this did not help me in any way during the interrogation. My arm was broken and my skull was fractured. To this day, I have a scar where I was hit over the head with the muzzle of a gun I was supposed to have had in my possession. My case was not helped by the interpreter, who twisted my answers in such a way as to incriminate me even further. Since I had said that I knew no German in order to give myself more time to think of the answers, I could not even protest.

There was no trial. The Gestapo had made their own arrangements with their colleagues in Auschwitz. Having realized that prisoners could survive over a year, especially if they were fit and healthy, the Gestapo would telephone authorities in Auschwitz to send the prisoners to Block 11, where they would be executed. Of the 926 members of the transport from Tarnów and Kraków that arrived in Auschwitz on April 5, 1941, only fourteen people survived. My closest friends from Tarnów were all executed on June 15 and 16, 1942. I can only speculate that I survived because my files had been sent to Berlin. After my arrest and transfer to Auschwitz, my mother wrote to Berlin to ask why I had been arrested. Later, the Tarnów Gestapo called her in. She was certain she would not be allowed to leave after questioning but, surprisingly, she was. The Gestapo first told her not to communicate with Berlin in the future; it appeared that Berlin had asked for my files. I am certain that the absence of the files is the reason I was not executed.

The motor pool commandant at Auschwitz, SS Untersturmführer K. Wiegand, lived in a house that also housed the motor pool administration. He was brutal not only to the prisoners but also to the SS drivers. During my four-year stay at the camp, I was in almost daily contact with him, and he unwittingly contributed to keeping up the morale of some of the prisoners in the camp. I had access to his living quarters, where he had a radio. I used it to listen to the news from London—"*Tu Mowi Londyn*" (Here London Speaks)—which I passed on to trusted friends. This played no small part in keeping our spirits up.

Wiegand was a peculiar chap. Once he beat one of the prisoners who was responsible for cleaning the house where he lived. When I asked him why he beat the prisoners who worked in the motor pool, he told me that he hated people who acted as if they were afraid of him. This piece of information came in very useful later, when a friend of mine and a Jewish prisoner saved themselves from Wiegand's anger by standing their ground and looking him straight in the eye.

There were certain unwritten laws in Auschwitz. Informers and those who stole food from their fellow prisoners were "dealt with." The person who had denounced us was sent to Auschwitz about eight months later. One day we got news that a transport from Tarnów had arrived, so we went to see the new prisoners as they stood waiting for roll call. There in the front row was the one who had denounced us. He had two black eyes, so he must have been beaten. He recognized us and asked me to help him write a letter to his mother, but before I had time to reply, my friend pulled me away saying, "Let's go. He knows what the rules of Auschwitz are." That was the last I saw of the fellow. In another case that I witnessed, we got news that an informer from Silesia had arrived. He was beaten with the wooden clogs we all wore until he jumped out of the window of the barracks and ran to the barbed wire fence, where he was shot by the guards.

It was Christmas Eve 1941, our first in Auschwitz. After the day's work in the camp motor pool, our group of about twenty prisoners stood ranked in fives waiting to go back to the main camp. We were waiting for Franek, who was often kept busy right up to the last minute. He was the camp specialist in the repair and vulcanization of tires. (Before the war he had been a wine taster with the firm of

Lipoccy.) We were all "specialists" in fields in which we may have had little experience before the war but that were now our only chance of survival. Next to me stood the ever-smiling Witek, who worked in the petrol station. (Before the war he had studied law.) I was feeling the cold, as I had just left the warmth of the motor pool's central heating boiler, which I tended in the winter months.

Snow was falling gently, covering the ground with a white shroud so that even the gray camp building near the crematorium and the barbed wire fence seemed to lose their ghastliness. At long last we moved off and after a few minutes' march entered the camp gate with its ironic sign *Arbeit macht frei* (Work makes you free). I hoped that the SS-men guarding the gate would be in a holiday mood and not search us as they sometimes did, because hidden under my jacket I carried a piece of Christmas cake and the traditional Christmas *opłatek* (wafer). The cake had been baked in a Polish house in the town of Oświęcim and had reached me by the most improbable means, by way of Janka, who worked in a drugstore in town. This twenty-year-old girl, at enormous risk to herself, supplied us with medicines, bandages, and food, as well as acting as our post office. Letters were sent and received through her because the monthly letter we were officially allowed to write was subject to the strictest censorship.

After evening roll call, Witek, Franek, and I went to our block, No. 9, where we were joined by the rest of our group from Tarnów. Among them were Fredek and his older brother Tadek, who worked in the nearby camp farm and supplied raw potatoes to those of us in the motor pool. Whole buckets of this priceless commodity found their way into the chimney ducts of the central heating boiler, where they were baked, serving as the main meal for the prisoners of the motor pool and the farm.

Others in our group included Jasiu and his brother Ignas and an elderly gentleman, Dr. T., who worked in the hospital and who before the war had been a surgeon and director of the Tarnów Hospital. Several other small groups of prisoners gathered in the room. Between the bunks, our group sat around a table with our bowls of tea and our daily ration of bread. For atmosphere, we lit a small candle and then we shared the *opłatek*. We shook hands because it was difficult to find the right words to say. Today and tomorrow were likely to pass quietly, but it was better not to think of the future.

The news from outside gave us no grounds for optimism. German successes on the eastern front and action near Moscow were confirmed by London. In any case, the huge number of Soviet prisoners—about eight thousand—and their mass extermination was evidence enough that for the moment the Germans acted without any scruples. My friends ate the small pieces of cake, chiding me for having dealings with one of the SS drivers in the pool. I did not answer because it was a very dangerous topic. Only Witek smiled, for he was the only one who knew where the cake came from.

Then we talked about the good days before the war—other Christmas Eves, holidays, dances. We all forgot the sad reality. With Witek we returned to the days when we sat on a terrace in Modlin, where we had admired the majestic beauty of the rivers Bug, Narew, and Vistula. With Jas we talked of the inter-school athletic meets where we had always excelled in throwing the javelin and the discus. Tadek talked of our walks in Kraków. Fredek reminisced about the marvelous cakes at Gajewski's and the boxing matches at the Officer Cadet School in Komorowo. Dr. T. asked me whether I remembered his daughter waving to us from a garden near the sidings where we were loaded on the train that took us to Auschwitz.

Quietly we started singing carols. The tune and the words of *"Bóg sie Rodzi"* ("God is Born") seemed to take on a strange magical quality and rose above the barbed wire, crossing the snow-covered fields, the rivers Sola, Vistula, and Dunajec and reaching our homes. There we knew that a place had been set for us at the table. Our mothers would be trying to preserve a semblance of normality while fully mindful of the tragic situation in which we found ourselves. Everyone would be talking and thinking of us.

From this dream world we were awakend by the camp gong announcing that the time had come for everyone to return to their blocks and for lights off. Our camp friends, our only contact with the past, said goodbye and left. Franek, Witek, and I remained.

Before we slept, we thought of all those most dear to us and dreamed of freedom and a better world. Over the camp a silent and holy night set in.

Janka, the girl who worked at the drugstore in the town of Oświęcim, was involved in organizing the escape route from Auschwitz as well as sending and receiving our letters. Our liaison was SS Sergeant Richard Bock, who helped many of us. He took great risks but was very astute and covered his tracks well. Once when he thought he was under suspicion, he started shouting and yelling at me as I was crossing the courtyard of the motor pool. At first no one knew what had happened, because he was generally friendly, but later he explained why he had done it.

He told me that when he was first sent to Auschwitz, he was so appalled by what he saw that he was determined to help someone. Of course he had to be very careful in his choice. He decided that I was to be trusted. Once, after the execution of my colleagues, I had to see my mother, to pass on this information and to discuss the plans for my possible escape. So Bock decided to go and see my mother. The meeting was arranged to take place in the apartment of my relatives above the Bank Polski in Kraków. I explained to him in detail how he was to get there, and he went with our letters tucked into his socks, inside his high boots. My mother was naturally horrified when she opened the door and saw an SS-man standing there, but she quickly calmed down when he introduced himself by saying, "I am Janka."

After the war, he was interned in the American sector of occupied Germany. When I heard he was there, I got in touch with friends who were in the American sector, and eventually he was freed. Richard Bock was later made an honorary member of the Political Prisoners Association in Europe.

After the war, Kocyan was a member of the Polish First Armored Division, which served as part of the Allied forces of occupation. In 1947, he settled in England, where he worked as a mechanical engineer. He kept in contact with Richard Bock after the war.

JUREK KOLARSKI

I was a young boy, only sixteen years old, at the time the Germans came into our village. They seemed to do the same thing everywhere in the vicinity—terrorize all the civilian inhabitants, Jews and Poles.

I remember that day quite vividly. It was September 1939. A German motorized unit came into town, shooting wildly at the people like we were animals. Many people of all ages, Jews and Poles, were wounded or killed. I ran into the cellar of a neighbor's house. I never remember being so scared. I heard a lot of shouting and screaming as the Germans herded the people into a nearby barn. When things got quiet, I left the cellar and saw with my own eyes as the Germans burned a large barn with forty or fifty people inside it. Poles and Jews died together there.

I was so horrified that I ran as fast as I could. As I left the village, I met a Jewish boy whom I knew. He was about my own age. He was walking casually along the road. I asked him if he knew what was going on in the village. He shook his head, so I told him. With tears streaming down our faces, both of us were lucky to reach some nearby woods for the night. We were frightened, hungry, and tired.

This Jewish lad and myself, who had never been close before the war because our parents frowned on it, now became friends. How ironic! As we were to learn later, both his parents and mine were killed that very day in the same barn.

He looked very Jewish and therefore could not leave the woods. The Germans would have killed him. It was I who went out to get food and water for us from some peasants who lived on the edge of the woods. I did not tell them that a Jewish boy was in the woods with me because it would have endangered these people if the Germans found out. It was simply better that they knew nothing about my Jewish friend. I learned later that this peasant family were shot for hiding Jews in their barn.

I don't remember exactly when it was—a short time after the Polish army surrendered to the Germans in October 1939—that I made contact with a small group that had organized not far from the village as a resistance force. Most of the members were young men like me. A few former noncommissioned officers of the Polish army ran the unit. I never really knew who was in charge because orders came from different sergeants at various times. The group was high-spirited and passionate in its desire to kill as many Germans as possible.

Only after I made sure that my Jewish friend would be welcome in the unit did he reveal himself. He ended up one of the best fighters in the unit, killing ten or twenty Germans with a rifle older than he was.

Many different partisan units sprouted up in those days. We were anti-Nazi and anti-Soviet. Many of us continued to fight the Soviets after the war, as I did, in guerilla operations.

The mortality rate was so high in our unit that when it came time to integrate with the Union for Armed Struggle, which later became known as the Home Army, very few members of the original unit were left. By then, my Jewish friend had perished in an attack that our unit launched against a German convoy. It was a massacre. There were about fifty or sixty of us. Little did we know that we were hitting a convoy of about three hundred Germans. Our unit was decimated. I was wounded in the arm and was lucky to get out alive. I don't think more than ten of us made it out of that catastrophe. But the Germans had heavy losses too.

Kolarski, a member of an anti-Communist group after the war, was killed in an engagement with Communist forces in 1948. This account is based on the notes and diary of Pelagia Łukaszewska, a former Polish–American social worker who visited Poland in 1947.

MARIA KOLATOR

I do not remember the Germans entering Warsaw in 1939, but a memory that remains with me to this day is the German parade before Adolf Hitler in the Polish capital, after the Germans defeated Poland in the September Campaign.

For some reason I can no longer recall, I had to go from Wola to Pius Street. There must have been some prior German warning about not going into Warsaw that I interpreted as applying only to the very center of the city, for I took a very circuitous route to my destination. I remember being struck by the emptiness of the city. There seemed to be no one around.

As I reached the extension of Jerozolimskie Avenue beyond the main railroad station, I stumbled upon the German parade. I stood quite alone. There was no one else on the street. No faces at the windows. No one in any of the doorways. Just Germans. I could not take my eyes off them. There were thousands of them. I was riveted to the spot, staring at the vast quantities of "iron" passing before me. The very long barrels of the antitank artillery particularly struck me. As I think about it, it was as if there were no troops at all, just the weaponry rolling by before my eyes. The whole episode had an eerie, unreal quality about it. No one came up to me; no one told me to move off. I do not know how long I stood there but I had to wait until they had all gone by. I watched without feeling. There was no hatred, no admiration; rather awe at the vast quantity of weaponry.

At the beginning there were very few Germans in Warsaw. The first one I saw in the Wola district was helping a blind orthodox Jew across the road. Since so much was said at the time about the persecution of the Jews, I remember thinking that despite all the rumors, perhaps the Germans were human after all. On one occasion, the Germans distributed bread to the civilian population of Warsaw. The bread was brought in huge canvas-covered trucks, and the Germans stood on them and handed the bread out, one loaf per person. The loaves were enormous and terribly heavy. I do not know what they were made of; the texture was very fine and the loaves quite flat, as if no yeast had been used.

At the time I lived with two friends, one of whom refused to go for the bread on the grounds that she was not going to eat anything the Germans offered. But the other girl and I decided to swallow our pride and went to get some. The German who handed out the bread accused the boy in front of me of coming up a second time and kicked him in the face. Despite this, I changed coats with my friend and went up for a second loaf myself. We had very little to eat, and we must have been very hungry, because we ate this bread even though it barely resembled bread as we knew it.

My family was in the Soviet-occupied part of Poland, and I decided to join them. I knew I needed a pass but when I went to the German authorities to get it, they said they were not issuing any more. So I decided to try my luck without a pass. At Siedlce, the Germans tried to dissuade me from going over to the Soviet side. When we finally got to the border, the Germans stood on one side of a strip of no-man's-land, the Soviets on the other. At certain times, the Germans opened their side of the border to let people through, so when they told me to go, I entered the no-man's-land. The Soviet troops, however, refused to let me cross into the zone they occupied, so I had to return to the German side. The Germans then refused to let me back in, and I was forced to wait there in no-man's-land.

Eventually, the Soviet guards let everyone in except one Jew who had remonstrated with them for not allowing us to enter after "we" had waited so eagerly for the Soviets' arrival. Because no one else in the group wanted to be associated with his remark, everyone had moved away from him, and the last time I saw the Jew he was standing there in no-man's-land surrounded by Soviet troops. On the train from Baranowicze to Sarny, we met a Jew who had decided to go back to the German-occupied zone. He explained to us that even if the Germans took what they wanted from him, they would allegedly leave him something on which to live, while the Soviets would take everything and leave him utterly destitute.

After being deported with her family to the Soviet Union in 1940, Kolator was later evacuated with the Polish Army under General Władysław Anders. She made it to England by way of Iran and Lebanon. She is married and has one daughter.

J. KOWALSKI

During the early period of the German occupation of Poland, my mother and I were more directly involved in helping and hiding Jews we knew than in the later stages of the war, when a very perilous environment had developed. However, even at that juncture I was able to make contact with the legalization bureau of the Home Army, which assisted me in providing identification documents for Jews. Thanks to these documents, Jews were able to live outside the ghetto.

It was extremely difficult, if not impossible, for Jews to find lodgings in the Aryan part of Warsaw. Jews became guests in our home for several days or longer, until another location could be found for them. It was a trying time for the Jews and their Polish helpers. Food supplies were limited. Our Jewish guests were forced to live in circumstances of extreme confinement in a restricted area; it could not be otherwise, since their Semitic appearance would sooner or later result in a tragic end to their existence.

Nazi agents, the *Volksdeutsche* and their collaborators, hunted Jews to where they lived to rob or arrest them or worse. One day the German police and their agents surrounded our home in the belief that they would capture Jews. But fortunately, I had been warned by a neighbor, a member of the Home Army, of an impending roundup. All of our Jewish protégés had been relocated elsewhere, and my mother and I cleared the house of any traces that would have suggested that we harbored Jews. We ourselves left the city until it was safe to return.

After 1941, perhaps even earlier, the Germans began to check the authenticity of the identification papers and employment cards of people they had rounded up in their periodic sweeps throughout the city. Fortunately, there were helpful Poles everywhere, including the Warsaw Population Control Office. Most of the time, those brave

Poles were able to sneak in duplicate documents for the false identification cards that had been issued illegally by legalization bureaus
to the "burned" individuals, both Poles and Jews, who were wanted
by the Gestapo. This arrangement saved many Jewish lives, including
those of two Jews whom I had helped previously.

A young Jewish man whom I had furnished with false identification
documents had been placed in the apartment of a Polish woman. The
young man, who did not look Jewish, felt safe and secure. But soon
after taking up residence there, he began an intimate relationship with
a promiscuous girl who immediately became aware of his Jewishness.
Perhaps more out of stupidity and carelessness than ill will, the Polish
girl told others of her discovery. Soon the information got to the
landlady, who immediately alerted me to the obvious danger for the
Jewish man and herself. There was not much time to find another
hiding place for him. We made desperate efforts, but the people we
approached were too frightened to help or did not have a suitable
place to lodge him. By this time, German arrests and executions of
those who dared to help Jews were commonplace in Warsaw. Finally,
almost miraculously, we found a place for the Jewish man and moved
him clandestinely to his new home. He had learned his lesson and
was very careful to stay out of further trouble for the duration of the
German occupation. He survived the Holocaust and settled abroad
after the war.

In their search for Jews and for Poles who helped them, the Gestapo
came to our home and arrested my mother. Fortunately, I managed
to hide in a secret spot where they did not find me. Before the Gestapo
left our home, however, they threw an explosive that caused me
permanent injury. With the help of two friends, I was later evacuated
to safety. But our family's property was confiscated. I never saw my
mother again. She was murdered by the Germans.

Early in 1944, a man believed to be a Jew, the brother of a member
of the Home Army, was caught in a roundup in the street and imprisoned by the German police in the ghetto camp. His brother and
some of his Polish friends were aware that I had been entrusted with
a large sum of money for safekeeping. They approached me and asked
me to save the Jew's life by paying a ransom through a trustworthy
mediator. I was confronted with an enormous dilemma: Should I give
up the fifty thousand złotys and save the man, or should I deny the

request because the money was not mine to give? There was not much time for me to deliberate on the matter. The next day a transport train was scheduled to carry the prisoner from Warsaw to an undisclosed destination, most likely Auschwitz or another death camp. I was unable to contact the owner of the money because he was out of the district for several days. I opted to dispose of the money without the owner's consent in order to save the Jew's life. Within twenty-four hours, the Jew was freed. He and his brother survived the Holocaust, but neither of them even contacted me to say thank you. (Incidentally, the owner of the money gave me only a pro forma reprimand, and the matter was closed.)

Several months later, I loaded up a droshky with about forty or fifty pounds of victuals, donated by a Polish farmer and intended for some Jews hidden by a Polish couple who lived on the right bank of the Vistula River. When I got to the Poniatowski bridge, two German policemen stopped me. They demanded to see my identification papers and asked suspiciously what I was carrying. Anticipating such a possibility, I had secured a bogus document stating that the goods were intended for an orphanage. The "magic" paper saved me from serious trouble, if not grave danger.

A friend of mine was not so fortunate. About the same I crossed the Vistula, he was on his way to deliver some medicines and papers to some Jews. He was stopped and arrested. Several months later he was executed.

With the exception of several Jewish people whom my mother and I knew personally, no one I helped was aware of my true identity. I also strictly observed the principle of putting out of my mind the names and addresses of those whom I had provided with false identification. Obviously, in the interest of mutual safety, it was wise for me and my Jewish friends to use fictitious names. This explains why, after the war, I heard from only a few of the forty or fifty people whom I helped to survive. To be sure, many of them died along with their Polish protectors during the Warsaw Uprising of 1944.

After the lapse of so many years, I do not recall all the names of Polish men and woman who were engaged with me in rescue activities. Some of them lost their lives during the German occupation. Some died after the war. Some are still alive. Like myself, these people did not help Jews for any future reward or publicity. They probably would not even want their names revealed. So let it be that way.

Suffice it to say that we did what we did because we strongly felt, as Poles and Christians, that—despite the Holocaust we ourselves experienced—we must remain faithful to the humanitarian tradition of our country. This was true of the overwhelming majority of Poles.

J. Kowalski is the pseudonym of a distinguished Pole who went on to earn his medical degree after the war. He emigrated to the United States in 1961 and now lives in Colorado.

KRYSTYNA KOWALSKA

During the war, I lived with my family and four other relatives at 3 Solna Street in Lublin. It was a three-story stone building almost in the center of the city. Next to us was a German club, so we saw a large number of Germans in the vicinity.

My father worked near the street called the Kraków Suburb. He had, as we say, golden hands. He could repair anything. Many of his clients were Germans. My father worked from six o'clock in the morning to eleven at night. Outwardly, he gave the impression of being overworked, preoccupied with his daily chores. This placed him beyond suspicion of any involvement in conspiratorial activities.

In 1942 my father brought home a twenty-year-old girl. He said that she would be our maid and that she had very good references. She went by the name of Stefania Grzyb. (Her real name was Ewa Rainer.) She was pretty and pleasant but very nervous. I remember how she flinched every time the doorbell rang.

One day my father returned home with a strange expression on his face. It turned out that the superintendent of our building, Mr. Sajdak, had asked him: "Do you know that you folks are keeping a Jewess in your apartment?"

My parents reflected a long time on how to extricate themselves from the situation. Did the superintendent know for certain that Stefania was Jewish? Did he just want to provoke my father? Or was this the prelude to blackmail, getting money from my father for hiding Stefania, under threat of revealing the information to the Germans? But my parents ruled out these suppositions. They conducted themselves as though there was nothing to be concerned about. Stefania did not look Jewish. She had false identification papers. When questioned by my father, she acknowledged her Jewish background.

At this time the anti-Jewish terror affected everyone, but it never occurred to my parents to get rid of Stefania. My mother was very pleased with her, and my mother and father told her to continue to act as a regular maid. Stefania went outside, shopped, and even went to town. She did not shun the neighbors.

Since I was a young child at the time, it would be difficult for me to say whether or not I was afraid. But from the perspective of time, I can see how much my parents risked. Roundups were the order of the day. The Germans were everywhere. In our apartment we had no hiding place. Yet because we conducted ourselves normally and Stefania acted so gallantly, no one suspected us.

In this way we lived right up to 1944, and even after the liberation Stefania lived with us for some time. Later she emigrated to Israel, where she lives today. She married an attorney and is known as Ewa Maj. Her first son's name is Rafal. Some time ago she wrote a letter of thanks to my mother, telling her how indebted she was.

Kowalska completed her education after the war and has been involved in school administration in Warsaw, where she now lives.

STANISŁAW KOWALSKI

On the evening of September 20, 1940, 250 prisoners from Pawiak and over two thousand people rounded up from the streets of Warsaw passed through the gates of the Auschwitz concentration camp. I was among them. We were greeted with beatings, yells, rifle shots, and the ironic inscription above the gate: Arbeit Macht Frei (Work Makes You Free). Speaking to us the next day, the commandant of the camp, Rudolph Hess, emphatically confirmed our status: "You are dead men on furlough. Your furlough ends here."

We were forced to sing a prison song, the first stanza of which went like this: "I am in the concentration camp of Auschwitz, which pleases me. Perhaps I will be here one month, perhaps a day, maybe a year, which pleases me very much." We sang the sarcastic words of this song while trudging to and returning from work.

Work in the camp was compulsory and difficult. It went on from daylight to late in the evening, with a one-hour break for supper. We had to work in a rapid rhythm. The SS-man, Kapo, or prison functionary who kept an eye on us prodded with a stick those who tried to change the tempo of our work. Every prison functionary and Kapo had the right to beat and even to kill an inmate.

The congestion of inmates in the barracks and the lack of sanitation created an environment for lice and other insects to spread contagious and infectious diseases like spotted typhus. The inadequate food, the lack of amino acids and vitamins, lowered our physical resistance to these diseases and to dysentery.

Those shadowy people whose skin barely covered their bones were known in prison jargon as Mussulmans. They were mainly the older inmates. Even they had to work, march in an even line, and sing the camp song. If they didn't, then bloodthirsty Kaduk, Hasler, or Palitzsch would hit them with a stick or spade to kill them. If they gave any sign of life when lying on the ground, the tormentors would kill them off by jumping on their chests.

Death, torture, beating, and harassment—that was the daily camp program. Those who could not endure this strain ended up hanging from the electrified wires that encircled the camp or were shot by guards from the observation posts.

In December 1940, the snow covered the ground in deep layers. The temperature was about ten degrees. The cold went through our bones. This weather lasted through the entire winter. I appreciated that my work was under a roof, and I sympathized with those who had to work outside. Among them was my friend Władek. The Germans had arrested us at the same time. I saw him often. He looked very bad, slowly turning into a Mussulman. He was a cigarette addict. He sold his own allotment of chunks of bread for three cigarettes. He showed no concern about his appearance or his bad physical condition. More than once I tried to talk some sense into him. Unfortunately, he did not react to my persuasion and pleas.

Every day, as usual, I kindled a fire to warm the chilled bodies of those who had to stand outside in roll calls. Christmas was near. It was my first holiday away from family and friends. Palitzsch and other SS-men often checked on us. Palitzsch, treading the stairways like a cat, tried to surprise us. We kept alert because we knew what a great blessing it was to work under a roof. For even the smallest offense, we could be forced to work outside.

Just before Christmas, my luck ran out. Just as I was cooking some potatoes for myself and friends, Palitzsch with his catlike step appeared in the workshop. "Attention! Take your hat off!" he screamed. When he gave the command, I was holding a baked potato in my hand and delayed taking off my hat. This did not escape his attention. He came up to me and checked my hand. Seeing the baked potato, he grabbed it and threw it into the fire. "You damned dog!" With these words his litany began. He had caught me in a prison offense. A tragic play began for me. First, exercises on concrete. I had to do pushups and frog jumps for several minutes. During that time, Palitzsch was busy hitting me with the handle of his whip wherever he could. He didn't hold back from kicking me hard. "Get up!" he yelled. Wobbly on my legs, I slowly straightened my beaten body with the last strength in me. Suddenly I receive a powerful blow in the face. As though I had been cut down, I fell to the floor with a bloody, pummeled face. The sight of the blood obviously satisfied his sadism because he finished his beating with the words: "You are lucky." He took down my prison number. I understood that this was not the end of the punishment for such a "great offense."

I was summoned from the barracks and brought to the prison office. The official in charge was a vigorous, sadistic ruffian, Lager-führer Zeidler. Count Baworowski, the prison interpreter, translated: "What kind of offense did you commit?" I told him that I had cooked potatoes. He wrote something in his report and told me to give up my room. For the next several days, I was very dejected. In my thoughts, I was already in a penal section.

The decision was made on Christmas Eve. On that day, work lasted only until the afternoon. I was called by the clerk of the block and brought to a group of men standing near the kitchen. There were about twenty "offenders" like me. They took us to Block 11—the penal section. There the notorious Krakemann, a caricature of a man, a fat tormentor and executioner, waited for us. He beat and kicked us, assisted by his Kapo collaborators. After this greeting, they escorted us to the garret block where we were to serve our punishment.

We had to take off our prison clothes. The first row of men placed themselves under horizontal poles where hooks were fastened. There weren't enough hooks for the second row, where I was. The Germans ordered us to squat with our hands behind our heads. In that position we awaited our turn. Meanwhile, the Kapos twisted the hands to the backs of those who stood under the poles. Then they bound their wrists with chains and hanged them on the hooks. There I watched as my friends suffered terribly. Their faces were full of suffering and pain. Some moaned, others screamed from the pain. There were those who cursed. My friend, Geniek, who was seized in a street roundup in Warsaw, suffered especially. I found out later that he had a ruptured hernia, which caused him awful pain. Cold sweat flowed over his face. He turned pale and prayed to God for help. The Kapos jeered at his agony, laughing and beating him. Geniek lost consciousness. They threw cold water on his face to revive him. Finally the punishment came to an end.

They removed the victims from the posts. Then a Kapo bound my wrists with chains to my back and hoisted my body upward. Instantly I felt a terrible pain in my shoulder blades. It was difficult to breathe because the diaphram drew up toward the throat. The muscles of my arms stretched out like strings, carrying the weight of my body. I lost feeling in my hands; my muscles stiffened. The slightest motion brought agony. I tried to hang there without moving, but the Kapos maliciously hit us across the face, swinging the body to make it even more painful. Hanging on the poles, subject to this refined torture, I wondered when my Golgotha would end. Time dragged. Finally, the longed-for moment arrived; they unfastened us. My weakened legs could not sustain the weight of my body. I weaved back and forth. My hands were numb. The pain in my shoulder blades was indescribable. My wrists were cut by the chains.

My friends helped us to put on prison clothes; we could not do it ourselves. The Germans took us to the ground floor of the block. There we meet Krakemann again. He insulted us with his sneering glances and smiles. This time he didn't beat us. He escorted us from the block. In my room, my colleagues greeted me on this sad Christmas Eve.

Władek O.—his real name was Wadek Olszewski—had been arrested with me and transported with a group of 250 inmates from Pawiak prison to Auschwitz. In July 1941, Hess announced that all inmates who were ill should present themselves for transport to a sanitarium. There they would have suitable treatment. Władek volunteered. On July 28, 1941, 575 prisoners were taken to a Konigsberg euthanasia center where they were murdered. Three weeks later, their clothes were returned to the block leader.

Kowalski earned a doctorate in medicine with a specialty in stomotology. This account was originally published in Polish as part of Kowalski's graphic description of his experiences in Auschwitz-Birkenau: *Numer 4410 Opowiada* (*Number 4410 Reports*) (Chicago: Contemporary Images, 1985).

WANDA LESISZ

In 1940, as a girl of fifteen, I joined the Home Army. I was trained first as a courier and later attended the first aid course at the Jesus Hospital in Warsaw. Until the Warsaw Uprising of 1944, my duties included carrying messages and orders between units and transporting arms and ammunition.

I lived with my mother, Leonia Gutowska, and my sister, Janina, at 5 Feliński Street, Żoliborz, Warsaw. The house was used as a hiding place for firearms and ammunition of the Home Army. Our home was also used to instruct boys and girls in military matters.

During the uprising, I was assigned to the 202d Platoon of the Twenty-first Regiment, and I carried out many dangerous duties in Żoliborz. After the Polish capitulation in October 1944, the Germans took me prisoner and sent me to Germany where I spent seven months in Camp Gross Lubars and Oberlangen. On April 12, 1945, the First Polish Armored Division liberated me and 1,735 other Polish women—soldiers of the Home Army. For my exploits in the Warsaw Uprising, I received the Cross of Valor, the Cross of Merit with Swords, the Underground Army Cross, and the War Medal.

One day in 1941, Mr. and Mrs. Teicher, a Jewish couple, and their young son, Piotrus, came to our house in search of a hiding place. They asked my mother if they could leave Piotrus with us until they found a more suitable place. Unfortunately, while they were out the Germans caught and killed them. Warsaw was a very dangerous place at that time. Mass arrests and public executions were commonplace. The Germans hunted the Jews everywhere. The Jews had to hide to escape being sent to a concentration camp and inevitable death.

Piotrus remained with us until the end of the war. During his stay with us, we had to watch him constantly so that he would not be seen by outsiders. During Gestapo searches of our home, we hid him in the attic. After the capitulation in October 1944, when the Germans evacuated the people of Warsaw from the city, we bandaged Piotrus's face. My mother explained to the Germans that the boy had been found wounded and that she did not know where his parents were.

In the period 1941-43, we also hid in our house a young woman, Teodozja, whose family name I don't remember. Her fiancé, who lived under a false name, was a Polish officer in the Offlag II C prisoner of war camp in Germany. His real name was Palenker. After the war, Teodozja married Palenker. I was in contact with her and still have some of her letters, in which she praised my mother for her bravery and for helping her and Piotrus.

In 1958 Teodozja emigrated with her husband and her daughter, Ania, to Israel. I have not heard from her since then.

After the war, my mother managed to trace Piotrus's family in America and Israel. Eventually he went to Israel, where he fought for his country. Four months ago, he telephoned my sister in Warsaw and promised to contact us, but so far I have not heard from him.

In March 1988, Lesisz and Piotrus Teicher were reunited in Israel, where she was honored by Yad Vashem for her bravery. Since the end of the war, Lesisz has lived in England; she is married to Oxford-educated Tadeusz Lesisz, who served with the Royal Navy. Lesisz's mother, Leonia Gutowska, died in 1956.

BARBARA MAKUCH

In June 1939 I graduated from high school and enrolled in summer courses to prepare myself for university studies in September. I was a happy eighteen-year-old blond girl, looking forward to a happy future.

I never returned to school. Instead, the war broke out in September, and we experienced the miseries of the German invasion. The entire country was cruelly destroyed by the German bombing and artillery. The Polish government had to evacuate abroad, and Poland ceased to exist as a free country.

Germany annexed the western part of Poland and converted the central and eastern part into the General Government, with the notorious Hans Frank as governor. The German regime started in a very barbaric way, killing thousands of people in mass executions, confining thousands in prisons and concentration camps, seizing thousands as hostages, and forcing hundreds of thousands of young people to work in Germany. The whole country was a labor camp in which the Germans exploited the Poles. A monthly salary was equivalent to a kilo of sugar or meat. Huge requisitions of food and industrial goods caused catastrophic shortages. The Germans closed educational institutions except for some elementary schools. They deported teachers and intellectuals; some never returned. The German army, military police, and Gestapo made their presence known in every town. Curfews, manhunts, expropriations, and expulsions characterized life in Poland during German rule.

As soon as the hostilities finished, I rushed to Sandomierz, where my mother and sister were spending their vacation. We could not return to our former home in Krzemieniec, where our family was well known for our anti-German attitude, so we decided to stay where we were. The place was pretty quiet. I found a job as an instructor in the local agricultural school. We decided to make our life there, waiting for the end of the war, which we believed would come soon.

Three and a half million Jews lived in Poland before the war. They led a decent, quiet, life—working, maintaining their own businesses, practicing their religion, and going to their own schools. During the course of centuries, some of them had integrated into Polish society and had become rich and educated. There were Jewish doctors, teachers, artists, and poets. There were also many Polish–Jewish marriages.

During the first weeks of the German occupation, the Polish people were horrified by the cruel treatment of Jews, despite the fact that the Poles were also being terrorized by the Germans. The Germans expropriated and humiliated the Jews. They forced them to wear the Star of David. Prominent Jewish people were forced to do humiliating labor, such as cleaning streets and hauling garbage. Slowly, Jews disappeared from the streets. The Germans put them in ghettos, separated from the Polish population by walls and barbed wire. They suffered incredible famine and shortages. Very shortly, Jews began to starve to death, especially children. The Germans refused the Poles entry into the ghettos, and Jews could leave only under the penalty of death. Germans chased the miserable escapees with dogs and with the help of the local *Volksdeutsch*.

After one or two years, the Germans started the systematic liquidation of all ghettos. The Germans sent the Jews to concentration camps such a Majdanek, Treblinka, and Auschwitz, where they gassed and cremated them. Some Jews were taken to deserted places where the Germans shot them, burying them in mass graves. Everything was kept secret; people were told they were going to a labor camp. Some believed this, but soon the sinister truth started to become clear. Yet it was still difficult to accept the truth. After all, the Germans had a reputation as a civilized people. Slowly the gruesome news seeped through the wall of secrecy. It was clear that the Germans had decided to liquidate three million Polish Jews; moreover, the

Germans planned the same fate for the Jews from other countries under German rule. It was also clear that the same fate awaited Polish Christians and people of other nations.

Since Germany was successful on all fronts, it was completely impossible to think about rescuing Jews. Helping Jews or hiding them meant death, not only for the Polish family but also for their neighbors, who were usually cruelly murdered. We must realize that the problem was extremely difficult. How could we save or hide millions of people, when their appearance and language betrayed them? Only those with a non-Jewish appearance could be saved. They could survive by changing their identity with falsified documents. The Poles saved thousands of Jews that way. But there was no hope for Jewish-looking people, the Orthodox, and the uneducated, who spoke broken Polish. Only a small number of them could be saved, hidden in complete secrecy by extremely courageous people. The risk was enormous because the Germans killed Poles who aided Jews.

However, there were many Poles who ignored the risk of death. The principal of the school where I was employed as an instructor, in Mokszyszów near Sandomierz, Mr. Polowicz, was a wonderful man. He accepted a Jewish boy, fourteen years of age, as a student in his school. Later the boy worked in the same school and lived in the school residence. He was there until the end of the war. Mr. Polowicz also employed Dr. Olga Lilien, a Jewish woman from Lwów, in the school kitchen. She is now 80 years of age and still lives there. She decided to remain there after the war, to be with the people who saved her life. Despite the escalation of the anti-Jewish terror by the Germans, Polowicz never lost his courage.

One summer evening in 1942, someone knocked on our door. When I opened it, a woman completely unknown to me entered the house. She had a little girl with her. She told us that she owned a store in the city but now lived in the ghetto with her husband. "We know that we are going to die. Please save my little girl." she said. Frightened, I looked at my mother, who looked at me in silence. How could we say no? The woman left after a while to join her husband in the ghetto, but the little girl stayed with us. She was a lovely child. She was very smart, no doubt taught by her mother. Her name was Malka but we changed it to a typical Polish name—Marysia. Marysia had blond, curly hair and little freckles on her face. She could pass for a Polish child. Our only fear was that she might betray herself during some interrogation, but she behaved wonderfully. We told the neighbors that she was my niece from Lwów.

We heard about German searches in the neighborhood. This development, added to our fear that somebody might recognize Marysia and betray her, convinced us to move with the girl to Lwów, where my sister lived. We took the train. It was the most frightening journey of my life. The trains were so slow that our trip, which in normal times would take no more than four or five hours, took five days, interrupted by the searches of the military police at every station. I sat there holding little Marysia on my lap and prayed silently to God to help us. Thank God we arrived safely, welcomed by my sister and her husband.

They welcomed us for a special reason. They were members of *Żegota*, a Polish organization created to help Jews. Thanks to them, I found a place for Marysia at the convent of the Felicjan sisters who took her into the orphanage. The sisters took care of many war orphans and thus helped to save many Jewish children.

My brother-in-law introduced me to *Żegota*. It was a huge conspiracy, helping Jews to survive the war by collecting and distributing money and forged documents, finding refuge for them, and transferring them from one hiding place to another. They recruited me as a courier. I traveled between the central office in Warsaw and Lwów, carrying documents and money. It was a very dangerous job, but I was excellent for the role. I was a little girl with light blond hair and blue eyes—almost perfect German looks. I was the last person the Germans would suspect. I traveled many times on my dangerous mission and was successful for a very long time.

But one day my fortune changed for the worse. I was on the train with huge packages full of documents and money. The Germans opened my luggage and arrested me. I denied the luggage belonged to me. Perhaps the Germans had some hint about me. After all, I traveled too much. They took me to the Gestapo prison in Lublin and later to the prison in Lwów, the cruelest prison in the city. I must have looked pitiful—a tiny person in a white summer coat, handcuffed and escorted by two armed military police with dogs. People knew what had happened to me, but nobody could help me. But I was lucky in my misfortune. A young man from *Żegota*, Jurek Fiderer, spotted me in passing. We pretended not to know each other, but I raised my handcuffed hands. I saw horror in his eyes. I was happy; I knew he would warn *Żegota*.

The Germans threw me into a little cell, which was, in fact, the washroom. It had a small window, a toilet, and nothing else. I continued to pretend that the Germans had arrested me by mistake. But they did not believe me. They tortured me. They beat me cruelly. I lost my teeth. My tormentor was a huge Gestapo man who put me

naked on a bench. He took a bottle of strong vodka and drank it all
to kill his conscience, if he had one. Then he took a huge hard whip
and started to beat me, fifty or a hundred lashes, I do not know.
When I lost consciousness, the Germans threw me back in my cell.
I woke up later on the floor. My back was bruised and bleeding. The
pain was incredible. But my indignation and my disdain for those
brutes were so strong that I decided not to give them the satisfaction
of a confession. I decided to die. I managed to send a message to my
mother, telling her where I was. I said goodbye to her and the whole
family, and to my friends. I was tortured so much that I wanted to
die to avoid the suffering. I had so strong a death wish that I stopped
eating the meager cup of soup they gave me once a day. I lost all my
strength. I could hardly move.

But then the Gestapo left me alone, and I wondered why. I found
out that the Germans had brought in a group of forty people from
the Home Army. They were interrogating and torturing them. Day
and night I heard the wailing of prisoners. The Gestapo had a torture
chamber in the basement where they executed the Poles. Strangely,
the misfortune of these people brought some relief to me because the
Gestapo had forgotten about me. I had a faint hope that they might
release me. Then my young body started to regenerate. I decided to
regain my strength and started to eat and move as much as possible.

In this misery, something beautiful happened to me. One day I
heard a knock from the neighboring cell. Somebody wanted to communicate. I returned the knock. To know that another human being
was there was a big comfort to me. I found a broken fork and started
to scratch the wall. My neighbor did the same. After a few hours, we
had made a hole through the wall. We introduced ourselves. She was
Ewa Gibalska, a twenty-five-year-old member of the unfortunate
Home Army group that had been arrested by the Germans. We spent
hours whispering to each other, until we knew each other's life stories. A doctor in Zakopane had adopted her. Her parents had perished
in World War I. One of the Home Army boys was her fiance. I was
so happy to find a friend in this death cell.

But happiness did not last long. One day I heard a door open
and shut. The Gestapo took Ewa for interrogation. She never returned. When I asked a guard what had happened to her, he did not
answer but pointed toward the basement. They killed Ewa, I thought.
Now I was sure I would die too.

In the meantime, my friends from Żegota worked for my release.
They paid an enormous sum of money to get me out of there. In
January 1943 I joined a group of people sent to Ravensbrück, a no-

torious concentration camp in Germany. It was a large camp for women. Approximately 135,000 were imprisoned there. They gave me a cotton uniform—a striped Nazi prisoner's uniform to be used for the summer and winter. Located in an overcrowded, unheated barracks, I received two meager meals a day. Ravensbrück was infamous because doctors used women as guinea pigs for their cruel research. Close to a hundred women underwent medical experiments; only forty-two survived.

My only comfort was information about the Germans' military setbacks and their imminent defeat. The possibility of my survival now became stronger. As the Russian army approached, the Germans ordered all prisoners to form groups. They ordered us to march in the direction of Hamburg, three or four hundred kilometers away. Only elderly and sick prisoners were left behind. The journey is hard to describe. Hundreds of miserable, emaciated women in striped uniforms were escorted by German guards and dogs. Many women died on this journey.

The day I especially remember was May 3, 1945, when we met American troops. I had a feeling that they did not know what to do with us; I suspected that they could not understand what kind of prisoners we were. They left us where we were, and the local people brought us food. Some prisoners died, eating too much after years of starvation. After a few days, our liberators told us we could go whenever we wanted. Nobody gave us any help or transportation. We were thousands of kilometers from our homes.

My only dream was to return to Poland to find my mother and sisters if they were still alive. I joined a group of twenty other women and we started our march. For more than a month, we wandered throughout defeated Germany in its ruins, with groups of German soldiers hiding in the woods and criminals at large. Mostly we walked, but occasionally we received lifts on cars or trains. The most comfortable part of the journey was on a coal car. Food was scarce, but sometimes people gave us soup or a few potatoes. But we were free, and were on our way home. Someone gave me an old dress, and I got rid of my striped rags. Finally I managed to reach Poland, and I found my mother and sisters. That was a joyous reunion. They assumed I had perished.

After a few weeks, I got a job at Połczyn Zdrój, a medical resort in Poland. I found an apartment in a doctor's home. I made friends with his family. I loved his old mother, who liked to tell me stories of her life. She told me that during World War I, she lived in Zakopane, a mountain resort in Poland. One day a pregnant woman came to their house and asked for help. She was a homeless refugee, and her husband was at war. They accepted her, and after a few days she gave birth to a beautiful baby girl, named Ewa. Finally the woman told them she had to go to find her husband. She left the baby at the doctor's home. She never returned, probably dying somewhere in the war. The doctor's family adopted the girl and raised her as their own daughter. At the beginning of World War II, Ewa joined the resistance like thousands of other young people. Later she disappeared. The doctor's family did not know what had happened to her. It was then that I interrupted the old woman, saying: "You told me about Ewa's birth; now I will tell you about her last days. The girl you are speaking about was Ewa Gibalska, my friend from the prison in Lwów."

Returning to my original story about my little protégé, Malka-Marysia: She survived the war at the orphanage, and her mother survived the concentration camp. Unfortunately, her father did not make it. Malka's mother returned after the war and was extremely happy to find her daughter. They emigrated to Israel and later to Canada.

Makuch became lifelong friends with Malka-Marysia and her mother. They invited Makuch to Canada, where she met her husband. After emigrating to Canada, Makuch was honored by Yad Vashem for having saved Malka's life.

HALINA MARTIN

Tarczyn was a small town. Rickety houses surrounded the square. Poor little shops, run by Jews, were inside the square. There was an ironmonger and an establishment that sold fabrics. Another tiny shop specialized in soap—bars of very poor quality. Here one could also buy matches and, from time to time, even candles. They had sold out of paraffin because the peasants had bought it all up. The poor wretched shopkeepers lived frugally, saving all their pennies. They hoarded them in the hovels at the back of their shops that served as homes. They never spent a single unnecessary penny. Money had to be set aside for sons and especially for daughters, who had to have dowries with which to get a good husband. Tailors sat bent over their needles. Shoemakers busied themselves over their wooden lasts.

Skullcaps, long robes, beards, and side curls characterized their world. All around them were the Germans, whom they trusted. It was tragic.

The center of life in Tarczyn was the mill. My father had bought it in partnership with Kramarski, Leszno, and Borensztajn. Each of these gentlemen had a large family. They worked conscientiously at the mill. They were proud owners. Kramarski and Leszno had shaved their beards and discarded their typically Jewish attire. Borensztajn, however, was adamant; he would do nothing that might go against his religion.

"You must sign the bills of sale with me. Otherwise, the Germans will confiscate the mill," I told them. Our discussions took ages. Whole days passed. Bad times were approaching, and the situation worsened all the time. I begged. I tried to explain. Kramarski was the most difficult to convince.

"I'm not giving up my 'epaulettes'—the thing that I am proud of. The peasants know I'm a miller; they treat me with respect."

"There will be no peasants in the ghetto. Why don't you just find yourself a farmer who will hide you. I'll pay him well every month," I said.

"That's a great favor. You want to pay? From the proceeds of my own mill?"

"There'll be no mill unless you sign the bill of sale. Even at this stage we'll have to forge the date," I told him.

This was my third encounter with the Jewish community and my partners. Even the two who had shaved their beards simply refused to listen. There was no rabbi among them. Nevertheless, I managed to find someone who knew the First Book of Samuel, and I asked him to recite chapter 8. The old man covered his eyes with his hand. He swayed rhythmically, speaking for a long time in a language that was totally unknown to me. Whenever he stopped, a groaning and a wailing filled the room; the noise rose with each verse. I pressed my own Bible to my heart and swayed with them in rhythm to the words. I had no way of knowing if he was actually reciting the chapter I had chosen. Would they understand at last? Would they grasp the gravity of the situation? The old man sat back in silence. I waited for everyone to calm down. I opened the book. I felt apprehensive, unsure in case I might offend their religious sensibilities by quoting from the Bible. But I had no choice:

. . . he will take your sons and make them serve
. . . he will take your daughters

. . . he will seize the best of your cornfields
. . . and you yourselves will become the slaves
. . . It will be too late, the Lord will not answer you.

[1 Sam. 8:10]

"You must believe me," I shouted. "You must trust me before it's too late," I appealed.

A few days later, Kramarski led a delegation into the mill. I was just drinking some strong black coffee that had been brought to me from the little Jewish restaurant—real coffee bought by a Jew from a German. The men would not sit down. I was asked not to talk too long, for precious time had already been lost because of me. What did I want? We started from the beginning, talking about how bad the ghettos were. They were overcrowded and disease-ridden. There was hunger. I did not have the courage to even mention the word "death."

"How do you know all this? Have you been in a ghetto?" they asked. "So what's this thing about ghettos? So people do business; it's not that bad. Why should it be any worse? Because they've beaten a few Jews? Who hasn't? Work? Who can't pay his way works! Put us in there? What for? Aren't there enough there already?" came a stream of responses. "Ssh," cried Kramarski. "Let her have her say."

"Hide whatever valuables you have," I said. "Give them to people you can trust before they're confiscated. Find yourselves a hideout. Now! Whilst there's still time and. . . . " I could no longer tolerate their suspicious glances nor those hands stroking their beards.

The Germans were clearing the area of Jews, but a torpor had set in on Tarczyn. A stubborn, hypnotic faith persisted that nothing could possibly happen here. I tried to avoid the mill. The trance-like atmosphere in the little town was frightening. Winter was on its way. The first snows fell thickly, consolidated by the frost. Then it happened. A telephone call from the Polish police station: "The military police are surrounding Tarczyn."

We set out from the estate in a cavalcade. Three pairs of horses were harnessed to the large sledges, two strong men to each sledge. Wrapped in a sheepskin coat, thick winter boots, a colored woolen shawl tied around my head, I rubbed my frozen hands. I felt a cold, nervous sweat running down my back. By the time we reached Tarczyn, only my men were pretending to do some work on the mill. The millers' belongings were strewn outside their homes. We rushed to the square. The Germans were everywhere. They pushed people into open trucks. They had been dragged out of their homes with nothing but what they wore at the time. I ran into the ironmonger's, brushing past the German who was standing there with the butt of his gun raised ready to strike. "Here!" I shouted at the Jew. "Here, see?" I thrust an old bill at him. "Here," I turned to the Germans. "I paid but he didn't deliver the goods. I won't let this go. Come on boys, load up."

The commander of the military police appeared. Beside him was Jarząbek, the commander of our own police force. He took the scrap of paper from my hand and without looking at it, he put it into the pocket of his uniform. "She's right," he reported to the German. "The lady of the manor is owed some iron girdles, a few cartons of nails, spikes, and horseshoes." While he talked, I slid my leg behind the counter and winked at the terrified shopkeeper. I whispered: "Put whatever you have of value inside my boot." Luckily, he understood. I ran to the mill and emptied the contents of my boot on the table. My men noted the owner's name and hid everything in the silo of rye while I went to the timber yard. I managed to run to the mill several times to deposit a few gold coins, some cheap jewelry, and a few creased green dollar bills. The Polish police camouflaged my comings and goings among the gathering crowd. Whenever they could, they barred the Germans' path, creating a general confusion that made it possible for me to reach a few unfortunate individuals. Amid the lamentation, the prayers, and the swearing that was going on in German, Polish, and Yiddish, we managed to thrust an eiderdown at some old woman or a blanket for a mother to wrap up her child. We drew the Germans toward an empty doorway, shouting, "Jude, Jude!" while at the other side of the house we pulled a terrified girl through the broken window. A hand over the child's mouth, a sack covering her, and then her rescuer ran with his human bundle into some quiet alley to look for safety.

The Germans shouted: "*Raus!*" There were more and more of us until eventually it was difficult to spot the military police in the chaos. Everyone shouted at once; it was impossible to distinguish any individual voice or word. Then the motors of three trucks were switched on. A few shots into the air, and everyone stood frozen to the spot. Suddenly someone pushed me against one of the Germans who aimed at the fleeing figure, and his bullet fell short on the trodden snow. I was on the ground, the navy uniform of Jarząbek towering above me. He helped me up and brushed away the snow and grit. The cart began to move. My flowered woolen shawl was on its way to the ghetto, wrapped around one of the babies. The colored woolen shawl was important. Later it would be cut into pieces by people from the ghetto who came to me for help.

There were two horrid faces on either side of me, while straight ahead I had a view of the back of the chauffeur's thick red neck. The ones beside me held their guns posed ready to shoot. I was lucky they had not handcuffed me. I sat between them, aware that at any moment I might be thrown first against one, then the other. I had to be careful not to jostle them, for they might beat me there and then. What could they want, damn them! There was no point in recapping all my sins. I wouldn't have enough fingers to count them. It was more important to see which way the car would turn once it reached the main road. If it turned right, it would mean that these men were from Gestapo headquarters in Warsaw, and that would be hopeless. If we went left, they were part of the Gestapo stationed in Grojec, where there would be some hope. The car jumped over the potholes at the entrance to the main road. I shut my eyes tight; a few seconds passed. By then, a feeling of relief swept over me. My bones felt the car turning towards Grojec.

I tried to talk to them but they replied: "Shut your mouth!" So that was that. Mentally, I was prepared for the worst. I hoped that my own people would have raised the alarm by now. But who would alert Warsaw? Apart from Bolek, no one at home knew about my secret contacts with the underground there. I had been taken from the fields, literally dragged off my horse. I wasn't carrying any poison. Bolek was in Warsaw; maybe they would let him know. How long could I last? How long would they keep me in Grojec? Would they send me to Warsaw before friends could help? Why hadn't they searched me?

I looked through the window of the speeding car, wanting to feast my eyes on the world before the prison gates closed on me. In the fields, people were bringing in the last of the harvest. We passed the white peasant cottages. "That's my work," was the thought that shot through my mind. "I stole the whitewash from under the noses of the Germans." I felt a little better, hoping that the inhabitants of those cottages would remember me. Maybe they would help my children. With this thought in mind I was led into the Gestapo building.

The Gestapo lackeys were always in a hurry. They jumped out of the car shouting, "Quickly, quickly!" Was I expected to hurry toward my death? I walked as slowly as possible despite their jostling.

One guard, then another, some steps, a door, and there behind his desk sat the Gestapo officer looking almost pleased to see me.

"Please sit down." The words were polite, but his tone was sharp. He barked something at the men who had brought me in. Three of us were left in the room—the officer, someone sitting at a typewriter, and I. I didn't know whether I felt hot or cold. My hands were sweating. The German lit a cigarette. Then, as if suddenly remembering his manners, he held the box out to me. I had a terrible desire to smoke, but I declined with a gesture of the hand. "Have you stopped smoking? Since when?" The bastard remembered my little performance with the cigarette at our first meeting.

He said: "Where's the Jew?" I almost asked, "Which one?" but instead I said, "What Jew?" "The one who escaped from the ghetto. The one you took into your house!" Now I knew what he meant. I saw my end.

He was lying in the bushes on the edge of the wood near the potato field. His head was hidden under an arm. I thought he was asleep, but Swietnicki assured me that he was unconscious. He was surrounded by reapers, women laborers, and stable hands, a whole crowd of people. He was slight. The bony arm that protruded from his tattered threadbare coat showed that he had been starved to the limit. His huge, grown man's shoes were well-worn. Flies settled around him. I gently rolled the boy on his back and lifted his hand from his face. The whites of his eyes were visible under the half-closed lids. The parted lips hardly took in any air. His nose was white, his complexion bluish; his neck was long and far too weak to support his head, which lolled on his shoulder. "How long has he been lying here?" I asked.

"Oh, well, Witek found him on his way to work."

"And you've only brought me here now? Have you no fear of God? Aren't you ashamed?"

"But the Germans shoot people for helping Jews." One woman started sniveling; another burst into loud tears. Swietnicki turned purple as he listened to my whispered orders. He took my horse, clumsily got into the saddle, and rode off. I waited for the cart and horses to arrive. I had the time to make a speech.

"You think you're afraid of the Germans? And who'll betray you?"

"*You?*" I pointed at each person in turn. "You, or maybe you? It's not the Germans you're afraid of, you're scared of one another.

Who's the informer among you—well, who?" They stared at the ground. The boy groaned. Thick saliva trickled down the side of his mouth. "Józka, wipe his lips with your rag." The terrified girl slowly knelt down beside the child. Her movements were hesitant, but suddenly she was filled with pity and began to cry loudly. "You wretch, you poor thing, there's no punishment good enough for those murderers," the women chimed in. The men took off their caps and scratched their heads uncomfortably. The cart approached. "Go to your work, all of you. I advise you to keep your mouth shut, or we'll all pay."

We couldn't bring him into the rooms. He lay in the hall. Gienia carefully took off his lice-infested rags. A colored scrap of material was attached with a safety pin under his jacket. It was a tattered piece of scarf, the one that had gone to the ghetto the previous winter. It was a cry for help from the ghetto. Linka gently washed the sores on his body with a large sponge and put some stuff into his hair to delouse it. Kit had led the children out of the house to spare them the unpleasant sight and us from the added danger of their childish prattle. Robert called the doctor. For the time being, we put a spoonful of warm milk mixed with a drop of brandy to the boy's parched lips. We gently massaged his heart. He began to regain consciousness. He shook and goose pimples covered his body. I left him wrapped in blankets; I was now able to go to the phone.

"Mr. Jarząbek," I said to the chief of police. "I'd like to invite you with one of your friends to dinner. . . . Do not thank me, it is my pleasure . . . and maybe you'd better warn your wife that you won't be back for the night."

"What's happened?" he asked.

"What could possibly have happened? We need your companionship. We're missing a partner at the table," I calmly replied.

I knew very well that Jarząbek had never held a pack of cards in his life. He understood; he asked no more questions but promised to come. The doctor arrived. A drip was set up. There were injections, vitamin pills, creams, and bandages. There was a lot of crying and pain, then a bit of food. The boy finally fell asleep in the side room. It was a fitful sleep, interrupted by the moans of nightmares.

In the late evening, a cart left the house. It was well lined with straw. A few planks were placed across it to hide the boy, and sacks of potatoes and vegetables were put on top. To all appearances, the police had requisitioned some smuggled goods. Mr. Jarząbek sat beside the stable lad, and the other policeman sat at the back of the cart with a bottle of vodka in his pocket just in case they met up with a

German patrol. This was the fastest turnaround to a safe place that
we had ever accomplished.

"How do you know it was a Jew? Maybe he was a tinker?"
"I'll ask you again. Where's the Jew?"
"How should I know? He ate well and disappeared."
"Do you know that helping Jews is punishable by death?"
"Jews, but not children."
"Don't split hairs with me. A Jew's a Jew and. . . . "
"Listen!" Thanks to my broken German, I could speak familiarly
to them all. "Listen, you, I'm a mother. For me, a child's a child
whether it be German, Turkish, Jewish, Chinese, or Polish. If I find
one lying in a ditch, I'll always feed it. You threaten death? Fine! I'd
rather not live in a world where a woman, a mother, can't help a
child. You can shoot me, hang me. Do you have children? Where?
Are they in Berlin? Under the falling bombs? Who's going to help
them when they're lying wounded in a ditch somewhere?"

The man at the typewriter rushed to take down all that I said.
The Gestapo officer moved from behind his desk. I thought it was all
going to end right then and there. Automatically I raised my hands
to protect my face. He passed by me. He opened the door and looked
out. He came back to the typewriter. He took out the sheet of paper
and tore it up, slowly. "Couldn't you be a little more discreet? A little
more careful? I'll order a car to take you home, madam, but this is
the last time."

"Thank you for the car. I don't like cars. But I want to get in touch
with my people at home, by telephone." He gave the number I dic-
tated to the operator and handed me the receiver.

"Send out the horses to meet me. I'm coming home, on foot."

Just at the corner of the Gestapo prison, I recognized a member
of the resistance. It meant that the underground alarm network
worked, and that they were watching to see what was happening to
me. The boy who was looking for me, took off his cap, looked up at
the sky, and as if pointing at something, raised his thumb.

Walking in riding boots is a very uncomfortable experience, even
when one has the feeling one has returned to life.

Martin studied mechanics at the University of Warsaw before the war. She
married in 1935 and had two daughters. An active member of the Home
Army, she participated in the Warsaw Uprising of 1944. Martin left Poland
for England in 1946 and has been involved in affairs of Polish emigration ever
since. Her husband died in 1972.

KONSTANCJA MARZEC

The event took place in Wolyn, on the outskirts of the small town of Różyszcze. One day my father brought home a sixteen-year-old girl from the woods. She was Jewish. Her name was Eugenia Katz. My family sheltered her in our home during the German occupation. After the war, she emigrated to Israel.

Quite often we helped other Jews who came to us for food; there was the late Mr. Dołgopoluk and others, whose names I don't recall because my parents never asked them.

I remember one young Jew named Geniek, who stayed with us for three months. In the region where we lived, many Jews were saved by Polish families, although every Polish family risked their lives in doing so.

Marzec, who is in ailing health, lives in retirement in Poland. She visited Katz and other Jewish friends in Israel in 1980.

LEOKADIA MIKOŁAJKÓW

Together with my husband and sons, I lived during the Nazi occupation in the town of Dębica, where we had a clinic. Next to our home were the local Gestapo and the criminal police. Opposite our home was the gate to the Jewish ghetto, established by the Germans in Dębica in 1940. Jews from far and wide were brought together in this ghetto. Here the Germans selected strong and healthy women over sixteen years of age and men over fourteen for work in the concentration camp in Pustkow. All working Jews, registered in the *Arbeitsampt* (Bureau of Labor) and other workshops, received basic medical care in a clinic offered by me, a qualified nurse, and my husband, Aleksander, a physician of great learning. Other residents of the ghetto and working families also received examinations.

In 1940 a Jewish woman by the name of Reich came with her son, Froimek, for an examination. She appealed to my husband to save her son from certain extermination. Froimek, who was physically weak, would probably have been shot by the Germans in several days on account of his unsatisfactory output at work. My husband and I decided to help Mrs. Reich and Froimek; he was registered at the *Arbeitsampt* as a messenger for the dispensary. From that moment, we helped the Reich family and other Jews many times with medicine and food.

In the meantime, there were two major liquidations of Jews. In the fall of 1942, the Germans began the complete liquidation of the Jewish ghetto of Dębica. With the aim of hiding at least some Jews from extermination, I gave Froimek the key to my home so that he could hide as many Jews as possible in the garage and in the office garret. More than once it also happened that I sent my own son to the ghetto to take Froimek the key, which he had forgotten. During the time of the liquidations and pogroms, Froimek brought us nine of his relatives to rescue. We took care of them in our home for five to seven days. With our consent, Froimek simultaneously began the work of adapting the garret of our home and the cellar under the garage as a hiding place for the Jews for a longer time.

In November 1942, my husband, Aleksander, found out that the Germans planned to finish the liquidation of the Jewish ghetto in the next several days. That same day, twelve of Froimek's relatives escaped from the ghetto and concealed themselves in our home. From that time until the liberation of Dębica by the Soviet army on August 24, 1944, twelve people were under our constant protection: Froimek's parents, two sisters, brother, brother-in-law, three cousins, uncle, aunt, and a five-year-old child.

In the beginning, they hid themselves in the cellar under the garage of our home and in an outbuilding, but during the day they stayed in the garage. In December 1943, the German criminal police entered our home, saying that they were requisitioning the garage for their own needs. They demanded at once the key to the garage. Anticipating that at that moment the Jews hiding in the garage were moving about, I induced one of the Germans to walk with me to the inside door of the garage, talking loudly in German, after which I feigned forgetting the key and returned to the house for it. I judged that the Jews in the garage had heard the German language and had hidden themselves in the shelter below the garage because after he unlocked the door, the German did not notice anything. That same evening, my husband escorted the Jews to another place in town— to the home of Mr. Kunysz, an eighty-year-old man, where they stayed in safety until the liberation.

During the time we sheltered this family, we gave them a large container of cooked food every night and at the same time carried away their trash. These deeds we performed secretly, keeping it even from the maid who worked in our home. Several times during the occupation, we survived inspections conducted by the Germans.

In addition to concealing the Reich family, my husband and I played our part in saving approximately thirty other Jews, offering them medicine, food, documents, and clothes.

My husband died on the day of the liberation of the town while ministering to a wounded partisan. The Reich family survived the war, and they now live in Brooklyn, New York.

Mikołajków, now retired, spent most of her life as a nurse. She was also active in community affairs, having served as a town councillor in Dębica.

WACŁAW MILEWSKI

I was fifteen years old when the war broke out. My father commanded the Third Light Horse Regiment. When the war started, they evacuated all families of army personnel by train to Parczew. From there we made our way to the outskirts of Kowel, where we learned of the Soviet invasion of eastern Poland. We retreated through Chełm, where the Soviets caught us. We stayed at Chełm until the Germans arrived. Then my mother and I went to Lublin, where we spent the terrible winter of 1939-40 in a room infested with bedbugs.

By the spring of 1940, all of our money was gone. We had to find work, so my mother and I decided to go to my uncle, who was the administrative director of a sugarbeet factory at Częstocice near Ostrowiec, in the Kielce region. There my mother worked in the office, while I worked in the factory. I also joined the fire brigade because in that way I could avoid being taken to work in Germany. The fire brigade was also a cover for the Home Army. I joined the Home Army and took the oath in 1941. Most of the time we just trained; lectures were held in private homes and in the refinery. But on several occasions between 1941 and 1944, we went on maneuvers in the Holy Cross Mountains.

On Friday after work, we all set out on the long march to the mountains. About dusk, we reached a village where our weapons were hidden, and we then marched throughout the night, arriving at the summit of the Holy Cross Mountains at dawn. There full-scale training took place. We participated in drills of all kinds and even shot our weapons on a rifle range. On Sunday the entire unit went to Mass. We stood in ranks in front of the church and generally behaved as if there was no German army in Poland. As far as I remember, the Germans never seemed to make their presence felt. On Sunday night, we started on the march back to Częstocice and arrived back exhausted on Monday morning, ready to start the day's work.

I was very fortunate not to be called up by the Home Army in the first mobilization for *Burza* [code name for the summer of 1944 and the Warsaw Uprising], because everyone who started out to go to Warsaw's aid was caught by the Germans. They called me up in the second mobilization and assigned me to Lieutenant Potok's unit. The men who had been in the unit for a long time were armed and dressed in uniforms of some kind. On the other hand, the new arrivals were a terrible mishmash. I wore several sweaters under a windbreaker. There were no weapons. Someone gave me a rusty rifle with a curved barrel to use. We slept on the bare earth in rough shelters made of branches.

One day we ambushed some Germans, killing an official and his assistants. The Germans started a systematic roundup, but instead of leaving the area immediately, Potok decided to remain. The German artillery attacked the center of our camp. Unfortunately, everyone who had remained in the camp, including boys as young as twelve years of age, were killed. Those of us who had weapons were some distance away at the time. As the Germans closed in on us, we argued about whether to try to escape or to hide in the trees. We became a discussion group instead of an army. I was in charge of a squad, and we decided to attempt an escape. The Germans were hiding in ditches that served as firebreaks. The confusion was incredible. No one knew what was happening.

As we approached, the Germans, obviously thinking we were also Germans, called out, betraying their positions. We threw grenades at them and thus succeeded in crossing three such ditches. At one point, we heard a noise and started to shoot, only to find we were shooting at wild boar. Out of twelve men in my squad, three got away. The Germans killed some of them, while the others decided to try their luck in the forest. As we reached relative safety, I saw that blood was pouring down my hand. I had been wounded in the shoulder but had not even noticed. I tried to decide what to do and where to go. I remembered that nearby there was an estate that sent sugarbeet to the refinery, so we made our way there. There someone tended my wound, and I stayed until my mother, who had found out where I was, came to fetch me.

After the war, Milewski and his mother fled Poland. They went to England in 1947, where he eventually became the head archivist of the Polish Institute and Sikorski Museum.

ANNA ORSKA

I was walking along the street in Warsaw with some friends in November 1943 when I was caught in a *łapanka* (roundup). I was nineteen years old. One moment everything was calm, the next moment there were piercing whistles on all sides, voices calling in Polish to take cover. But it was too late. I ended up in a labor camp at Buków. There were Poles, Italians, and Russians there. The Italians were treated abominably. One officer who had tried to escape was kept immersed in water up to his armpits. I used to take him food.

One of the most memorable events of my life occurred in 1944, when the Germans started to be more careful with their ammunition. We were still at Buków. Shortly before the Warsaw Uprising, the camp was transferred to the vicinity of Wadowice, to an estate belonging to the Szczerbiowski family, and then, after the uprising had started, to the Sudetenland. At Buków, the street was visible from the camp. One day I saw a woman crossing the road leading a small child by the hand. Suddenly an SS-man went up to her, grabbed the child, and threw it against a wall, killing it instantly. He shouted, "We have saved a bullet!" I could not forget that sight for many years afterwards.

Another event that has stayed in my mind involved the camp commandant, Sonderführer Erich Steinman. One day there was a roll call. We all wondered whether the uprising had started, because normally roll calls were held only if there had been some German military success. As we waited, Steinman drove into the camp in his Opel and showed off the dead body of a woman who had been shot and tied on the car's bumper. She had been a very beautiful dark-haired Jewish woman, dressed in a superb navy blue georgette dress. I had never seen a dress like that worn on the street; it was so beautiful. Still, Steinman was not as bad as his deputy, Jeschke, who could be merciless. On the other hand, the camp doctor, Dressler, who was an Austrian, helped everyone a great deal.

Toward the end of 1943 but before I was taken to the camp at Buków, I was walking along with a friend, Mrs. Kazimierczyk, near Treblinka. She said she wanted to show me something. Suddenly she said, "Look!" But I had already seen. The ground was literally moving, although the mass graves had been covered over. The story was that only one person out of every four was shot. The rest of the victims were buried alive in the graves and could not get out.

The end of the war found Orska in a German camp near Prague. Like so many other Poles, she made her way to the Polish Second Corps in Italy and was evacuated to England in 1946. She attended college, married, and later worked for British Caledonia Airways.She is now retired.

HALINA OSTROWSKA

I was born in Pińsk, where my father was the headmaster of a high school. He came from Podhorce, east of Lwów. After his arrest by the NKVD on March 23, 1940, my mother, grandmother, and I decided to go to Podhorce. The journey took us about a week, traveling dressed as peasants. Unfortunately, my father's family could not put us up, as our presence would have been dangerous for them. So we lived the best we could, hiding during the day in stables and barns. During the summer months we hid in the forest, going to friends at night to eat and to wash. Conditions were appalling. We lived this way for nearly two years, until the German attack on the Soviet Union in June 1941.

We had spent the night before the German attack in a barn on a hill, its rear entrance hidden by a ravine and the forest. From the front entrance we saw fires and explosions in the vicinity of the main Lwów-Kiev highway through Brody, which had been built by Polish prisoners of war. We saw strings of tanks along the road. At this stage we had no idea the Germans had attacked. After about an hour, around midday, we heard the roar of tanks in the village. Then we heard a few shots; the Germans had arrived. Some time previously, Soviet tank troops had entrenched themselves around the village of Podhorce Górne, which was inhabited mainly by Poles, in contrast to Podhorce Dolne, which was largely Ukrainian.

We thought the Germans had come to deport us, but now it was obvious that they had come to defend Brody and the Lwów-Kiev highway. The Germans attacked from the direction of Olesko. Since all the Soviet tanks faced in the opposite direction, they were unable to swing their guns around in time. The result was a massacre.

The Germans then continued on to Brody. This was the first wave of the attack. We did not see any more Germans for several weeks. During that time, we were left entirely on our own. There was no police, no authority of any kind. The Poles protected their village, the Ukrainians theirs. This situation lasted until the end of autumn.

Then the Germans arrived and started to commandeer supplies of food. In November, I was called into the office of the military police in Olesko and told I would be sent to work in Germany. People who did not own any land in the area were the first to be sent as forced laborers to Germany. Since we were refugees, I belonged in this category. I was sixteen years old at the time. At the police headquarters, the children of the Bobrowski family, who had also been called in, and I were seen by a member of the commission charged with requisitioning supplies of food and labor. His name was Henryk Lenz. He turned out to be half-Polish; his mother was Polish, and he came from Łódź, where he had been forcibly conscripted into the German military police. (Some time later, a distant relative of mine helped to get false papers for himself and Lenz, who died in the Warsaw Uprising of 1944, fighting on the Polish side under the name of Henryk Leśniewski.) Lenz told me and the other children not to worry and said that as long as he was in Olesko, we would not be sent to Germany. He suggested that we go back to school, so my mother sent me to a school in Złoczów, eight kilometers away through the forest.

In 1942, I was called in to the *Arbeitsampt* (Bureau of Labor) in Złoczów and this time I was told that I would have to work at least half of every day; otherwise I would be sent to Germany. Thanks to friends, I got a job as a messenger at the architect's offices of Eduard Wyklicky, who had branches in Vienna, Lwów, and Złoczów. They engaged mostly in designing the interiors of SS and Gestapo houses and apartments. Wyklicky himself was an Austrian, a member of the Nazi party and a most unusual man in many ways. He was a very big man with a fondness for tweed jackets, so he looked like an Englishman. I worked from 6:00 a.m. to 12:00 noon. Since the Germans had introduced Soviet time in these territories, it was very dark when I left for work during the winter months. Many of Wyklicky's employees were Polish or Jewish; he did not employ any Ukrainians. All architectural plans were drawn by Jewish architects. The secretary, Krysia, was also Jewish. Despite Wyklicky's protests, she was later arrested by the Gestapo and disappeared. All the Poles and Jews employed by Wyklicky were very well looked after. We were given food and even allowed to take bread home to our families.

Wyklicky was very friendly with SS Haupstürmführer Warzog, head of the Gestapo for the district of Złoczów. Warzog spoke perfect Polish. He was very good-looking and had the habit of tapping the top of his boot with his whip. As far as I know, he never mistreated any Pole or Jew, at least not on Wyklicky's premises.

Warzog occasionally had private parties at his house, to which we were sometimes invited, together with officials of the Jewish council and the Jewish police. I went once, unwillingly, with an older friend of mine. This friend had married a Jewish doctor before the war and was now hiding him at home. It never occurred to me how potentially dangerous the situation was. Probably it was because of my age, but I was taking an enormous risk, and my mother was terrified. Anyway, we went. A blond, Polish-speaking woman opened the door and assured us that no harm would come to us in that house. Judging by the way Warzog addressed her, she must have been his housekeeper. He told her to make sure that no one left hungry. What is more, we were all given a parcel of cold meat to take home.

All the Jews employed by Wyklicky lived in the ghetto and came to the office every day wearing the required Star of David on their clothes. At the beginning, the ghetto was very well organized, and the Jews brought us cakes and bread from the ghetto bakery. Wyklicky's Jewish lawyer, Dr. Maks Pomeranz, and the chief architect, Mr. Margulis, noticed that I had no shoes, so they made a rough guess as to my shoe size and had a pair of shoes made for me in the ghetto. I had no coat, either, so they also had a coat made for me there. In return, I went on foraging expeditions into the countryside, walking many kilometers through the forest to get onions, garlic, milk, cereals, eggs, and other provisions for the ghetto. I used to take a four-wheeled cart to carry the goods. Money had little meaning at this time, so I took articles to barter for the food—a ring, a length of cloth, whatever there was.

In 1942, conditions in the ghetto deteriorated. My forays into the country became increasingly dangerous. Armed bands roamed the forests. The Ukrainians were very well organized, but there were also the *Bataliony Chłopskie* (Peasant Battalions) and Soviet soldiers who had evaded capture by the Germans. To be quite fair, most of them were just bandits who had committed their crimes in the name of one or another Polish or Ukrainian organization, giving them a bad name in the process. They stole everything they could lay their hands on. Jews who escaped from the ghettos were hunted. But anyone they chanced upon in the forest was in great danger. We avoided all human contact on our expeditions. During one search for food, we saw a Polish village near Wronki completely destroyed; its inhabitants were impaled on fence posts and half-burned. My companions and I fled in terror.

The year 1943 was terrible. Conditions in the ghetto were appalling. Our situation worsened too. The ghetto was constantly surrounded by Germans. The Jews died of hunger, cold, typhus, and beatings. Those Jews who worked for Wyklicky were lucky because they worked and got food. But one day the German police came to the office at about 11:00 a.m. and ordered us out into the street. We were forced to watch in horror as trucks took the entire Jewish population with their families from the Złoczów ghetto, surrounded by SS and extermination squads, to an unknown destination. Later we heard that the Germans had executed them near Wronki. People who lived nearby said the earth moved and blood seeped through the soil of the mass grave. The stench of death hung over the entire place.

The Germans spared Wyklicky's employees. The previous day the employees had not been allowed by Wyklicky to leave the office building. Instead, their families had been brought to the office, where they spent the night. The next day they were taken to Lwów by truck to work in Wyklicky's offices and factory there. About five hundred people were rescued. In that world of savagery and corruption, many of them managed to survive the war. (I met Dr. Pomeranz again after the war in Wrocław, where he lived until he emigrated to Israel with his Polish wife.)

We had to live from day to day, with the determination to keep going until tomorrow and to manage to survive the war. During the winter of 1943-44, the German retreat was in full swing. Carts and cars full of wounded soldiers and stolen goods passed through Złoczów. Wyklicky's offices were now entirely transferred to Lwów. He offered to take the Poles to Lwów, but my mother decided it would be better to stay in Złoczów as long as we moved into an apartment house where mostly Poles lived. At the time, we were living in an apartment house where there were many Ukrainians, and almost every day we received written threats signed by the UPA, a Ukrainian terrorist organization, pinned to our front door.

The German army now took over the administration of the area. The Gestapo disappeared. Only special SS units remained, and they had little time for the civilian population. The *Arbeitsampt* closed and so did the shops selling rationed food. We heard gunfire. The Soviet air force bombed Złoczów every night. Just before the *Arbeitsampt* closed, the Germans sent me to an army vehicle and tank repair unit. This was an independent unit stationed near the front lines. I was to serve as a translator in the unit's hospital.

The commanding officer was Hauptman Durkopf. He was a typical German officer who had served in World War I and was now employed behind the front lines. In civilian life, he owned a factory near Hanover that manufactured sewing machines and bicycles. Russians in German uniforms, many of them descendents of the Volga Germans, staffed the unit. Their women worked in the kitchens as auxiliary staff. Most of them did not speak German. The hospital doctor, Dr. Heinz, came from Opole. He assured me that my family and I would be fine as long as I was with the unit, and all I needed to do was to translate for him. He was very good to me and to the Russian soldiers. After I had been with the unit for about a week, he called me in and told me that I would have to be present when he examined the soldiers for venereal disease. It was a terrible experience.

Again we were well looked after. We ate the same food as the soldiers. The Germans told me to bring a large container with me and it was filled in the kitchens for me to take home. Ladlesful of different vegetables went into the container, which my mother later separated. On the way home, we passed by the sentries, but no one ever stopped us from taking the food out. Only our pockets were searched. I took home enough to feed not only my mother and grandmother but also some of our friends.

The unit's telephone exchange had been manned by two sergeants. When one of them was transferred to the front line, I had to work alternate shifts in his place since my German was very good. The exchange was protected by metal walls and windows with metal shutters and could also be entered from Durkopf's office. I worked during the day, and the sergeant worked the night shift, sleeping close by while I worked.

Naturally, they did not trust me. One day I mistakenly disconnected a call from the front line before it had finished. The unit's political officer, whose call I had disconnected, rushed in brandishing his revolver. He called me "Polish pig" and accused me of sabotage. Durkopf managed to defuse the situation. Later he asked me whether I had disconnected the call deliberately. I assured him that it had been a genuine mistake since I had assumed the conversation was finished. He accepted my explanation but warned me to be careful in the future. That man in a German uniform had saved my life.

I stayed with the unit until the end of April 1944. There were not many Ukrainians around by then, so we had no fears on that score, but everyone was afraid of the Russians. The unit was transferred to Zimna Woda. I was told to go with the civilians who worked for the unit and to take my mother and grandmother with me. But my mother decided to stay in Złoczów. After a few days in Zimna Woda, I decided to go back to Złoczów and try to persuade my mother to come to Zimna Woda. I was given the necessary permission and set off, traveling on German trucks. After six or seven changes, I reached my destination. Złoczów was in ruins, but I found my mother alive. She had managed to survive by hiding in cellars. By now my permit had expired, so together with my mother I went to the military commandant's office to get another permit. We arrived to find a long line of people clutching bundles and waiting for permits. No one could go anywhere without a pass. The Germans reserved the trains for troops, and civilians could travel only if they had a permit.

While we waited, the Gestapo surrounded the building and took away the military commandant. Then they herded all of us into the town square, where we stood for some five hours under guard. Men and women, young and old, were put into separate groups. They separated me from my mother. At about 5:00 or 6:00 p.m., a special SS unit gave us passes and allowed us to leave as long as it was on an "official" route. We then found out that the military commandant had been half-Polish and had helped his countrymen the best way he could.

By now, the Germans were in full retreat; their trucks did not stop for anyone. So we set off for Lwów on foot. We arrived on the night of April 30–May 1. That night the Soviets bombed Lwów heavily. They destroyed the main railway station. The Soviets also dropped leaflets saying that this was their way of celebrating May 1 and that the Polish army was fighting alongside the Soviet army. I remained with the vehicle and tank repair unit until it was ordered to retreat.

They offered to take us along with them but my grandmother, mother, and I decided to stay in Lwów.

We survived the Holocaust and the horrors of the war. Above all, we wanted to return to our home in Pińsk but it was not to be. These are my personal experiences relating to a few Germans who remained human despite the orders they had to carry out. This does not mean that the Germans as a whole did not behave badly, as they did elsewhere in Poland. All around me there were reprisals for acts of sabotage. The Germans hanged hostages from balconies. They executed people in the street and sent them to concentration camps. It was just my good fortune that none of these things happened to me.

Ostrowska left Poland in 1956. After obtaining political asylum in Germany, she worked for the American Seventh Army near Stuttgart. In 1957, she went to England, where she married and for many years worked for Fregata Ltd. She is now retired.

FABRIOLA PAULIŃSKA

The year was 1943 when a Jew made himself known to me. He had been an officer in the Polish Thirtieth Cavalry Regiment. He asked if he could spend a few days with me at my home in Warsaw. During the day he could rest because I was gone most of the time, either taking care of people in the ghetto or working in the underground. He stayed with me for several weeks, until my residence was threatened by a police check. Then I had to bid farewell to my Jewish visitor.

I visited the Warsaw ghetto. I noticed that wealthier Jews did not help the poorer ones. Picture this: There were plenty of bread and rolls on display, while outside, under the shop window, Jews died of hunger.

With my own eyes, I witnessed Jews being loaded on buses and transported away.

There was a gardener who had a home near Narutowicz Square. He hid several Jewish families. What betrayed him was the amount of milk supplied to the home. To be sure, he and the Jews he sheltered were shot by the Germans.

Paulińska, a former officer in the Polish Army, emigrated to England in 1947. She married a pharmacist and is the mother of three children. Now a widow, the 77-year-old is active in Polish affairs in England.

STEFAN PETRI

When the war broke out, I lived with my wife, our sons, and my wife's family on Halicki Street, now called Barburki Street, in Warsaw. During the first months of Hitler's occupation, I built in my home a small hiding place in the cellar. Access was through a cabinet in the laundry room. Being an engineer by education, I executed this in a comparatively short time. This secret place was to serve me and my family in case of a threat to our lives.

In 1942, when the Germans began the liquidation of the Warsaw ghetto, I decided to hide in this secret place a Jewish family by the name of Szapiro—Kaufman and Ela Szapiro, together with their sons, Jerzy and Marek. I had known the family of Dr. Szapiro before the war. I decided to hasten to their assistance because this was my obligation.

In the spring of 1942, the four of them escaped from the ghetto and with the help of a mutual friend, Irena Wroblewski, hid themselves in a tollgate in Praga, a suburb of Warsaw. Late at night I escorted them along side streets to my home on Halicki Street. From that time they had to spend the day in the secret hiding place, but at night they could be in the apartment.

One day someone reported to the Gestapo that I was hiding fugitives from the Jewish ghetto. The Germans appeared at my home. They conducted two detailed examinations, attempting by beatings to compel me to reveal the place where the Jews were concealed.

During the searches they used dogs, but even the dogs were unable to uncover anything because in the apartment and in the cellar I had placed a preparation of nicotine, which blunted their sense of smell.

After the intrusion of the Gestapo, I realized the high probability that the hiding place would be uncovered during subsequent searches; many people knew about it, too. During the absence of other residents, I constructed another hiding place for the Szapiro family in 1943.

This time the hiding place was located under the cellar. Under the first cellar, I dug out another one. The access was under a workbench with locksmith's instruments in the upper cellar. In the floor of the upper cellar were found ideal movable boards, opening the way to the hiding place.

The Szapiro family spent the night in the apartment, but during the day they sheltered themselves under the cellar. This situation continued from April 1943 to July 1944. From July to September 11, 1944, the day of liberation of the Praga section of Warsaw from the Germans, the Jews remained constantly in their hiding place.

The sons of Kaufman and Ela Szapiro live to this day. Marek lives in the United States, and Jerzy Szapiro is a professor of medicine in Warsaw.

Petri worked in communications after the war. He died in 1987.

ADOLPH PILCH

During the time of the Warsaw Uprising, in August and September 1944, I was commander of the Palmiry-Młociny Regiment, one of the largest units of which was the Kampinos group, whose commander was Major Alfons Trzaska-Kotowski, known by the pseudonym Okoń.

On August 21, our security forces around Modlin informed us that the commander of a Hungarian detachment had asked for permission to pass through the Kampinos Forest to the south, to reach Laski. I sent an officer to explore what was going on. I received a report indicating that this was a detachment of Hungarian Jews, numbering around two hundred, who were escorted by twenty armed soldiers. The commander of the convoy was Lieutenant Zelinka Sandor Josef.

I agreed to let them pass on the condition that the armed escorts lay down their arms on a wagon, which would be guarded by our partisans. When the detachment arrived at our location in the forest, the Jews were separated from the escorts and received food. Everyone was very hungry. I was able to speak freely with them. They were for the most part around fifty years of age; there were not many young ones. They included industrialists, directors of businesses, bankers, and professors.

When the Jews were asked if they would like to get rid of their guards, they excitedly said no because they did not wish to be responsible for their lives. When asked if they wanted to remain with us, only a few indicated agreement. But when the detachment left, the Jews started to come out of hiding. Forty-six of them stayed with us. They were divided among various companies and squadrons and became regular soldiers.

Unfortunately, the uprising was coming to a close and the Germans began the liquidation of units in the Kampinos Forest. Major Okoń decided to move the group to the south, to the Kielecki Woods. En route to Jaktorow, the group was destroyed. Over 200 men were killed, and approximately 150 were taken prisoner. About 250 joined smaller groups in the south, and over a hundred returned to the Kampinos Forest.

One of the Hungarian Jews, Stevan Istvan, who was about twenty years old and came from Debrecin, came with us to the south. He participated with the unit in several battles. Later he got sick and we left him for treatment near the village of Adamów. This was not easy because he did not speak Polish, and any stranger could see that he was not a resident of the village. And this was dangerous. He waited for the arrival of the Soviet army, receiving from us a pass in three languages—Polish, Russian, and Hungarian. The pass indicated that he was a Polish partisan and requested help to return to Hungary. We were not able to find out what happened to his countrymen whom we had assisted.

Many times I asked myself what had happened to Istvan. Did he get back to Hungary? Then in 1968, in a Warsaw periodical, *For Freedom and Nation*, there appeared an interview with Istvan Garami, by then doctor of economics and director of supply of Budapest's department stores, on the theme of his struggle and adventures in Poland in 1944. He praised us highly, commenting on how humane we were and singling me out as the best partisan commander he had met.

My former partisans in Poland established contact with him, and from that time he often came to Poland with his wife to join in annual festivities commemorating those days. After receiving his address, I wrote him a letter, to which he replied with the salutation "Dear Comrade Dolina" [Pilch's *nom de guerre*].

Pilch left Poland in June 1945 and arrived in England a month later. He was a member of the Polish army until 1948 and later became a consultant in work simplification for large mechanical concerns. He is now retired.

IWO CYPRIAN POGONOWSKI

I was born September 3, 1921, in Lwów, Poland.

In December 1939, at the age of eighteen, I was imprisoned by German authorities on the suspicion of attempting to join the Polish army in the west. I was a political prisoner of the Germans for over five years. For those five years, I witnessed and experienced the atrocities of German prisons and camps.

From December 30, 1939, to August 7, 1940, I was held in a number of German prisons on Polish soil. The Germans debated whether to classify me for immediate execution or for gradual extinction through exploitation as a slave, working on a starvation diet. One way or the other, the Germans intended to eliminate me, because I was a member of the Polish educated class and therefore considered a potential enemy of the German state.

I witnessed transports to execution sites, such as in Jasło, where the Germans ordered execution by firing squad of eighty-six out of 122 inmates.

The Germans often obtained confessions by torture. The Gestapo used especially brutal torture on those who were arrested as a group. Admission of anti-Nazi activities by one man was enough to condemn to death all of the men who had been arrested as a group.

Severe flogging with wire-reinforced, hard rubber clubs was administered to shoulder blades and buttocks; often the Germans knocked out a prisoner's teeth with the butts of handguns. I saw the soles of an inmate's bare feet burned on a hot stove. My cell mate, Joe, a Polish-American from Cleveland, Ohio, lost consciousness several times during repeated beatings and mutilation of his shoulder blades. One time he did not come back from the debriefing session, during which the Germans apparently murdered him. His few possessions were removed from the cell.

Every day I saw in the overcrowded prison cell the swollen and discolored flesh of my fellow inmates who were under current investigation.

The Germans classified me for transport to a concentration camp. They brought me to Tarnów. The transport of five hundred men were partly survivors of Gestapo investigations. However, most were there without any specific charges having been brought against them. They were simply to make up the number of five hundred educated Poles to be shipped to slow death.

The Germans used a cavalcade of trucks to transfer us from prison to a cattle train. They pointed a machine gun at the five prisoners placed on a bench at the rear of each truck. The prisoners did not know whether the trucks were going to an execution site or to some other prison.

At gunpoint, the Germans crammed us into cattle wagons without toilet facilities. The next day the train arrived at Auschwitz, which was so congested it could not take any more inmates. Two days later the train arrived, via Wrocław-Breslau and Berlin, at Oranienburg, Sachsenhausen.

From August 10, 1940, to April 20, 1945, at the Oranienburg-Sachsenhausen concentration camp near Berlin, the Waffen SS soldiers made the pale-faced prisoners disembark. Several of us had bayonet or bullet wounds inflicted during the transport. After days in the closed-up wagon, I straightened and stretched in the sunshine. My posture attracted the attention of an SS-man behind me. He knocked me out by hitting me in the back of my head with the butt of his rifle.

With our shaved heads, we had to stand for days in the sunshine, making our bare skulls swell to the point that many could not open their eyes. A man named Owczerk scaled the electric wall and ran away. We had to stand for days until he was caught. He had to show the SS-men how he did it.

My first job was to unload, without gloves, cement bags brought on a barge. After three thousand bags, the skin was gone from my fingers. I had to load rapidly because the carriers ran by, driven by the blows of the Kapos. Many of them were so severely beaten at work that they were unable to work. The able-bodied had to carry their friends back to camp.

We were exposed to the elements eighteen hours a day. The majority of the men died within three months. Many were priests, lawyers, and other professionals. The starvation diet dulled our senses and sensitivity to the murders that we witnessed daily. My two close friends, young Polish Army officers, were debilitated by wounds suffered in the September Campaign. They could not tolerate our utter and hopeless degradation: one after the other, they committed suicide by grabbing the electric wire fence. Another close friend of mine fell down from exhaustion. He died while two of us kept him standing, so that he would not fall on the frozen *Appel Platz* (roll call area).

The integration of German industry into the Nazi extermination effort was evident in the presence of civilian technicians called *Polieren* (quality control foremen). They had the power to order beating unproductive inmates to death to enforce productivity.

I witnessed in the Klinkerwerk labor group a Polier who threatened death by flogging the next day to a Pole nicknamed Gacek. I saw the desperate man getting his left arm broken by other inmates to simulate an accident. Admission to the hospital saved Gacek's life by getting him out of reach of his civilian German tormentor. Later he went to work in another labor squad. I do not remember him among the survivors of the camp.

I worked over two years in the clay pits of Klinkerwerk. It had some of the worst working conditions in Sachsenhausen. Eventually, Klinkerwerk became a separate camp, which was heavily bombed in April 1945. There I saw inmates' bodies roasted with incendiary bombs. The corpses were carved up by desperately hungry men who committed cannibalism.

My friend Paul survived the longest among the Jews in Sachsenhausen. His shinbones were broken and set experimentally; the major shinbone was connected to the minor one, leaving the other two stubs unconnected. Paul had to be X-rayed every few weeks so that the Germans could follow up their experiment. I remember many cases of such "scientific" experiments, performed mostly on Polish Christian inmates.

I was sick with scurvy and tuberculosis, my molar teeth had crumbled from malnutrition, and my weight was down from 190 to ninety-six pounds. In this condition, I barely survived the "sports" exercises routinely ordered by the Germans to finish off the sick and useless. The Germans coerced us during "exercises" to roll in one direction on the ground until most of us vomited and hemorrhaged at the same time.

Sachsenhausen concentration camp ended in the death march to Brandenburg. It lasted twelve days, during which some six thousand inmates died.

Educated in Poland, Belgium, and the United States, Pogonowski came to the United States in 1950. He has written several books, including *Poland: A Historical Atlas* (New York: Hippocrene Books, 1987). He is also an inventor and holds numerous patents.

MARIA RADECKA

At about 2:00 a.m. on July 17, 1943, four Lithuanian policemen came to arrest me at my aunt's apartment. I insisted that I could not get dressed in front of them. They allowed me to go into my aunt's bedroom to get dressed. Since most people tended to assume that everyone belonged to some clandestine organization, my aunt suspected that I might be a member of the Home Army. She asked me if I had hidden anything that was incriminating in the apartment, to which I replied in the negative. I got dressed and returned to the living room, where I sat in an armchair and waited for the Lithuanians to search the apartment. Meanwhile, one of them told my aunt in Lithuanian to get what bread and bacon she had in the house and give it to me. Needless to say, that sounded very ominous.

I was taken away to Gestapo headquarters, which was quite close to my aunt's apartment, surrounded by armed guards who warned me that if I tried to escape they would shoot me. I told them that I had no intention of trying to escape because my arrest was a mistake. While I was led away, I was aware of what a beautiful, clear night it was.

At Gestapo headquarters, I was in German hands, a matter of some importance because the Germans were much harder to bribe than the Lithuanians. The Germans took away my handbag and put me into a small, stuffy cell. As the door closed behind me, I heard a voice asking what was happening in town. I thought it was somebody who recognized me, but it turned out to be someone who simply wanted to find out who had been brought into the cell.

It was Saturday morning. Since the Gestapo did not function on Saturdays or Sundays, I thought I would not be interrogated until Monday. This turned out to be a mistaken idea. I was called in for questioning that morning. I knew German, but I asked for an interpreter anyway, to give myself more time to think of answers. I was kept in the underground cells of Gestapo headquarters for three weeks—one week of solitary confinement and two weeks in an ordinary cell. Conditions were appalling. Cockroaches dropped from the ceilings. They denied food parcels to me. No one even knew I was there.

During this time, I was interrogated three times for periods of four to five hours at a time. They asked the same questions over and over. I was a courier between Wilno and Warsaw, and the courier whose pseudonym was *Czarny* (Black), who worked on the same route, had been arrested by the Germans and had divulged my name. They told me that if the answers I gave did not agree with what was being said about me in Warsaw, I would be taken there for a confrontation and would most likely end up in Auschwitz. Although I was questioned interminably, I was not beaten. Somehow I guessed that I would not be mistreated when my interrogators said that Poles always accused them of beating and torturing people, implying that the accusation was a totally unfounded one.

Once during questioning, one of my interrogators said something that infuriated me. I blazed with anger. But when I saw the look of triumph on his face, I decided to change my tactics and to be very meek, whatever the provocation. I had never before realized that it was possible to alter the expression of one's eyes. But I did so during the remainder of my interrogation.

After this, they took me to the main prison of Lukiszki. The food was very poor, but at least the Germans allowed the inmates food parcels every week. Perhaps the most humiliating aspect of life in the prison was not being allowed to go to the toilet without a guard standing at the open door. We were allowed to go to the toilet at 5:00 a.m. and then about 5:00 p.m. Facilities in the cells were strictly limited. Some of the older prisoners suffered terribly because they were unable to adjust their needs to these strange hours. One of the cures for this was to smoke a cigarette immediately upon waking in the morning.

But nothing was pleasant, from the poignant graffiti on the cell walls telling of torture and giving the dates of their writers' executions (the Germans never quite succeeded in obliterating them), to the moans and screams of inmates who were beaten or mistreated by some of their fellow prisoners. In the cell next to mine, there were some sixteen- and seventeen-year-old couriers from the Home Army. They suffered greatly. The Germans locked up political prisoners with ordinary criminals and prostitutes. Many of them were belligerent; fights broke out and food parcels were stolen. They locked me up with a woman who had murdered her husband, cut up his body, and salted the pieces down in a barrel to sell as meat.

I was in a cell with Barbara Dudycz, whom I called Basia. She headed a group called *Kozy* (Goats), the internal liaison of the High Command of the Wilno district of the Home Army. The Germans sentenced her to death, but this had been commuted, thanks to judicious bribery. She was always cheerful and good-humored. Her idea was to put a particularly aggressive criminal prisoner in charge of our cell. This was a marvelous idea because the woman who was selected was so pleased with the "honor" that she kept everyone in the cell in order. What was most important, our precious food parcels were safe.

The political prisoners stayed in the same cells, whereas the other prisoners were moved around. The prostitutes were, on the whole, very friendly. I recall one girl who was so delighted when the Germans moved her back into our cell that she threw her arms around me as if I were her long-lost friend. Another had a wooden leg and stomped around the cell singing a popular song, "Carioca."

Fridays were the worst days because that was the day the Germans executed prisoners. Not only did the Germans execute political prisoners, but they also killed ordinary criminals convicted of stealing German property. The Lithuanian wardens and wardresses would enter the cell with a list of names. We knew by their very bearing why they were there. After someone had been taken away for execution, none of the other prisoners ever had much of an appetite.

The Lithuanian prison chaplain was known to be a Gestapo agent. Basia and I never understood why so many political prisoners persisted in confessing to him. They maintained that because he was consecrated, he could not possibly divulge what had been confessed to him, and it was impossible to convince them otherwise.

The Germans denied political prisoners the right to have visitors. But by a curious coincidence, I saw my mother once during the four months I was there. My father was a prisoner-of-war in Murnau, and periodically he sent my mother money orders. They were usually in my mother's name, but for some unknown reason, after my arrest, my mother received a money order made out to me. Since she was unable to draw the money, she went to the Gestapo with a friend who spoke German and asked what to do. She was told that there was absolutely no problem because they would send a noncommissioned officer to accompany her to Lukiszki prison, where I would sign the order, and she would then be able to withdraw the money. That is precisely what happened. She was accompanied to the prison by a Polish-speaking soldier, and I signed the money order. The same soldier was present when the Germans released me, and he told me on that occasion that he seemed to bring me luck.

Radecka managed to escape postwar Poland with false papers. In October 1946, she went to England, where she married.

TADEUSZ ROSICKI

I will never forget February 25, 1941—two hours past midnight. Warsaw is asleep—a dark, gloomy night. A foreboding silence permeates the air. . . . I had gone to bed quite late and I had just fallen asleep. Suddenly, I am jolted out of my sleep by the sounds of steps made by heavy boots and then the shrill sounding of the door-bell. One . . . two . . . three . . . followed by violent banging on the door. I jump up, fully awake with a lightning-like thought crossing my mind. Gestapo! The banging continues. My mind springs to action.

Quietly, without switching on the light, I tiptoe to the kitchen and head towards a secret hiding place, from where I recover a small box. Small, but not insignificant—it contains incriminating evidence, names and addresses of the members of the underground organization to which I belong.

Under no circumstances can these be permitted to fall into the hands of the Gestapo. Neither can this happen to the special report which, I remember, is also in my possession. It is in the pocket of my jacket hanging in the closet. But time is running out. The intruders are now banging at the door not only with their fists, but also with the butts of their guns.

I get a sudden idea. Why not dispose of the box by tossing it into the air vent opening in the wall? The job completed, my thoughts turn to my family, which is by now fully awake and yet unaware of what is going on. I try to keep them calm by walking to the door slowly, pretending not to be alarmed. I ask in Polish, "Who is it?" "Open the door!" comes back a response in German. I open the door and find myself in a spotlight coming from four flashlights. I also see four guns pointing in my direction. Another order is issued: "Get dressed!" I see now the men behind the voices: four tall, powerfully built Germans in Nazi uniforms. I throw an overcoat over my shoulders and immediately hear the next order. "Hands up and don't move!" They ask for my name and my date of birth. The barrels of their guns are pointed at my head while they are pushing me and ordering me to rush. But I don't; I have all the time in the world.

At this point I really don't care. I hate each and every one of them. They invaded my country; they are killing my people; they are hurting my family and destroying my countrymen. I feel an upsurge of patriotism and rebellion against what I see as Evil. My job now is to protect my family and my fellow Poles who could be incriminated by the report that I had no chance to destroy. It is in the pocket of my suit, in my closet. What am I to do? They are watching me like vultures. They are searching me. They are watching my mother, my brothers, and my sister; they don't even permit them to get up from their beds. They forcefully stop me when I attempt to say good-bye to them. I am leaving my family with tears in my eyes. Will I ever see them again?

I am prepared for the worst. But my mind is still on the incriminating report. Will I be able to save my friends from a horrible death, my friends who have trusted, and relied on, me? I ask the Nazis for their permission to fetch my hat from the closet. Permission is granted. I go to the closet and swallow the report, which is written on a tissue-thin paper. God has been kind to me. I return with my hat.

Leaving my sobbing family behind, I am escorted by the SS men at gunpoint to a car which awaits us outside. I take a deep breath and thank God for making it possible to do my job. The Lord will also protect my family. But will I ever see them again? I light up a cigarette but one of the Nazis knocks it out of my hands. I am no longer permitted to smoke. I am taken to the police van.

They give me a push and I find myself inside a dark van; the only sound I hear is the clattering of handcuffs. Are my friends here? Yes, I am correct, the two men I joined in the van are my colleagues from the underground. The third person, a young woman, Krystyna, turns out to be a liaison worker who recognizes me, for we have met before. She whispers, "Remember, you are doing this for our country—for Poland." She raises my spirit; now I am no longer frightened. I have no fear of anything and am ready to go through any torture. My country is now more important to me than my own life, and I will gladly die for Poland.

Before long, I find myself in the notorious prison Pawiak. They separate me from my companions and, within half an hour, take my personal data and search me thoroughly. Next, they escort me to a prison cell. They switch on the light and I see human misery at its worst. Ten prisoners, their faces bloody and swollen—faces twisted in pain. The scene is frightening but I regain my strength when I recall the words Krystyna whispered to me as I entered the van . . . "Remember, you are doing this for our country—for Poland.

Cell No. 7 with its eleven prisoners is immersed again in darkness as the light is switched off. Things quiet down. I lie down to sleep on the bare floor. I have no covers to protect me. It is a freezing February night. The darkness of the night envelops me. This is my first night as a prisoner, a man torn from his family and home. The uncertainty of the future looms heavily in the darkness of the night. I remain fully awake; I pray to God to give me strength and I prepare my defense. Exhausted, I finally fall asleep.

I wake up to the cold reality of prison; it is still the morning of February 25, 1941, the day of my arrest. I look around and see bodies of eleven men, including myself, who are lying in a neat row, elbow to elbow. The cell is very small and I soon find out that it is difficult to get up without disturbing one's neighbor. The daily routine begins: We get a slice of bread with a mug of black coffee to start the day, and a bowl of soup in the afternoon to finish it. Nothing in between.

We get about 30 minutes of daily exercise in the prison yard. The exercise is leapfrogging: We are ordered to jump up and down, with knees bent and arms extended. It is exhausting. Many of us are weakened . . . and keep falling down to the ground, out of breath. Whenever this happens, the victim is kicked viciously by an SS-man and ordered to get up. When he does, he is clubbed mercilessly for good measure. We run out of breath by the time the "exercise" is over, and we need a long time to recuperate. Back in our cell, we hear the never ending cries and moans of the victims who are being interrogated. My cellmates are being plucked from the room one by one. Either they return staggering and frequently bloodied, or they are never heard from again. New prisoners come and go, yet the cell is always filled to capacity. All day long we hear the cries of people who are being tortured. Days, then weeks, pass by. Spring is near.

April 1941. Just before midnight, six weeks after the night I was taken prisoner, we are awakened by a commotion in the prison halls. Suddenly, the door to our cell swings open and a gun-wielding guard marches in shrieking *"Laufschritt!"* ("Run!"). We jump to our feet and run out into the hall, where we are joined by scores of other prisoners who are streaming out of their cells. They order us out of the building, into the prison yard, and onto the street. As I cross through the gate,

I am blinded by the glare of the spotlights. They prod us into a bus that is already waiting, and I notice that other buses are lined up behind it. Scores of SS-men, their carbines poised for action, are lining the sides of the street. As soon as the bus is filled to capacity, we start rolling and the next one takes its place. Except for a few select ones, Pawiak is now almost empty of its victims. Among those left behind is a Polish priest, Father Maximilian Kolbe, whom I am to meet again under different circumstances.

The bus is crowded. We are ordered to kneel down, which is difficult. All follow the command, except for one man who remains standing since there is no more kneeling space left for his long legs. An SS guard hits him with the butt of his gun, and we all huddle together to let him fall to his knees. I look at his bloodied head and I recognize the well-known Polish actor, Zbyszko Sawan, a tall and handsome man of thirty-six. We become friends later. Another prominent Polish actor, Stefan Jaracz, is also riding with us. Both men were taken hostages after the execution of a Nazi collaborator, Igo Sym, by the Polish resistance.

We move through the streets of Warsaw, in a motorcade of buses . . . surrounded by a detachment of SS-men who ride motorcycles. The special motorcycles have a passenger seat which is occupied by a Nazi holding a gun, ready to shoot. They know what they are doing. With the many prominent Polish prisoners riding in the buses, there is an ever-present threat to the Nazis that the Polish resistance might try to ambush the convoy and free the prisoners. The ride seems long, but we finally come to a stop. We are ordered to debark and, as I get out, I am again blinded by the intense glare of lights. We are at a railroad station, but I am unable to recognize which one. We are surrounded by what seems like thousands of SS-men armed to the teeth.

They herd us into cattle cars, in which we continue our odyssey. They are windowless and filthy. The pungent odor, left behind by its previous occupants, is unmistakably that of pigs. But what is even worse, there is not enough sitting space for all of us and we must take turns sitting and standing. The ride feels like an eternity. We are surrounded with darkness, and the only way we can see changes from night to day and to night again is through the little crack in the door. Our only glimpses of the outside world are at the infrequent train stops during which the buckets, our only luxury, are emptied by the railroad workers. They open the door from the outside, and what we see are not regular railroad stations. Instead, the train stops at sidings in the middle of nowhere. Where are we going?

I am hungry, thirsty, and dizzy, but I try to forget the reality by talking to my fellow prisoners. Still, thoughts are crowding my mind. What can I expect when we arrive at our destination? More of hunger, thirst, and abuse to which I was subjected during the six weeks at Pawiak? I see before my eyes pictures of the bloody, tortured human beings, which were ever present at Pawiak, and I wonder how many of my underground friends, who might have since been captured, could withstand the tortures without naming others. I pray to God to give me strength to withstand all that might come or to die, rather than to incriminate my friends.

I estimate that we have been on the road for about thirty-three hours. No food, no water, just raw fear. I am dizzy to the point of fainting. Suddenly, the train stops. The door swings open and someone barks a command, *"Raus, die Polnische Schweine!"* ("Out, you Polish swine"). I am caught off guard at the door with the bucket in my hand and we are both pushed out by the crowd surging from behind us, anxious to follow the order. The stop is Auschwitz. What we face is a detachment of SS-men who are yelling at the top of their lungs, while holding vicious barking dogs on leashes.

They order us to run. We do, until we reach a building where our transformation into full-fledged Auschwitz inmates takes place. They take away our clothes and equip us with striped prison gear—pants, jackets, and caps. Each jacket is adorned with a triangular patch of cloth with a letter *P*—for Pole. Our color is red, as contrasted to the green worn by criminal prisoners. We also receive strips of cloth with a number. The number is to be placed under the triangular patch and on the side of the prison pants. Mine is 13470, and it will become my identity from now on. Clad in our new garments, we are directed to one of the blocks, where we are greeted by our future block leader, who wears a green colored patch on his jacket. He is a criminal prisoner who, I soon find out, is nicknamed Bloody Aloiz.

Still thirsty and hungry, we are ordered by Bloody Aloiz to stand in a military-like formation of five rows and to follow his commands. He begins with a "hats on" and "hats off," which we are expected to follow immediately. As one of the shortest prisoners (I am only 5 feet 5 inches), I find myself in the first row and get the brunt of his viciousness. I am exhausted and I make mistakes; I grab my hat either too soon or too late. He slaps my face repeatedly until it bleeds, and when I fall to the ground he kicks my chest and my stomach. I feel dizzy but I sober up when I hear the voices of some of my fellow inmates who urge me softly in Polish to immediately get up and not to look at Aloiz squarely in his eyes, a mistake for which he would surely kill me. They are old-timers who already know his ways. I get up; I am through the initiation ceremonies.

At long last, we are given a bowl of soup and a slice of bread. This is followed by speeches that are delivered by the block leader and the SS-men. They exhort us to work honestly, to obey orders, and to maintain cleanliness. Now we get an issue of blankets. They are filthy and crawling with lice. They point to our beds—the bare floor. At the onset of darkness, we hear the sound of a gong, which announces bedtime. But it does not mean permission to go to sleep. For at least thirty minutes, we are ordered to sing German songs such as "Schoene sind Fraüleins 16 and 17 Jahre alt" ("Pretty are the six-teen- and seventeen-year-old girls"). I finally go to sleep, praying to God again.

I sleep fitfully and wake up to the sound of a gong which an-nounces the new day. I see one prisoner fall to his knees and begin to pray. But God is banned from this valley of death, and Bloody Aloiz does not wait long to let the man know it. He is now running toward his new prey, who soon begins to crumble under the cruel, indiscriminate blows. While hitting his victim, Aloiz yells with fury that he is a non-believer and he sneers at God, for where was He when Aloiz needed Him in his years of imprisonment? He leaves his victim bloodied and groaning.

Now they tell us to get undressed. It is time to wash up after the night and face the day's work. They chase us out of the building, naked. . . . The day is very cold, and wet snowflakes are falling to the ground. Outside, we see buckets of water, but there is only one bucket for about fifteen prisoners. We wait our turns while the water gets murkier and murkier. Even so, not everyone is lucky enough to get to the bucket, for the time is limited. Later during my stay in Auschwitz, I learn to appreciate the value of my fast legs, I am usually one of the first to reach the bucket. As we find out later that day, the population of about ten thousand Auschwitz prisoners is serviced by only one water pump and one latrine.

Our cleansing done for the day, we are herded back into the building, permitted to dress, and then receive an issue of Dutch-made wooden clogs carved from a single chunk of wood. No socks. Next, we are summoned for a roll call, and we assemble in front of the building. First we are counted by the block leader, then by an SS-man, and later we stand on alert. This takes about thirty minutes. We get a mug of black coffee and a slice of bread. We are told to get ready for work, but first we must get our assignments.

It is my first morning in Auschwitz. We are assembled in front of Block 7, waiting for our work assignments. One of the SS-men issues an order, "All doctors, priests, engineers, executives, and students step out!" I am caught off guard; what shoud I do? I know that they want to identify the Polish intellectuals and potential leaders for their sinister reasons and that admitting that I was a university student will not help me. But I also know that they can check on my personal data and that to be caught lying will bring instant death. I step out, along with about thirty others.

We, the select group, receive special treatment. Each of us is given a wheelbarrow and a shovel. We are led to a pile of sand, then commanded to load the wheelbarrows and to run with them. As we run, we pass SS-men who are stationed every fifty or so yards and who yell at us to hurry. Those who slow down to catch their breath are kicked and hit with clubs. As soon as we reach our destination in a distant area of the camp, we are ordered to empty our cargo into ditches and run back for another load. I run back and forth from morning till night. The routine never varies, but the cargo does: It changes from sand to rocks, then to sand again. The ditches never fill up; I notice after a while that there is another group of prisoners who are frantically digging up what we bring in. The purpose of this labor escapes me.

At the end of the first day, my feet are covered with blisters and I am exhausted. I try to lighten the load by attaching the ends of a heavy wire to each handle of the wheelbarrow and by placing the wire around my neck, like a yoke. However, I abandon this idea after I get bleeding cuts in the skin of my neck. Days pass, and by the end of the week I feel that my end is near. Yet, my mind refuses to give in to my battered body, and I refuse to die.

I find out from Łukasiewicz, when he is brought to Auschwitz several weeks after my interrogation, what had happened. He is only in his late twenties, but as the head of an underground organization, he has been a prominent figure in the Polish resistance movement. He tells me that he had been captured while transmitting information through the underground radio that was installed in the attic of his fiancée's home. This occurred in the winter of 1941, shortly before my arrest. He was careful not to keep lists of his current collaborators, but one of the names he overlooked was mine, written in secret code. They took him first to Gestapo headquarters where they tortured him by twisting his bones, driving nails under his fingernails, and burning his body with hot iron. Weakened by the abuse, he gave them my name, as well as the names of a few of his other collaborators. As he talks, I begin to understand why they have not executed me yet. It is simply because he told the Gestapo that the only contacts we had were prior to the war, and that his reason for recording my name in code was his habit of keeping all names of his old acquaintances in code, so as not to endanger their lives because of his personal involvements. Since he did not mention our meeting in the fall of 1939, there was no discrepancy between what they got from him and what they extracted from me during my interrogation. I feel I have gotten another reprieve from death. Lukasiewicz is relieved from his misery later in Auschwitz; he is executed in front of Block 11 by the notorious Palitzsch in the winter of 1944.

At this point, the overwhelming majority of Auschwitz prisoners are ethnic Poles. The wholesale extermination of Jews comes later and there is only a sprinkling of them among the inmates of Auschwitz. From what I find out later, any groups of them who are brought to the camp during this period are immediately put to death. We Poles are united in our suffering by our common memories and our patriotism. We help each other as much as we can, sharing an extra piece of bread or potato. Each day new victims from all walks of life arrive. Some, like myself, are charged with underground activity; others are innocent bystanders rounded up on the streets, plucked out of their homes for no apparent reason, or collected in churches while worshipping. Even a clergyman's garb does not assure immunity. We are waiting for tomorrow, to be free. But, as much as I want to be free, the thought of escape never crosses my mind. Not because the odds are high that I would be shot to death, but because I know that if I tried, others would suffer. I know they would immediately capture my entire family and that I would endanger fellow inmates. The majority of escapees are those imprisoned for criminal activity.

July 1941. A prisoner escapes from Block 14. Many thousands of us are ordered to stand on alert in front of our blocks. We get no morning rations and we are exhausted. It is a hot day, and the sun beats down with a vengeance. We are frightened and many succumb to exhaustion. Many "natural" deaths occur that day. The most frightened are the residents of Block 14, for everyong knows that ten of them will die as retribution for the escape. And everyone knows that death for the victims will be slow.

We have been standing on alert during the evening roll call when, suddenly, two uniformed officials appear before our tired eyes. Palitsch, the tall one, is accompanied by another who is much shorter and speaks in a squeaky voice. The squeaky voice belongs to the commandant of Auschwitz, Karl Fritzsch. With a smile, Fritzsch points his finger at ten residents of Block 14, one after another. All ten are Poles. When he reaches the last one, a middle-aged man whose name, I find out later, is Franciszek Gajowniczek, the man cries out in anguish, "Oh, my wife! Oh, my children." I hear him and my heart goes out to him. Before I catch my breath, I see a frail man raise his hand and step out. I recognize the name: He is Father Maximilian Kolbe, the Polish priest whom I had met at Pawiak.

I see the action, but I am not close enough to hear the dialogue, which is reconstructed for me later by those standing next to the priest . . . . Commandant Fritzsch, taken aback, asks Father Kolbe: "Who are you and what do you want?" The answer is simple, "I am a Catholic priest, and I want to take the place of this prisoner." He points to Gajowniczek. Fritzsch is momentarily stunned and motionless. However, he quickly recoups and motions Gajowniczek to return to the ranks. They lead away the ten victims, including Father Kolbe. We all know by now that the escape was successful.

Next morning I hear that the victims were stripped and thrown naked into one of the death cells. With room only to stand, they get no food and no water from that day on. Some linger so long as two weeks, and I hear through the grapevine that even the executioners are impressed by the courage of the frail Polish priest. He leads the dying in prayers and, while the others wail in pain, he never complains. They tell me that the voices are getting weaker and are slowly fading away. I hear the details about the final hours of Father Kolbe, who was one of the last to die, only after the end of the war. He and two other hostages, who were still alive after two weeks, were given a lethal injection by Hans Bock, a criminal offender who held the post of a supervisor.

Fall 1941–Winter 1942. I am still working at the carpentry shop, but I am at the breaking point. I am starving. My stomach and guts hurt, my legs are giving out, and all I can think about is food. I am obsessed with the thought of filling up my stomach, even if it would be the last thing I do in my life. I feel dehumanized, almost like an animal. I am losing hope and, one by one, I am losing my closest friends.

The Roman Catholic Church recently canonized Father Kolbe.—Ed.

Rosicki was liberated in Germany by General George Patton's Army on May 2, 1945. In the immediate postwar period, he worked for the Polish Education Department in the American and French occupation zones. In 1949 he emigrated to the United States, where his most recent interests include painting and sculpture. He is the author of *My Fifty Months in Nazi Camps*, published privately in 1984, in which this account appears.

MARIA RÓŻAŃSKA

I was married to a regular officer in the Polish army. I had been a primary schoolteacher before my marriage. My husband came back to Przemyśl after fighting in the September 1939 campaign and later decided to go to Hungary. He succeeded with the aid of an official pass, which allowed him to go to Piwniczna, on the border with Hungary. I stayed in Przemyśl with my mother and four-year old son, living in the house we owned. We had a succession of people living there—Germans, a Czech, and a *Volksdeutsch* family.

I lived by selling off my possessions. At one point I gave school lessons to a peasant's child in return for skimmed milk, and I generally coped as best I could. My mother's pension was two hundred złotys a month. We did not see meat for the duration of the war; pork cost 450 złotys for a kilogram, and that could only be obtained if you had the right connections. One day I managed to get some butter, but I did not have enough money for bread. Normally we ate a thin barley gruel for breakfast. Coffee was also made from barley. We knew something about herbs, so we used to collect a whole variety of different herbs and dry them for tea. This tea was so delicious that both my mother and I continued to drink it after the war.

Life was very hard. The Germans gave us nothing. The ersatz bread contained everything but flour. The bakers said if people knew what was in it, they would not eat it. I sold or bartered everything I had. The peasants did not want money, only goods. So I got rid of my husband's clothes, jewelry, bicycle, and anything else I could. When my son caught scarlet fever, I had no money at all. I went to the market and, under the nose of a German soldier, sold something for 240 złotys. With that, I went to the country and bought some cheese, butter, and eggs. On the return journey, I was caught by German and Ukrainian soldiers. I thought I would end up in a concentration camp. They asked me for my *kennkarte* (identification card), saying, "You know this [buying food in the country] is not allowed." I told them that the food was not for me but for the German who is living in my house, which was not strictly true, as he was not there at that particular time. Luckily, they let me go and did not investigate further. I came home trembling. One day I walked twenty-five kilometers to get some milk for my son, rushing back to get home before the curfew. If a Pole was caught, the food was confiscated, although older soldiers, especially those from the Rhineland, often turned a blind eye to our activities. One German once remarked that he wondered how we Poles managed to live if they did not give us anything and forbade us to buy any food as well.

One day the Germans searched our house. Someone had written an anonymous denunciation to the Gestapo. Two officials in civilian clothes, both of whom spoke Polish, came to the house and showed me the letter, which said that I hoarded barrels of butter and lard while they, presumably the writer's family, had nothing. I saw my mother's neck turn scarlet. I burst into tears. I was always terrified of what would happen to my mother and child if I were taken away. Anyway I told the officials that my house was at their disposal. They searched but found only the few potatoes and cabbages I had stored in the cellar. Then they left, saying that they had to carry out the search because they themselves were being spied on.

Eventually I was called up by the *Arbeitsampt* (Bureau of Labor). The office was full of Ukrainians and Volksdeutsche. I was very worried that I might be sent to Germany. But a friend used to bribe the girl at the *Arbeitsampt* to put my card at the back of the file. I was put to work sewing coats instead. I had no idea how to sew anything, let alone coats. I did not know which piece went where. Fortunately, a girl who had been a servant before the war helped me. The main problem was that I was paid one hundred cigarettes a month, so that not only did I no longer have the time to get food, but I did not have any money either. I was weak from lack of food and sheer worry. In the end, I stayed away from work for two days. The father of the German who owned the shop where I worked happened to live in my house at the time. He was furious with me and yelled at me that all Polish women are lazy and that he would have me shut up in a camp. As usual, I thought the end had come.

On another occasion, a German pastor from Poznań came to see another German who was billeted in my house. He also claimed that Polish women did not want to work, whereas wives in Germany had to work. By this time I had had enough. I told him that at least German wives earned something for their work. I asked him who was going to find food for my son if I was away all day. I also told him that I did not care if he went to the Gestapo. The pastor told me not to be afraid; he would go with me to the *Arbeitsampt*, and maybe they would let me off. I did not want to be seen walking along the street with a German, so I arranged to meet him at the shop, where he managed to get my hours reduced to half a day. The pastor was only in Przemyśl a short time because very soon afterward the German retreat began.

The worst thing was never knowing what would happen. As a result, we were often in tears. We called it a war of nerves. In many ways, relationships with Poles were more difficult than those with Germans. At least with the Germans, we were always careful. I knew two Poles who were executed by the Home Army. One of the Germans . . . was a Captain Hittler. He warned me not to let anyone know that my husband was in the West, because "my people" might denounce me to the Gestapo.

When the German-Soviet war started, we spent a week in the cellar because the front moved back and forth. My mother had saved scraps of bread for some time during our stay in the cellar. We ate the bread, even though it was worm-ridden by then.

Różańska was a schoolteacher after the Soviet army occupied Poland. Later she left Poland illegally with her son and joined her husband, who was then in Italy. She now lives in London.

ZDZISŁAW M. RURARZ

The German occupation of Poland has influenced my life dramatically. As a matter of fact, I still live in the aftermath of it. Living now in the United States, under the death sentence passed upon me in absentia after my defection as Poland's ambassador to Japan, I can truly blame the war of September 1939 for all my miseries.

I was nine years old when Poland was attacked by Germany on September 1, 1939. Evacuated from Pionki, near Radom, where I was born, I would not see the place of my birth again for thirty years.

As for the occupation itself, which ended for me on January 19, 1945, I barely survived it. Together with my parents, I lived in the county of Konskie, where my grandparents and other relatives lived. They lived in the village of Furmanów and later in the little town of Radoszyce. From the beginning of the war, the area was a battleground among Polish partisans, beginning with the legendary Major Hubal, whose detachment I saw. But there were other figures, like Ponury, Nurt, Szary, and Barabasz and many others.

It was in Furmanów where, on Sunday, April 11, 1940, I saw the Germans "pacify" the nearby village of Skłoby. After the Germans lifted the siege of Furmanów, I ran with my friends to Skłoby, some five kilometers away, where we could see the smoke billow into the sky. When we arrived there, I saw only burned houses and women and children lamenting the execution of 215 men. The youngest males who were executed by the Germans were fourteen years old. I did not see what went on in the village Hucisko, but I learned about its so-called pacification too.

Throughout the occupation, I saw many German atrocities and battles between the Polish partisans and the Germans, who were aided sometimes by Vlasov's troops the the Ukrainians. I even saw the daring Polish attack near the village of Grodzisko where the partisans, on September 2, 1944, bayoneted many Germans to death.

But all that was not as shocking to me as the following episode. In October 1942, I lived in Radoszyce. It was inhabited by perhaps fifteen hundred Poles and two thousand Jews, who were packed into the ghetto across the street from where I lived. To enter the ghetto was punishable by death. The same punishment was meted out to Jews who attempted to leave it. I saw many Jews killed for no reason by the Germans. I also heard about some Poles who were killed for trying to help the Jews. That probably led me several times to enter the ghetto with potatoes, bread, and other food that my mother would give me to bring to the Jews. Although we were very poor, we shared what we had with them. No money was ever demanded for the food. Once, at a time when I was studying German on my own, I saw in one Jewish home a German textbook. I asked the Jew, a watchmaker, to sell it to me. He gave it to me instead.

A few Jews sometimes risked their lives by crossing the street to enter our home for food. They always received something. The most frequent visitor was a Jewish girl whom we named Irena. She would always stay with us for hours, then before the curfew return to the ghetto where her parents, sisters, and brothers lived. Once, however, when she was darting across the street, a German named Gustav Stroebel, a sadist, saw her. He rushed after her. Scared to death, she told my mother what happened and my mother managed to lead her to a hiding place. When Stroebel broke into our house, waving his gun, he told us in broken Polish that a Jewish girl was in our house and that if we admitted it, we would be saved. If we didn't admit it and he found her, he threatened us with death. We did not say a word. He made a thorough search, hit my father in the face, and left. During the night, Irena returned to the ghetto, although we did not ask her to leave our home.

This was only a foretaste of what I saw a few days later. Maria Zielińska was a very poor woman who lived in our neighborhood. Her husband was in a German prisoner of war camp. She had two sons—Teodor was one year older than I, and the other one, whose given name I forget, was one year younger.

I never knew why the Germans arrested her. Freitag, a German official, claimed that he saw a Jew either enter or leave Mrs. Zielińska's place. The Jew was arrested by Freitag and admitted on the spot that Mrs. Zielińska had provided him with a hiding place. Freitag shot the Jew and arrested Mrs. Zielińska.

Soon afterward, the bell tolled in the marketplace. It was used for fire alarms. Together with my friends, I rushed to the place to see the firemen stationed there go into action. Instead, I saw something else. Under the escort of four helmeted German military police, commanded by Lieutenant Korth and the commander of the Polish Blue Police, Mrs. Zielińska was led into the courtyard. She was followed by her weeping sons. There were about fifty spectators, mostly children, women, and the elderly. I was there, too. The cortege stopped. The bell was ordered to be silenced. Then Korth spoke and Serwata, the head of the Polish Blue Police, translated. Mrs. Zielińska was to be shot publicly for helping the Jews! Indeed, in a few seconds she was led by one of the military police, Ebner, to a nearby fence in front of one of the houses. He tied one of her hands with a wire to the fence. With her free hand, she tried to cover her face. We all drew closer. Her sons sobbed. The Germans raised their rifles. "Feuer!" shouted Korth. The volley hit Mrs. Zielińska, and she slipped to the ground, hanging by the hand tied to the fence. Everyone was stunned. Nobody could move. Only after some time, when the Germans were about to leave the scene, her sons rushed to the body. Soon a horsedrawn cart appeared and Mrs. Zielińska was carried away.

To what extent this execution deterred many in Radoszyce from hiding any Jews, I cannot say. Soon the Germans evacuated the ghetto, and I do not know how many Jews from Radoszyce survived. But one thing was certain: To conceal a Jew could lead to death. Had Irena been found in our home, my family would have shared the fate of Mrs. Zielińska.

As for Lieutenant Korth—I cannot remember his first name—he was a high school teacher of Latin from East Prussia. Later promoted, he left Radoszyce and perhaps survived the war. More than half of the military police—but not Stroebel—later perished. Following a heavy battle between the partisans and the Germans on September 2-3, 1944, Radoszyce was burned to the ground, and more than thirty people died. Had the partisans not freed several hundred others, they would have been killed too.

Rurarz was a high-ranking official in postwar Poland. He served as advisor to Edward Gierek and as Polish ambassador to Japan. He now lives in the United States.

EUGENIA ŚWITAL

My husband, Stanisław, received his medical degree in May 1939, three months before the outbreak of World War II. The war began at the time he was an intern in the Wolski Hospital in Warsaw. After signing up for service with the regional draft board, he worked from September 1 to November 1 as a physician in military hospitals in Lublin and in other localities.

After his return to occupied Warsaw, he applied for work as a physician with the municipal Department of Health and Welfare. Nearly one month later, on December 10, he became a member of an underground organization, *Polska Niepodległa* (Independent Poland), that later became a part of the *Armia Krajowa* (Home Army). As a soldier of the Home Army, he conducted courses on sanitation, gave medical attention to participants in many armed actions, and treated soldiers in the resistance movement.

Until the creation of the Warsaw ghetto in November 1940, Stanisław Śwital cared for the medical needs of the Jewish people who had been driven out of villages and towns near Warsaw by the Germans. His friend, Janusz Korczak, noted educational theoretician and writer of Jewish origin, presented Stanisław with one of his books and thanked him for his dedicated work as a physician.

When the Germans enclosed the ghetto of Warsaw with a wall, it did not keep Stanisław from his activities as a physician among the Jews, profiting from the regular pass he had received as a public health physician.

During the sixty-three days of the Warsaw Uprising, which broke out on August 1, 1944, he held the position of deputy to the chief health physician of Warsaw's Home Army. After the collapse of the uprising, he returned to his family in Boernerowo near Warsaw, where he worked at a small hospital.

On November 15, 1944, a young woman, unknown to my husband, came to him and showed him a short letter signed Bartosz. Dr.

Lesław Węgrżynowski, his superior in the uprising, went by that pseudonym. Węgrżynowski asked for assistance in a matter that the young woman was to explain to my husband.

The young woman explained that she had come to my husband to get his help for a group of insurgents—five men and two women— who, to escape captivity, had hidden themselves in the cellar of a one-story house on Promyk Street, in the Zolibórz section of Warsaw. Since this building was important to the Germans to rebuild their defenses, there was a high probability that the insurgents would be discovered and murdered by the enemy. The woman, who revealed herself later as Alicja Margolis, was a liaison officer of the Jewish resistance movement. She got through German positions by a stroke of luck. In Grodzisk Mazowiecki, she had contacted Dr. Węgrżynowski about the matter.

Stanisław Śwital decided to take action to rescue the people. He proposed the matter to seven of the staff of the hospital. All of those who discussed the matter privately with him replied affirmatively to the question: "Are you prepared to die?" In the end, he selected five of them.

After providing the volunteers and Margolis with certificates and arm bands of the Red Cross, Śwital sent them out with two pairs of stretchers to Promyk Street in Zolibórz with the aim of bringing back the insurgents. In case the Germans stopped and interrogated them, or if they passed through German outposts, the rescuers were to explain that this group of Red Cross workers operated under the orders of a German officer who, during his visit to the hospital in Boernerowo, had ordered that the sick people at the Promyk Street address should be taken away.

The circumstances favored the complete success of the action. At twelve o'clock the Germans who worked on fortifications in the area went to dinner. The brave rescuers were Każimierz Sylkiewicz and his wife Maria, Barbara Kinkiel, Zbigniew Ściwiarski, Janusz Osęka, and Alicja Margolis.

The rescued group of insurgents turned out to be survivors of both the Ghetto Uprising and the Warsaw Uprising. There were both soldiers and commanders, one of whom was Marek Edelman of the Jewish Fighting Organization. The others were Icchak Cukierman ("Antek"), Celina Lubetkin-Cukierman ("Celina"), Marek Edelman, Tuwie Borżykowski ("Tadek"), Julian Fiszgrund ("Julek"), Zygmunt Warman ("Zygmunt"), and Teodozja Goliborska, the only Christian Pole in the group of survivors. They remained as patients for several days in the hospital in Boernerowo; later, they were transported to other places, one of them being a hospital in the village of Jelonki close to Włochy.

Dr. Marek Edelman, who received his degree in medicine after the war, recounted that he had met his future wife "when she came with a patrol organized by Dr. Śwital from the Home Army to lead us out of a bunker in the Żoliborz district." He added: "We'd been left there, on Promyka Street, after the general Warsaw Uprising in 1944— Antek, Celina, Tosia Goliborska, and I, among others—and in November they sent this patrol around to fetch us." (Hanna Krall, Shielding the Flame: An Intimate Conversation with Dr. Marek Edelman, the Last Surviving Leader of the Warsaw Ghetto Uprising, *trans. Joanna Stasińska and Lawrence Weschler [New York: Henry Holt, 1986], p. 82.)*

In September 1981, Stanisław Śwital received the Medal of the Righteous Among Nations, together with a certificate from Yad Vashem, for his work in rescuing Jews. He died on July 10, 1982. His widow, Eugenia Śwital, lives in Warsaw.

ELZBIETA SZANDOROWSKA

At the time of the German occupation, my mother, Janina Szandorowska, took boarders in our apartment at 11 Wiejska Street. When the Germans created the so-called German district in Warsaw, we were forced to move out. We moved to 11 Wielka Street. My father, begin a Polish military officer, had to stay in hiding and lived at another address. My mother ran an eleven-room boarding house, and we gave shelter and help to many Jewish people. We provided them with food and false documents.

As a rule, those living with us under assumed names did not leave the house for security reasons. They were afraid of being recognized by the Germans on the streets. The fact that they stayed with us did not guarantee them complete safety, because three or four times a week the Gestapo or the Blue Police searched our house. To avoid being surprised by sudden searches, one of the Jews whom we sheltered was responsible for observation duty on the balcony. Quite often Salomon Justym was responsible for this observation duty. His assumed name was Andrzej Jarosz.

Justym received false documents from my mother. . . . In Warsaw, Justym, his friend Beno Bursztyn, and Bursztyn's wife moved into an apartment at 39 Panska Street. The flat was closed from the outside by a padlock.

I was responsible for providing them with food. I was able to enter the apartment only when those who were hiding inside gave me the key. They lived without electricity and had to stay away from the windows. One day the neighbors smelled smoke coming from the supposedly empty apartment. They informed the janitor. After a few days, the janitor and the police tried to enter the apartment through the windows. The Jews who were hiding there were able to escape over the balcony and through the apartment next door.

After this, Justym moved into our apartment on Wielka Street. He hid himself in a very small recess in one of the rooms, covered by wicker baskets. He was able to move around the house only during the night.

The tasks in our house were divided as follows: My mother took care of so-called internal matters, providing us with food and sleeping places, while I was responsible for external matters—maintaining contacts, bringing information, and providing medication, money, and documents. To make it possible for the Jews whom we sheltered to maintain contact with their families, I secured permission from German authorities to correspond with people abroad.

When a house search took place, our Jewish tenants hid in the attic until the danger was over. Once there was not time to go to the attic, so they were forced to hide inside the house. The daughter of one of the Jews hid under the covers of a bed; I told her not to move or give any other sign of life. The girl obeyed me and did not move during the entire search.

In May 1943, the Germans arrested seventeen people in our boarding house, including my mother and the rest of our family. They took us to Gestapo headquarters on Szucha Avenue. Throughout the entire night, I taught Christian prayers to one of the Jewish girls who been arrested. The next day the Germans were in a very good mood because they had found diamonds sewn into the trousers of one of the Jewish men. So they allowed my family to go free the next day. They freed a couple of Jewish people, too, because they had extremely convincing documents and they had passed the so-called religion examination, which consisted of reciting Catholic prayers.

My mother's explanation to the Germans had been that she was unaware that some Jews were living in her apartment. When we got home, I realized that one of the Jewish women who had been arrested had left her documents in the house. I took them to the Gestapo, endangering my own life, and persuaded one of the guards to give them to one of the Gestapo interrogators. Lack of documents meant automatic death. A six-year-old girl, Basia Cukier, automatically brought the death sentence upon herself by refusing to say her prayers in the presence of the Gestapo, in spite of my mother's appeals.

My mother many times traveled by train—on two occasions to Lwów—to take care of matters for Jewish people. The first time she was responsible for moving the child Piotr Kamiński, one and a half years old, to Warsaw. He had been taken away from his Jewish mother and was staying in a Ukrainian orphanage in Lwów. The child had very Semitic features, so he was called "Jewish-like." My mother engaged a porter at the railroad station to carry the boy because he was too exhausted and weak to walk on his own. She was afraid that he might be recognized so she took him to the end of the train. He suffered from diarrhea, and she had to care for him the whole time. In Warsaw, he was cared for by Dr. Janina Żeligowska, who put him into the hospital. In spite of great efforts to save him, the boy died after a short time in the hospital.

The second time my mother went to Lwów was at the request of a Jew, Arthur Stala, who wanted her to recover two kilograms of gold that he had hidden there. After he had gotten his gold, Stala rented a room from a Blue Policeman. One day he came back to us, asking us for another favor. He was afraid to return to his room and he asked us to recover his gold once again. This time, I was the person involved in helping him. I entered his room, using his own key, while the wife of the Blue Policeman had gone shopping. I recovered the gold from the stove and from under the window. The owner of the gold thanked me by giving me three white tulips.

When I try to evaluate my activities during the occupation, I realize how important they were. In whatever I did, I was always motivated by my humanitarian attitude. Helping Jewish people took almost all of my time. Therefore, I was unable to attend secret school classes conducted by the Polish underground.

On July 31, 1944, immediately before the outbreak of the Warsaw Uprising, I was able to help Beno Bursztyn and his friends escape from Pawiak prison by a secret underground tunnel. I provided them with candles, batteries, and blueprints of the sewage system of Warsaw's City Center. After they escaped and left the sewage canals, I gave them food and clothes.

In the immediate postwar period, Szandorowska was involved in hospital work. She later became a librarian, with a special interest in old books. She collaborated with Maria Bohomos in preparing a catalog of Polish collections of books printed before 1501. She is now retired.

KRYSTYNA SZOMAŃSKA

When I think about it, the German occupation was horrible. The Germans threatened us with the death penalty for so many things. Our lives were at risk all the time, but for some reason I was not afraid. My friend, Zofia Rontaler, and I both worked at the theatre in the Łazienki Palace and had a pass that protected us if we were caught in a *łapanka* (roundup). We were both in the Home Army. We did everything together.

I remember a visit to my parents, who lived in Jasna. I limped along on my sprained ankle as snipers took potshots at passersby from rooftops. Somehow I was convinced I would be all right, just as I was convinced that nothing would happen to my parents as long as I visited them.

I knew Halina Schulzinger, a Polish Jew, before the war began. She was the friend of an acquaintance of mine. I had seen her two or three times. She was married to a German Jew, Jakub Schulzinger, who lived in Leipzig. She had left Leipzig before the war with her daughter, Jola, to come to Warsaw. Her husband remained in Leipzig to settle some business matters, and he then also came to Poland. At one point my mother hid him in a sofa bed while the Germans searched the apartment. Eventually Jakub was caught in a roundup He was taken from the train between Kielce and Warsaw—not because he was Jewish, because he easily passed for a Gentile with his blond hair and blue eyes. He was seized with everyone else on that train and simply disappeared. I cannot recall how Halina and Jola got in touch with Zofia Rontaler and me, but I think they must have come to visit us. I had exchanged my large apartment for two studio apartments, where Zofia and I lived.

As far as I recall, my dealings with Halina Schulzinger and her daughter took place between 1941 and early 1943. For a long time they managed to remain outside the ghetto. We found them lodgings, and sometimes we got them out to the countryside. In the end, they were taken to the ghetto. Halina was a pianist and by then used her maiden name, Neuman. In the ghetto, she supported Jola and her mother by sewing rabbit furs for German soldiers. Together with my father, I went to the ghetto. I had to climb over rooftops to see what was going on. I went there twice.

As conditions in the ghetto deteriorated, Halina and I decided that we had to get Jola out. Since work parties of Jews left the ghetto during the day, we decided that it would be best to get Jola into one of these work parties, and I would snatch her away from it once she was outside the ghetto. Halina managed to get word to me that there was a work party going to Mokotów on a certain day and that Jola would be in that group. I took a cab and followed the work party, which was guarded on all sides by German soldiers. At one point, I simply walked up to the group, took Jola by the hand, put her into the cab, and took her home. Looking back on the whole episode, it seems utterly improbable. Jola lived with me until I found her a place in a boarding school run by a Polish woman, whose name I do not recall, in Leśna Podkowa. Jola lived there on false papers. My friend and I visited her there from time to time.

Meanwhile, Halina Neuman got out of the ghetto on her own. She managed to bribe her way out. She also paid the cost of Jola's schooling out of her own funds. After leaving the ghetto, she lived under a pseudonym near Napoleon Square with false papers provided by the Home Army. She had had all her belongings scattered among various places in Warsaw, but by this time she had gathered them all together in her lodgings. Suddenly, during her absence the Germans searched her apartment. My friend Zofia went to the apartment, broke the seal, and brought all of Halina's things to her own apartment. After a few days, we found Halina new lodgings. In the meantime, I had been questioned by the Gestapo, but I was fortunate because they brought me back home in a short time. We kept in touch with Halina until the uprising, but after that we lost contact with her until after the war.

Zofia Rontaler and I also helped several members of the Wdowiński family, who were also Jewish. Mrs. Wdowiński survived the war and moved to New York, where she died. Another member of the family lives in South America. They used to spend the night at our flat sometimes. Individual members of the family usually lodged for the night, though sometimes the entire family did so. It was obviously extremely dangerous for all of us when the entire Wdowiński family was there. We arranged for Mr. Wdowiński to have a nose operation. Through our contacts in the Home Army, we supplied the family with false papers. Since Home Army meetings were held at our flats and we had Jews staying there, Zofia and I had to keep the caretakers of the buildings on our side. We must have succeeded, because we were never denounced by anyone and we survived the war.

After the Warsaw Uprising, Szomańska was imprisoned at Zeitheim, which was liberated by the Soviets in 1945. She escaped from the Soviet occupation zone and made her way to Italy; from there she was evacuated to England. She attended the Sir John Cass College of Art. In 1981, she was honored by Yad Vashem for having rescued Jola [Schulzinger] Hoffman.

ZDZISŁAW SZYMCZAK

Before the outbreak of the war in 1939, I worked in Warsaw. Being a student at the Warsaw Polytechnic, I was a member of the Communist party, which was dissolved in 1938. During this time I had many friends and acquaintances of Jewish background who, during the time of the occupation, found themselves in the ghetto. This does not mean that my help to the Jews during the occupation was limited to people of leftist backgrounds. I was motivated above all else by humanitarian sentiments.

The aid that I organized for the Jews had a three-fold character, first of all moving Jews to safe places. Often through my mediation, people found shelter with partisan units. The point of contact for moving Jews was my own residence at 15 Granica Street in Warsaw. During the occupation, nearly 100 people passed through my apartment. To avoid provocation of the Germans, those Jews who came to my home first called upon people whom I knew and in whom I had confidence. That same day or the following day, the Jews were moved to other apartments in City Center, Powiśle, or Wola. These apartments were specially prepared with secret tile stoves on rollers, in the event of a German search. The Jews were also moved often to the apartment of my in-laws at 43 Królewicz Jakub Street, where in a one-family dwelling two secret places to hide Jews—one in the cellar and one in the loft—had been built.

Warsaw citizens are searched by German soldiers during the occupation.
Courtesy of the Polish Institute and Sikorski Museum.

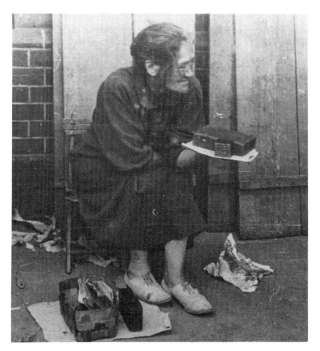

Left, street trading. Below, looking for relatives. Both courtesy of the Polish Underground Study Trust.

Above, expellees from the Zamość area. Below, Warsaw after the uprising of 1944. Both courtesy of the Polish Underground Study Trust.

Above, counterfeiting papers in the Wilno area. Below, small-scale sabotage by Polish youth. Both courtesy of the Polish Underground Study Trust.

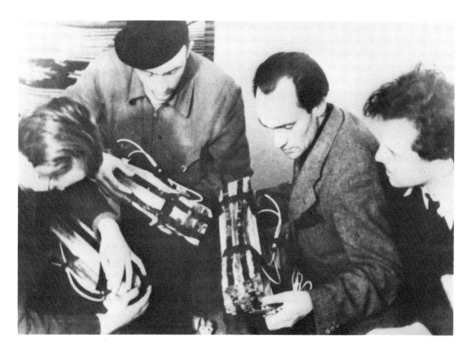

Above, a commander of a special "diversion unit" of Poland's Home Army examines a mine before blowing up a railway bridge in April 1944. Below, weapons training in the 77th Infantry Regiment of the Home Army. Both courtesy of the Polish Underground Study Trust.

Above, Polish policemen condemned to death by a German court in Poznań for the alleged crime of maltreating German minorities before the war. Below, Poles executed by the Germans in Lublin. Both courtesy of the Polish Institute and Sikorski Museum.

Above, hostages about to be executed east of Kraków. Below, victims of a mass execution. Both courtesy of the Polish Institute and Sikorski Museum.

Above, prisoners of war after an execution in the Lublin region. Courtesy of the Polish Institute and Sikorski Museum. Right, victims of German terror in Poland. The living are made to walk past the dead. Courtesy of the Polish Underground Study Trust.

My wife and I arranged to divert the attention of neighbors when providing food for those in hiding. Many who were hidden in the home of my in-laws later found themselves with partisan units who operated in the Kielce woods.

Second, I helped to provide food to Jews who lived in the ghetto, even during the Ghetto Uprising. After the end of the Ghetto Uprising, I received from Mieczysław Kadzielski (the name he used during the occupation) information about the location of a camouflaged bunker in the ghetto. Several Jews in a group were hiding in the bunker. I decided to help this group out of the ghetto. To gain entry to the ghetto, I hired myself out for several days with a group of transport workers who worked for the Germans. This groups' task was to carry away industrial machinery from the ghetto. I assumed the risk, convinced that there was no other possibility to save the people in the bunker. During the time of my work in the ghetto, I detached myself from the other workers, with the agreement of the supervisor, and went to the address of the bunker. All I got there was information that Kadzielski had moved to another bunker and would indicate later where he was. After several weeks, a fifteen-year-old Jewish boy, Little Jurek, a member of Kadzielski's group, came to my apartment. He had gotten out of the rubble of the ghetto through the sewers and he brought news of Kadzielski's location. Together with my friends, we decided to help Kadzielski and the people who were with him get out through the sewers. At a designated manhole exactly at midnight we would take them out. We leased an apartment near the entrance to the sewer, where we would immediately be able to get to the survivors. We anticipated using armed guards. The escape was successful. Kadzielski stayed first in the apartment on Królewicz Jakub Street and found himself later in Zalesie Górne near Warsaw, where he was hidden by Father Iliński, a member of the Home Army, in the home of the Matysiak family.

In my third way of aiding the Jews, it often happened that I traveled by train to escort Jews to Warsaw. On one of these trips I went to Częstochowa to escort the twelve-year-old niece of Mrs. Kadzielski. After several days, we moved her to the house in Zalesie Górne. This girl calls herself Ola Harland now and lives in Paris.

During the entire occupation, although I was registered as living at 15 Granica Street, I tried to be there very rarely because I was being pursued by the Gestapo. The Gestapo possessed documents concerning my prewar Communist activities at the Warsaw Polytechnic. I succeeded in avoiding arrest three times. Since I myself was being pursued by the Nazis, it seemed reasonable for me to help the persecuted Jews.

Little Jurek now calls himself Jerzy Płoński and lives in Israel. He often comes to Warsaw as a representative of Israel to celebrate the anniversay of the Ghetto Uprising.

Father Paweł Iliński lives now in Warsaw. The daughter of Mieczysław Kadzielski, who was born after the liberation, lives today in Paris under the name of Elizabeth Ganthier.

After the war, Szymczak received an engineering degree in photogrammetry and geodesy, fields in which he was professionally active until his retirement. In the spring of 1989, he is to go to Israel to be honored by Yad Vashem for his role in rescuing Jews during the Holocaust.

WENCESLAS WAGNER

Jadzia was one of several young Poles who during the German occupation lived a very intensive life. She differed from most of her peers in that she had access to a very roomy house, of pricelss value at the time of the conspiracy in which Jadzia and her circle spent most of their time.

In the morning, she was an attentive student who took commercial courses at the Lipiński School. In the afternoon, Jadzia became one of the uncounted cogs in the Polish underground machine. In the evening, in the company of her friends, elated that they were still free (and satisfied with having fulfilled their patriotic duties), she played bridge or danced the waltz and *kujawiak* to the music from a record player.

She lived in a beautiful old home in Warsaw's Old Town on Wąski Dunaj Street. She had the entire house to herself. Her parents, who lived in Radom, had been evicted by the Germans and lived with her grandparents in the county of Kielce, where her younger brother lived. The middle brother fought with the partisans in the Holy Cross Mountains, and the oldest brother was an officer in England. Most of the family was registered as living in the home on Wąski Dunaj Street, which enabled Jadzia to avoid unwanted tenants sent by the government.

It was clear that Jadzia's home, from the beginning of the con-spriacy, had become a "joint." Gatherings and meetings took place there; it was the point where the clandestine press was divided for distribution; several parachutists from the West spent the night there; the home sheltered boys who had been forced to leave their homes or had been wounded in action; it was there that foreigners were directed—those who ran away from prisoner-of-war camps or work camps; there arms and ammunition were hidden.

All of Jadzia's friends were aware that she was on her own and overwhelmed her with appeals to use the place for all sorts of social events. Jadzia never refused. Even when her commanders repri-manded her for the danger in having five or six gatherings in different rooms at the same time, everything remained the same.

On a warm May Saturday in 1944, Jadzia's daily schedule was similar to that of other days. Morning: study. Afternoon: conspiracy. Evening: a dancing party. On that day more young people than usual filled the place. In the evening, more than twenty people were invited, and one of the afternoon meetings was especially crowded—the last meeting, a Mass for a group of young men who were about to be sent beyond the Bug [to Home Army units in eastern Poland]. There were eighty people, more or less. The rules of the underground al-lowed no more than seven people to congregate in any one place.

The arrivals at the meetings at Jadzia's home were facilitated by the fact that, in addition to the regular entrance, it was possible to enter the home from the neighbor's attic; half of those who arrived received instructions to use this entrance. However, on the narrow streets of Old Town, it was impossible to escape the attention of the neighbors, who knew that there was always a great deal of activity at Jadzia's. It was fortunate that the sound of dance music frequently emanating from her window gave her the image of a fun-loving miss, and almost nobody in the area would have thought that she did more than study and dance.

I arrived at Jadzia's around 6:00 p.m. to help her with the last-minute preparations for the party. I arrived on time. In one room, a few stretcher bearers practiced folding and unfolding stretchers. In another room, they were about to finish the distribution of commu-niques and leaflets. The lads who were to go beyond the Bug had left an hour earlier.

For a brief moment, no one from the underground was there. But in each room they had left their tracks: communiques from London, newspapers, a package of bandages, and other hospital equipment.

We haphazardly threw everything into drawers and closets, and began to place hors d'oeuvres and liquor on the table.

In no time, the young people began to gather—punctually—because it was necessary to go home before the 10:00 p.m. curfew. Out of the dozen or so young men present, maybe three were in hiding, another three had false identification papers, two had no papers, one was an escapee from a concentration or prisoner of war camp, and the remainder, including me, had their documents in order.

By 7:00 p.m. the party had reached its peak. Through the open window, tango and fox-trot melodies flowed across Wąski Dunaj Street. In the dining room, one toast after another was offered to the demise of Hitler, Himmler, Frank, Fischer . . . there were enough of them to last the entire night. All of the activity took place on the third floor.

Suddenly I heard something like footsteps on the stairs inside the house. I looked below and went cold. Several Germans armed with automatic weapons—which was not unusual, but this was a strong formation—were marching upstairs, one after another. It was too late to warn anyone, or to escape through the fourth-floor attic to the neighbor's house and into the street.

In a few seconds, the noncommissioned officer leading the group stood before me. Before he said a word, I shoved under his nose my papers, authorized by German authorities. "This is a small gathering to celebrate the birthday of the lady of the house," I said, "a little liquor, some dancing, and several nice girls." At the same time in the "dancing room," the Germans were ordering the dancers against the wall.

White as a sheet, Jadzia appeared before the noncommissioned officer. We understood clearly that after even the most casual search or checking of documents, almost no one would return home. She looked up with her innocent blue eyes. "Why do you gentlemen want to hurt me?" she asked like a naive child in broken German. "Don't you see, gentlemen, that this is my birthday—aren't we allowed to dance a little on this occasion?"

The German officer looked into the living room and then at the abundantly set table in the dining room. "Don't you realize that you have to have a special permit for such a large gathering?" he said severely. "Is this the time for a party?"

"I did not know how many, if anybody, would come," Jadzia lied, "just as I did not expect you to come, gentlemen. But perhaps now that you are here, you would like to toast my health?"

The German looked longingly at the liquor and glasses, then at his goons, who awaited his orders. He thought for a moment, then waved to one of them. "Come, let's take a look around." They entered the dining room. Jadzia and I followed them. She wanted to fill the glasses but the noncommissioned officer would not permit it. "We don't have time, we must go elsewhere."

Elsewhere. Thank God. As long as he did not open a single drawer. The flat did not look anything like the underground establishment it had been just a few hours before. Now it had liquor, tortes, recorder and records, and a few bouquets of flowers.

It is better for the Third Reich that the young folks play and have fun, even though the time is not right, the German probably thought to himself. It is better than the serious young people who have a lot of stupid ideas in their heads like blowing up transports, killing Kutschera, Hoffman, and so many others. Let them drink, the German would have thought. [Gen. Franz Kutschera, known for his cruelty against the Poles, inaugurated street executions in Warsaw. The Home Army killed him on February 1, 1944.]

The German police went through all of the rooms in Jadzia's apartment, not touching anything. After a while they were already on the stairs. "Have fun," the noncommissioned officer said to Jadzia, "but do not arrange such large parties in the future."

After the unexpected guests left, there was silence for several seconds. We never had a better time than that evening at Jadzia's.

In Paris, *chèvre* (goat) is a good cheese, which is gaining popularity in the United States. In Warsaw, *Kozia*, meaning goat-like or goat's, is a small street that runs in a somewhat slanted way from Castle Square nearly parallel to the great thoroughfare, *Krakowskie Przedmiescie* (the Cracow Suburb).

Soon after the execution of the German General Kutschera by a squad of the Polish underground, I was delegated to deliver some secret documents from Warsaw's Old Town to Mokotówska Street, a considerable distance away. The town was full of German patrols. Executions of hostages, seizures of people for forced labor in Germany, home arrests of inhabitants, and street searches were routine events. German occupation forces pursued their goals by the use of terror, tried to uproot any resistance, and took revenge whenever they could, imposing their barbaric rule on the entire population.

With my package of documents, I traveled through Old Town, endeavoring to reach the center of the city. On every corner were

Germans. After a few attempts at other routes, I decided to take Kozia Street. There was no other possible way.

I looked at the short street from one end to the other. Everything seemed to be quiet and in good order. There were no Germans in sight, only the usual traffic. I proceeded, looking to the right and left. There was nothing suspicious. During the occupation, I learned how to observe the entire scene while turning my head as little as possible.

I reached the intersection. Again without turning my head, I spotted a German patrol just beyond the last building on the street on the left. There were three soldiers. One of them was searching a passer-by whose arms were held up over his head. Another soldier was standing opposite with a machine gun trained on the frightened person, and the third was looking around in search of another victim.

As soon as I emerged into the street, he saw me. Taking a step in my direction, he made a sign for me to appproach: "*Komm!*"

I had only a split second to decide what to do. To stop could only bring disaster. My papers would never reach their destination, and I would end up in the hands of the Gestapo on Szucha Avenue. Then, if I survived the tortures, I would probably die in Auschwitz or some other concentration camp. How should I cope with the situation? Crossing the street, I continued forward at the same pace. Should I proceed faster, it would indicate that I had noticed the patrol and wanted to escape. Seconds seemed like hours, but if I showed any emotion, I would make myself suspicious.

Will they pursue me? Will they shoot? I approached the other side of the street, but nothing happened. I did not turn my head in the direction of the Germans, so that it could be assumed that I simply did not notice them and had not heard the request to stop. Of course, I was more than eager to disappear as soon as possible, I made an effort not to rush, while looking straight in front of me. One step, then another, and a third step. I reached the other side of the street. Everything seemed all right. Nobody followed me, no shots were heard. Only then did I turn my head to see what was happening.

Instead of me, the Germans had stopped a man who had been walking on Kozia Street a few feet behind me. For the soldiers, one person was as good as another. After all, it was impossible for them to stop and search everyone. The man stood against the wall of the building with his arms up in the air. The Germans aimed a machine gun at his heart. I did not learn the final outcome of this encounter. To linger there was inadvisable. It was also dangerous to take a street-car, because the Germans frequently entered from both sides, making escape impossible. I continued to walk. Half an hour later, I delivered the documents to their destination.

Of course, it is hardly possible to speak of any enjoyable experiences connected with war, foreign occupation, and an uprising. From the very beginning of hostilities, when the Germans invaded Poland without any warning or declaration of war, on September 1, 1939, until the last days of military action, one terrible event followed another. Certainly a successful, well-accomplished mission, brings some satisfaction, but it is impossible to speak of real pleasure. A normal human being, serving his country as a soldier, does not enjoy killing a member of the enemy armed forces. He just fulfills his duty.

In Poland, every day during the German occupation brought sad news: either German victories, advances, and bombings, or executions and deportations to concentration camps, or forced labor in Germany.

Anyone could be arrested, imprisoned, tortured, and killed by the Gestapo at any time, either for any reason at all or for no reason whatsoever. The permanent atmosphere of tension and fright was too much for some. Nervous breakdowns were frequent. However, they were preferable to falling into German hands.

The list of my friends remaining at large dwindled. I myself had some close calls, but I managed to survive the occupation, uprising, camps, and a march across Germany. From March 23, 1945, I was in my fourth camp—Sandbostel. When Allied armies advanced in the direction of the camp, the Germans decided to evacuate us. Hundreds of us were driven along the roads toward the East. However, in this area the Germans furnished cattle cars to transport those prisoners who were too weak to make it on foot. The Polish camp doctor was commissioned to select these so-called weaklings.

The doctor found me in poor condition, and I thus qualified to ride in the train. The Germans placed me in a freight car along with others, and gave me a piece of bread. They padlocked the cars and the convoy started on its way. It was April 18, 1945.

The Germans did not tell us where we were going, but we realized that it was to the East. Of course we did not like it. The possibility of falling into Soviet hands terrified us, especially after our expectations of being liberated by the western allies.

For about an hour, the convoy quietly rolled eastward. We looked at the German countryside, which was becoming green under the sun of the spring. In larger settlements, some buildings showed the effect of the war—destruction or damage caused by bombs. In the fields there was not much life, but there were some agricultural workers. All Germans able to bear arms, including young boys, were called to military service. Those who remained were old or crippled. They supervised the work of the slave laborers from the conquered countries, many of whom were Poles.

Then, along with the rattle of the railway cars on the rails, we heard the distinct buzzing of distant airplanes. We knew what it meant. In Sandbostel, we often saw Allied planes on their way to bomb German targets. High in the skies, small silver birds in orderly formations flew toward Berlin, Munich, or other strongholds of our oppressors. It was always a most welcome sight. It was usually followed by a furious series of shots by German antiaircraft artillery, but I had never seen an Allied plane being shot down. "It will be hot, somewhere," observed one of the prisoners. Little did he know that he would soon experience one of the hottest moments of his life.

Soon after the sound of the Allied planes faded away, we heard other airplane motors moving in our direction. The sound came closer and closer. "Small German planes," someone said. A moment later the noise was directly above us, coming from a very low altitude. We also heard machine-gun fire. Suddenly, the convoy stopped. My neighbor uttered a cry and grabbed his leg. A bullet had hit him in the thigh. We realized what was going on. Allied fighter planes were machine-gunning the German train, not knowing its contents.

The German crew escaped into a nearby field but we were confined in the padlocked cars, unable to defend ourselves or to let the Allied pilots know that they were shooting at prisoners of war. The bullets continued, striking others of my colleagues.

The irony of this situation was monstrous. We had lived through all the horrors of war and occupation and had somehow survived. We knew that at any moment we could have been arrested, imprisoned, tortured, and killed, but we knew that whatever bad happened to us, it would come from our enemies. Now we were completely defenseless against an attack by our own allies. The possibility of being killed by Polish or Western aviators became more likely with the passage of every Allied plane over us.

With the strength of despair, we began to storm the padlocked door of our prison. One of the planks seemed to be weak. We kicked and pounded on it. Little by little, it began to give way. One kick, then another, and a hole appeared in the door. It was too small to jump through, out of the car. But a few moments later, our continuous attacks made it larger. Soon we were on the track, waving to the Allies to make clear to them that sick human beings, not war material, were being transported.

Soon the planes flew away. We tried to help those wounded in the attack. The Germans, scattered in the field, returned to the convoy, and the trip resumed. Before long, we reached the suburbs of Lübeck, where I spent the last days of the war in the barracks of Bad Schwartau, originally built for the German army. We were liberated by the British on the Polish national holdiay—May 3, 1945.

Wagner, professor of law at the University of Detroit was educated in Poland, France, and the United States. He is a distinguished scholar and author.

HENRYK WERAKSO

In 1941 Lieutenant Kacper Milaszewski, known by the pseudonym Lewald, began to organize the Union for Armed Struggle (later the Home Army) in the county of Stolpce (strictly speaking, the communities in the region included Derewno, Naliboki, Rubieżewicz, and part of Iwieniec). He selected me as his adjutant, in which capacity I served during the organization and early operations of partisan units under his command in the Nalibocki Forest (the Seventy-eighth Infantry Regiment and the Twenty-Seventh Cavalry Regiment).

When we had our framework ready, we began to penetrate German offices and place our own people there, with the aim of gathering and transmitting news about German actions. The most valuable information was transmitted by Hipolit Samson and J. Borysewicz, both of whom the Germans later put to death. They told us which ghettos would be exterminated and when it would occur.

In the spring of 1942, we learned that the Germans planned to liquidate the Rubieżewicz ghetto in June. Lieutenant Milaszewski immediately sent me to Rubieżewicz to relay this information to the Jews. The Rubieżewicz ghetto was not enclosed by a wall or barbed wire, allowing the Jews to walk freely around the town. They depended on the generosity of the Polish people for their food; the Germans did not give them any means of living. My first conversation was with Rabbi Pentelnik from Derewno and his daughter, Nieszka, a former schoolmate. The rabbi advised me to talk with Bratkowski, the former commander of a unit, called Talbot, from Derewno. Upon my return, Lieutenant Milaszewski was clearly pleased with my trip to Rubieżewicz.

After some time, we received information about a plan to liquidate the ghetto in Stolpce. The ghetto was wired and well guarded. We knew that the Germans used ghetto labor for slaking lime and working in the sawmill in Nowe Swierznie, two and one-half kilometers beyond Stolpce. I was sent to the quarry under the pretext of buying lime. I met Jewish acquaintances and relayed the news of what awaited them.

As they filled the bags with lime, three Jewish women asked me if I could take them along with the lime and carry them to the woods. I replied that we would try it and asked them sit in the wagon. At the gate, the German police stopped us and sharply asked me where I was taking the women. I replied through an interpreter that the Jews had asked me to carry them to Stolpce, where they would pick up certain items from their abandoned houses and then return to work. The Germans conferred with each other. Eventually a German sergeant approached me. He expressed agreement, on condition that I hand over my German identity card, which would be returned to me after I brought the Jews back to work. At first I excused myself on the grounds that I lacked the time to bring the women back and could not see what I would get out of it. He replied that I would receive something. I readily handed over my identity card because that was not my real name on it anyway. We moved away as the Germans waved us on. I responded with a friendly wave too.

After I crossed the railroad track, I did not travel over the bridge by way of Stolpce. I chose a longer road on the left side of the Niemen. After one kilometer, I threw the bags of lime into the ditch, and away I went with my Jewish charges. (This incident would be confirmed by a former resident of the Stolpce ghetto Mrs. R.N., who now lives in Manchester, England.)

In July and August 1943, action against the partisans began in the Nalibocki Forest. Several German divisions, aided by thousands of police, participated in the operation, code-named Herman. At this time our detachment numbered about 650 men under the command of Lieutenants Milaszewski and W. Parchimowicz. For several days we did not fight due to the overwhelming strength of the Germans, who drove us deeper into the forest. In the forest, we happened upon a Jewish partisan camp that the Germans had not yet reached. We had a cordial meeting. We had no provisions, but they had spare food. On the same day they had baked bread. They shared what they had with us. For us this was, indeed, manna from heaven. We learned that their detachment numbered a few hundred, primarily from the ghettos in Rubieżewicz and Stolpce. I recognized many of my colleagues among them.

Werakso emigrated to England in 1947 and for eighteen years was associated with the textile industry. In 1967 he opened his own travel agency in Manchester and Bradford. He has been retired since 1985.

HENRYK WOLIŃSKI

From February 1, 1942, to the middle of January 1945, I was a soldier in the Home Army. I worked in the Bureau of Information and Propaganda of the High Command. There I was in charge of the Jewish Office. My pseudonym was Wacław and later Zakrzewski, though within Jewish organizations I was always known as Wacław. The Jewish Office of the Government Delegacy was organized at the same time as the Jewish Office in the Home Army. The director of the Jewish Office in the Government Delegacy was Witold Bienkowski, of the pseudonyms Jan and Kalski, and his successor, Władysław Bartoszewski, was known as Ludwik and Teofil.

From the early days of February 1942 until September 1942, I had no contact with an official representative of the Jews in the Warsaw ghetto. The liquidation of the Warsaw ghetto began on July 21, 1942, and continued until the middle of September 1942. At that time, more than 300,000 Jews were transported, under the guise of being relocated for work in the East, to Treblinka, where they were murdered. In the Warsaw ghetto, approximately sixty thousand Jews remained. Of that number, about half were there legally, to work in the factories.

Until September 1942, my activities centered on making contact with personal friends who lived in the ghetto and on collecting information, which flowed to me from Warsaw and other areas of the country, especially from Polish railroad workers on the Warsaw-Treblinka line. After July 21, 1942, they supplied me very day with the number of transports and the numbers of people carried away. By the end of September 1942, the residents around Treblinka reported a terrible odor of burned flesh that emanated from the area.

Until his arrest on June 30, 1943, all this information went to the commander-in-chief of the Home Army, Stefan Grot-Rowecki.

I know that my office was not the only source of information about the ghettos that reached the High Command of the Home Army. In addition to the Jewish Fighting Organization and the Jewish Coordinating Committee, there were, after all, smaller Jewish organizations in Białystok, Częstochowa, Kraków, Będzin, Wilno, and Lwów and in the camps in Oświęcim, Poniatów, Majdanek, Sobibór, and Treblinka. In the midst of these organizations was the Jewish Military Union, organized by officers and noncommissioned officers of the Polish army, participants in the September Campaign. I did not have contact with these organizations, but General Tadeusz Bór-Komorowski, both before and after the arrest of General Rowecki, undoubtedly had a wider range of information.

After the defeat in September 1939, Polish anti-Semitism calmed down, deadened by the common misfortunes of the war and the occupation. The atrocities of the occupiers in their dealings with the Jews, more intensive in the early days following the capitulation of Warsaw, met with the opposition of Polish society, which gave generous assistance in hiding Jewish children and adults. The attitude toward the Jews of the Union of Armed Struggle and afterward of the Home Army, was free of anti-Semitism. Never, not in the slightest way, did I witness signs of anti-Semitism, either in the High Command of the Home Army, or in the Bureau of Information and Propaganda. If someone before the war had been an anti-Semite, he did not reveal it during the war, but, on the contrary, helped Jews as much as possible. To be sure, what I have in mind is the average, decent individual Pole.

It is untrue that the Home Army, especially officers designated to cooperate with the Jewish Fighting Organization, had no interest in extending assistance to the Jews and were in fact anti-Semitic. The help of the Home Army to the Jews was truly self-sacrificing.

That was also the opinion of Jurek (Arie Wilner) and Borowski (Adolf Berman). I deny that anti-Semitism was the reason for the limits on military aid given to the Jewish Fighting Organization by the Home Army. The help given by the Home Army was small in relation to the needs of the Jewish Fighting Organization, but it is necessary to measure the possibilities available to the Home Army at the time. They were not great. Arms were in short supply even for the soldiers who fought in the Warsaw Uprising of 1944.

Let me return for a moment to the subject of anti-Semitism among officers of the Home Army. One time Jurek complained to me that an officer of the Home Army, with whom he was in contact, had admitted that he was an anti-Semite. I asked Jurek whether I should intervene. He didn't want me to do it. I returned to the subject in a subsequent conversation. Jurek informed me that dealings with that officer (I don't remember his pseudonym) were conducted on a level of mutual respect and friendship. The two of them even conducted one of the transports of arms to the ghetto, Jurek as guide and the Polish officer as chief of the transportation detachment.

General Rowecki urged that aid to the Jews be organized as soon as possible; he commanded that military aid be dispensed to the Jewish Fighting Organization, which he recognized as a paramilitary organization. Monter (General Antoni Chruściel), a high-ranking member of the Home Army's High Command, gave the Jewish Military Organization military help within the bounds of possibilities.

My contact with General Rowecki was close enough for me to exclude the possibility that he was an anti-Semite. With Monter I discussed several times establishing regular cooperative actions between the Home Army and the Jewish Fighting Organization. I had similar conversations with Chirug (Major Stanisław Weber). Neither in words nor certainly by actions was there ever a hint of anti-Semitism.

Let me explain that in addition to my official duties, I established, on behalf of the High Command of the Home Army, the nucleus of an organization that extended protection to the Jews of the Warsaw ghetto. At the time of the Warsaw Uprising on August 1, 1944, 283 Jews were being sheltered by members of the High Command. In addition to financial help, our unit provided refugees from the ghetto with suitable documents.

I once lived with my family in the same apartment (Al. Niepodległość, No. 227/33) as Mrs. Ewa Brzuska, an old but vigorous woman who sold vegetables and other agricultural goods. One day Jewish children appeared on the street in front of the building. There were several of them. It was always the same: The residents of the building protected them and offered food or help. The facts about such care and benevolence are not adequately understood . . . because the threat of death existed for their protectors as well as for the Jews themselves. The same penalty threatened Mrs. Brzuska, who not only fed Jewish children but allowed them to sleep in her shop. One day one of the Polish Blue Police came to Mrs. Brzuska's shop and accused her of hiding Jews. In the presence of her customers, Mrs. Brzuska heaped verbal abuse upon him as only a Warsaw shopkeeper can. The policeman desisted from further inquiries and left. The event was most sympathetically commented upon by the residents of the neighborhood, among whom there were surely some prewar anti-Semites.

I knew Mr. and Mrs. S., who took in a Jewish girl, Halinka, from the ghetto. Halinka's mother, one of the many agricultural laborers forced to work in the area of Wilanów, left the group and brought her child to Mr. and Mrs. S., begging: "Mrs. S., take my Halinka. She is polite and knows how to bless herself and says her prayers."

Mrs. S. allowed her to stay: "We have enough. We have enough for ourselves and her. Without money." They did it in a Christian way; after all, these were religious people. Mr. and Mrs. S. died in the 1950s.

Were there signs of anti-Semitism in Poland? Of course there were. But compassion, protection, and aid dominated the attitude of Polish society during the war.

My first contact with Jewish representatives of the underground in the Warsaw ghetto occurred in October 1942. I found out from Jurek about an earlier attempt by the Jews to contact the Home Army. I did not know when the attempt was made, who sought to make contact, nor who was reached. However, I immediately reported the matter and asked for an explanation of the circumstances. The unsuccessful attempt to reach the Home Army cannot be defined as "interference" or as a deliberate withholding of help. I don't know who tried to contact the Home Army nor whom that person approached. I learned only that the person who was approached was a civilian and that he did not want to assume the task of making contact with the Home Army.

The representatives of Jewish organizations in the Warsaw ghetto—Jurek, Borowski, and Mikołaj (Leon Feiner) never in my presence made any accusations about the earlier unsuccessful attempt to contact the Home Army. They themselves made contact with me through Gorecki (Aleksander Kamiński, later professor at the University of Łódź). Before the war, he was a leader in the Scouting movement, director of a troop of minority children in the Union of Polish Scouts, and an opponent to anti-Semitism.

Privately, I protected various Jews over the course of four years—more than twenty-five of them. Jews who fled the ghetto found a transition shelter in my apartment for periods lasting from several days to several weeks.

Woliński, who had a remarkable career in the Home Army, was highly regarded by both Polish and Jewish leaders in the underground conspiracy. Educated in law, Woliński lives today in Katowice, Poland.

MARIA ZAGÓRSKA

During the time of the German occupation, I lived with my husband and three children in the Bielany section of Warsaw. We lived at 78 Szreder Street, next to a German airfield. From 1942 to the moment of the outbreak of the Warsaw Uprising in 1944, eighteen people of Jewish background passed through my home.

One of the rooms in the apartment was occupied by the Polish poet Tadeusz Holender. Mrs. Kott, whom we knew before the war, came to live with us in 1942. She came to Warsaw from Lwów. During her stay with us, she used the certificate of my sister-in-law, who was of Tatar descent. In 1943, Mrs. Kott had a dangerous experience on a journey to Skierniewice, near Warsaw, where she was stopped as a Jew. The Germans brought an anthropologist of Jewish background and, on their orders, he gave her the required examination, which turned out negatively for her. Her life was therefore saved. Mrs. Kott lived with us right up to the outbreak of the Warsaw Uprising. After the failure of the uprising she went through Lomianki, to a village, and later to Kraków.

For some time, Danuta Grossfeld stayed in my apartment. She had been recommended to me by my friend in Gdynia. Mr. Tenenbaum and his wife and father-in-law also lived with us for several months. They turned up in my apartment in 1943, immediately after fleeing from the Warsaw ghetto. They were all dressed in white aprons—the uniform of physicians—which were indispensable to fool the ghetto guards. Kitel, Tenenbaum's father-in-law, was very stained with the fresh blood of his wife, who had been shot by the Germans during the flight from the ghetto.

For several months, Janek Wilk, a thirteen-year-old Jewish boy, also hid with us. When asked by neighbors about his descent—he had a very Semitic appearance—I replied that he was my nephew. To camouflage the fact that Wilk was Jewish, he accompanied my family to Mass in the Catholic Church. Despite these precautions, bad neighbors threatened to report me to the Gestapo for hiding Jews in my apartment, so early one morning in 1944, we conveyed Janek and Tadeusz Holender to the home of Mrs. Zołotarew on Ikara Street.

Several times during the occupation, Jews spent several nights in my apartment after having been recommended by acquaintances. Later they went to the homes of my friends. My friends and I organized these secret removals. One of those who never refused to hide a Jew was the Polish writer, Jan Dobraczyński.

False documents for Jews had to be arranged, sometimes even a Catholic wedding. This was necessary for Jews who hid under assumed names and rented rooms in the same building where I lived.

During the Warsaw Uprising, my husband and I found ourselves in various insurgent detachments. My unit, commanded by Konstantin Radziwiłł, was taken prisoner. I had served as a liaison officer.

After the liberation of Warsaw in 1945, I returned to my apartment which, except for my husband's library, I found utterly despoiled.

Mrs. Kott survived the war and departed for the United States. I maintain constant contact with her. Janek Wilk also survived the war and lives at present in the German Federal Republic.

Fluent in several languages, Zagórska worked as a translator for the Union of Polish Writers. Ten years ago, she was honored for rescuing Jews during the war. She now lives in retirement.

JANUSZ ZAORSKI

In 1939, I was evacuated with my family to Wilno. We crossed the Lithuanian border after the Soviet occupation of Lithuania. Since we were refugees, the Soviets automatically interned us. Because I was seventeen years old, the Soviets permitted me to live outside the internment camp and to continue my studies at the local gymnasium. From the beginning, I took an active part in the Polish underground movement, carrying messages back and forth between my father, who was commandant of the internment camp in Wilkowiszki, and the center of the underground movement in Kowno, as well as the Polish and British legations there.

After the transfer of internees to the interior of Russia in June 1940 and the German invasion in June 1941, I worked in the post office in Wilno. The head of the postal services was Napiwotzki, a member of the Nazi party who came from a Polish family that had settled in the Rhineland. At this time, the Germans called up all young men of my age for auxiliary service with the German army, and the majority from the Wilno area ended up in Leningrad. I managed to avoid this service because Napiwotzki told me not to go to the assembly point to which I had been assigned. I did as he suggested, and fortunately there were no repercussions.

Later I was to go to the post office training school at Magdeburg, Germany, in preparation for duty in the eastern territories. I refused this "offer" but doing so meant that I had to leave my position in the post office. Through the resident agent of the Polish Intelligence Service, Sylwanowicz, I managed to obtain alternative employment on estates taken over by the Germans.

Later I managed to get a visa to enter the General Government and arrived in Warsaw on September 1, 1942, with instructions to make a report to the Polish authorities on the internment camps in Lithuania. My cousin had recommended me for membership in the underground army. On the second day after my arrival in Warsaw, I joined the Union for Armed Struggle, took my oath, and made my report.

That evening I was invited for dinner by relatives who lived in an apartment at 16 Pius Street, where, as it turned out, the Polish underground movement had been started by General Michał Tokarzewski. Also present at the dinner were two men whom I had never met before. They asked me many questions about the state of affairs in Lithuania and Wilno, and since I did not have the slightest idea who the men were, I answered their questions very evasively. However, my aunt's assurance that they were entirely reliable led me to "let off steam." I told them everything I knew, using the real names of all the people involved. One of the men then suggested that I join a "special" unit, but I declined the offer because I had already taken the oath in another organization.

I saw one of the men, who wore a small moustache, several times later, but I never had the slightest idea who he was. It was only after the Warsaw Uprising of 1944 that I discovered him to be General Stefan Grot-Rowecki, who headed the Union for Armed Struggle, later known as the Home Army. My cousin, Ela Pradzyńska, was

Rowecki's courier and reputedly the last person to see the general alive.

Rowecki was betrayed to the Germans by Ludwik Kalkstein, Eugeniusz Świerczewski, and Blanka Kaczorowska. Arrested on June 30, 1943, Rowecki was sent to Sachsenhausen, where he is believed to have been executed.—Ed.

After the Warsaw Uprising, Zaorski was imprisoned at Stalag 11B Fallingbostel and later worked in a copper mine in Bad Harzburg. As the Allied armies approached, he and other prisoners managed to disarm their German guards. Zaorski was a member of the patrol that was met by the United States Third Army. Later Zaorski joined his father in Italy, and they later moved to England, where he worked several years in the hotel business. Retired, he now lives in London.

MARIA KONTOWICZ ZAREMBA

At the time of the German occupation in 1939, I worked as the administrator of several residences in the Praga district of Warsaw. In 1939, Mr. Mitelberg, a Jew who owned several buildings in Warsaw, came to me and proposed that I look after a house at 273 Grochowska Street that belonged to him. I agreed to the proposal. Not long afterward, eleven other Jews came to me with proposals that I administer residences that belonged to them. In this way I became the legally certified administrator with appropriately drawn documents that also served for German authorities.

I had an unwritten agreement with the Jewish owners that I would provide financial help to them from the rentals paid by the tenants of the properties. The residences that I administered in Warsaw were 257, 267, 269, 273, 275, and 283 Grochowska Street; 56 Złota Street; 24 Zabkowska Street; and 20 Stanisław August Street.

Because of my work, during the entire time of the German occupation I was able to keep in touch with Jews and their families, who lived under assumed names in the buildings administered by me. Being in charge of registration cards and other types of administrative records, I willingly expressed agreement to the leasing of an apartment by a Jew—under a false name, to be sure. More than once

I registered Jews at addresses where they never really lived. I did this often without the knowledge of the residents at those addresses. During the occupation, the registration card was an important document to German authorities.

As I took part in the resistance activities of the Home Army, not only did I know of the existence of stores of arms and ammunition in the houses under my administration, including the house next to mine, but I also had access to false documents. Jews who came to me received documents prepared on underground presses, most often *kennkarten* (identification cards). They naturally had to have a prior recommendation by one of my friends; there was always the fear of a German provocation.

Often I also sheltered Jews. Most of them were recommended to me, but often they were anonymous. In addition to a place to sleep in one of the houses administered by me, they also received food. In these circumstances, Mr. Reichman came to me. He even wrote a poem about me, which I delivered to a museum.

My Jewish friend and her children lived with me in my apartment on Stanisław August Street for many years during the occupation. To everyone on the outside, she appeared to be my relative from outside Warsaw. I not only maintained very strong bonds with Jews during the occupation but also socialized with them.

I was very friendly with a Jewish family by the name of Gersznabl who lived next to me on the same floor. One day someone denounced Gersznabl as a Jew, which caused him to flee from the apartment to the woods near Waszyngton Avenue, where he lingered with his wife in the potato fields for many months. Later he came to me. One day while he was staying with me, a German official knocked on the door. I was ill in bed. He accused me of hiding a Jew and then searched the apartment. Gersznabl had hidden under my feather bed, which the German probably suspected, but he left my apartment after I staged an attack of vomiting. A short time later, Gersznabl left my apartment.

I also helped Gersznabl in 1944, when I persuaded him to disguise himself as a railroad worker and go to a crowded shelter. Staying outside was dangerous, particularly considering the explosions caused by Soviet bullets and bombs when the Soviet army was attacking German positions around Warsaw.

A great number of Jews survived the Nazi occupation, living more or less openly in the houses I administered. I met several of them after the war; I maintain contact with some of them to this day.

Zaremba, who lives today in Warsaw, received the Righteous Among Nations Medal, presented to her in Jerusalem by Yad Vashem.

WITOLD ZŁOTNICKI

It was an autumn day in 1943, just before curfew. I was taking ammunition to a temporary storage place in someone's apartment. As I entered the gateway of the building, a civilian armed with a revolver stopped me. In typically German fashion, he screamed at me to stand still and put my hands up in the air. I could see a few other people in the same posture. From the caretaker's flat at the end of the gateway came shouting and screaming. It was obvious that a German-style interrogation was taking place. I stood very nonchalantly with one hand up in the air and held my briefcase full of ammunition in the other. To make matters worse, I wore army boots and trousers.

A very smartly dressed elderly gentleman and a lady, obviously his wife, stood next to me. As he looked at me, the man casually tore up some papers. Our guard, a Ukrainian Gestapo agent, did not see this, as he had walked over in the direction of the caretaker's flat. The gentleman then turned to the guard and in fluent German told him that he worked for the town authorities of Grodzisk and was afraid that he would miss the last train. The guard demanded to see his documents; after examining them, he let the couple go.

I sensed that the guard was unwilling to let anyone else pass but otherwise might be willing to negotiate. Since I had documents to show that I worked for a German firm, I approached him and in Polish said that I worked for a German enterprise and that I wanted to use the staircase near the caretaker's flat. Ignoring my briefcase, the guard looked at my papers and commented that I lived on Puławska Street, about six kilometers from where we stood. I answered that if he cared to look outside the courtyard he would see that there were no streetcars running on Marszałkowska Boulevard and that I would not be able to get home before curfew. It was, of course, a lie, but I realized that he would not be too keen to go outside to check and risk leaving us unguarded. He asked me whether I wanted to go to the staircase. When I replied in the affirmative, he returned my documents without taking the five hundred złotys I had left in them. His reaction on seeing the money had been a slight smile. He told me to go, but quietly.

Off I went, scratching my head while I pondered how to cope with my next problem. I knew that there were three armed men in the flat where I was headed and that they would all be aware of what was going on downstairs. When I arrived at the door, I knocked and very quietly said that I was Lieutenant Witold, that there was no one with me, and that everything was fine. I begged them not to do anything silly. The door opened slowly. Three gun muzzles and three pairs of eyes appeared. Then the door opened fully. They asked me how I had managed to get away. While I told them, I showed them the contents of my briefcase. The strain was so great that all of us started to laugh and could not stop.

It was a nice sunny day, March 30, 1943, fairly memorable in the annals of occupied Warsaw. Officer Cadet Sas (Janusz Kulczycki) came for a 3:00 p.m. appointment with me, known as Second Lieutenant Witold, then deputy commander of B3 Company of Baszta Regiment. He came to the premises where I worked, the EOS business establishment on the corner of Marszałkowska and Królewska Streets. The business sold glassware, china, lampshades, even toys. Ever since prewar days, my aunt, Stanisława Złotnicka, had run the establishment. Since I worked there, I had fairly good papers. . . .

The premises, well known to the Warsaw underground movement, housed the secretariat of the clandestine Law Department of Warsaw University, and the headquarters of B3 Company and its arms cache. The password "To Mr. Witold" had long ceased to frighten either the male or the female employees. I shall recount two of the happier incidents.

One day, just as liaison Helcia (Helena Glaschmit) handed me the book *Manual of Fighting in Towns*, by General Stefan Grot-Rowecki, two Gestapo agents and a Mr. G., whom I knew, entered the outer office, where we stood. I threw the book down on the desk. Neither the Gestapo agents nor Mr. G. paid any attention to the prominent title but entered the inner room. . . . After ten or fifteen minutes, the Gestapo agents left. Mr. G. apologized for the intrusion but explained that he had some matters to attend to. He was, of course, involved in the underground and worked for the city authorities, from whom he later acquired the plans of the school on Rozana Street for B3 Company.

The second incident was the visit of Major Burza, the commander of B Battalion, who carried a small package to the business establishment. Since I was absent he decided to wait, not wanting to leave the parcel with anyone else. On my return he explained why. The small package, bearing a label from a box of matches, contained two kilograms of plastic explosives, more than enough to blow up several of the surrounding buildings.

Some time before the March day in 1943, I had packed a Thompson submachine gun—the sort used by American gangsters during the prohibition era—together with some magazines in a large box. I wrapped it in brown paper, ready to take to a demonstration for a few platoon commanders of B Battalion. The demonstration was to take place on premises . . . on the corner of 6-Sierpnia Street and Niepodległość Boulevard, opposite the German hospital.

After a long wait, Sas and I caught a streetcar and went to the front platform of the third car. Both of us had pistols in our coat pockets; I had a Vis, he a Parabellum. Everything looked quiet and normal. Suddenly a ring of German military police surrounded the streetcar. All of Marszałkowska Street was cut off by a crowd of Gestapo. With wild cries they rushed into the streetcars and started to throw everyone off, including the engineer and conductors. They were forcing everyone to stand with their hands above their heads against the walls of the surrounding buildings. Still in the car, Sas and I looked at each other, and in a decisive manner I growled that we would stay where we were: "*Stoimy.*"

The other streetcars were empty; the military police started searching the people they had thrown off. We just stood. The officers of the military police and the Gestapo agents looked at us in passing; someone must have given us permission to stay in the car. With wooden faces, we watched the goings-on for fifteen minutes. At last the streetcar personnel got back on, and very slowly the streetcar moved off in the direction of Zbawiciel Square. As we crossed the cordon, we noticed the glances of the Germans, but no one questioned our presence in the empty cars. An amazed conductor came up shakily to us, took one look at us and our parcel, and went to the rear platform as fast as he could.

We later found out that punctually at 3:00 o'clock the counter-espionage department of the headquarters of the Home Army had shot two Gestapo agents who had arrived from Kraków—Second Lieutenant Boehme and a Staff Sergeant. That brought out the military police and the Gestapo a short time later.

Despite our frayed nerves, Sas and I arrived at the appointed place for the demonstration. There were no instructions for assembling the Thompson, so we toiled over dismantling it and putting it back together again. We found the letter *S* on one part of the submachine gun. Since we were used to German weapons, we decided this was the safety catch. To be certain that this was so, I turned the barrel toward the wall and there between me and Officer Cadet Janusz I loosed an honorary salvo. The ricochet flew past my ear. (I later carried it as a talisman.) At the sound, the sentry in front of the German hospital stopped for a moment, then calmly moved off again. On the floor above, in the apartment of Second Lieutenant Bożydar's courier, someone fell off a chair. Sas and I returned to the glassware shop in complete silence and without further mishap. A glass of vodka in the office behind the shop restored our good humor, and we laughed, perhaps a little too loudly.

In the middle of September 1944, a few weeks before the end of the Warsaw Uprising, B3 Company tried to hold off a German attack from the area around Czerniakowska Street. The company was quartered about one kilometer away from the front line, and there the less seriously wounded and recuperating members of the company stood sentry duty. Sentries had to be posted because the Gestapo had started to send prisoners from Szucha Boulevard—under the threat that their families would be shot—across the front line to bring the Germans information about the positions, weapons, and morale of the Home Army. There was no guarantee that some of these people would not carry out the tasks allotted to them by the Gestapo and so the sentries were essential.

Late one evening, after a day of heavy fighting among the burning buildings, I inspected the exhausted sentries and dozed off with the Second platoon for the night. I was awakened by a tug on my sleeve. My numb hand reached for the holster of my Vis pistol. Disjointed words came to me: " . . . a woman . . . sentry . . . shot." After a while I understood. I pulled out a crumpled pad, scribbled a few words to my second in command, Second Lieutenant Negus (Stanisław Potorecki). I awoke my messenger, fourteen-year-old Private Tadzik (Tadeusz Wodzyński) and explained where he was to take the message. Then, together with my courier, we started to make our way back to company headquarters. We had to go very carefully because no longer did war end at 21:00 hours, and heavy mortars are an unpleasant thing.

The Germans worried that we Poles might counterattack under

cover of darkness, so we paid great attention to any movements at night.

Dawn was starting to break as we reached the headquarters of the Third Platoon. I entered a dark room lit only by a carbide lamp, which threw shadows on the walls. In a corner, Private Y crouched. He was bandaged. He held his head in his hands. I knew him to be a courageous soldier. Two officers sat at the table. A step away from the table sat an old man, about seventy years old, staring uncomprehendingly straight ahead.

Private Y jumped up and reported to me. The officers introduced themselves. I did not have the courage to extend my hand to the old man. The military policeman started the inquiry with the sentry, Private Y. The boy stood at attention in the prescribed manner, the muscles of his face tense as he tried to control his sobs. "After curfew . . . the footsteps of two people. I called out stop three times . . . the footsteps came closer . . . I fired. . . . "

At this moment the elderly man shook himself and seemed to come out of a trance. In a tired, desperate voice he choked out that the soldier told the truth: "It was our fault. I too was once a soldier in the Tsar's army." In the next few minutes, choking back his tears, he told us the rest: "We stayed later than we had intended to with some friends in a cellar. We knew that it was past curfew, but we still ventured out. It was very dark. In a short time, we heard the voice of the sentry. My wife was a bit deaf, so I explained what the sentry was saying. After the third warning we stopped. Suddenly my wife left me and took a few steps forward saying that it was a Polish soldier. He fired. She did not suffer. Next month would have been our fiftieth wedding anniversary. I will somehow have to live alone."

Our very sincere, though restrained, condolences sounded rather hollow in the light of the carbide lamp. I asked the man whether he would agree to a delegation of couriers at the funeral. He nodded in agreement.

I took leave of the officers. At that moment I hated them. They were just as dirty and tired as I was. But they looked as if they had had just a little more sleep, and I was jealous of that. I recalled Sergeant Cyclops's lecture, "When It Is Permissible Legally and Finally to Kill a Man." Somehow, this time it did not strike me as very funny.

After a talk with Private Y, which seemed to calm him down a little, I gave him six hours off-duty. He did not take advantage of it; I saw him three hours later in position in a burnt-out ruin on Dolna.

I left that stifling room. It was already light. Sleep had gone to the devil. The first mortar shell exploded. The next German attack had begun.

Wounded in the Warsaw Uprising, Złotnicki was imprisoned at Murnau. Later he joined the Polish Second Corps in Italy. He went to England in 1946 and worked for London Transport until his retirement. He is a member of the Polish Home Army Ex-Servicemen's Verification Commission.

BIBLIOGRAPHY

In comparison with the fate of the Jews, the Polish experience during World War II has not been well covered by books and articles in the English language. The following list of books dealing with the Poles under German occupation is not comprehensive, but it does represent some of the major sources in English on the Polish wartime experience.

Bartoszewski, Władysław. *The Blood Shed Unites Us: Pages from the History of Help to the Jews in Occupied Poland*. Warsaw: Interpress Publishers, 1970.

————. *Warsaw Death Ring, 1939-1945*. Warsaw: Interpress Publishers, 1968.

Bartoszewski, Władysław, and Zofia Lewin. *The Samaritans: Heroes of the Holocaust*. New York: Twayne Publishers, 1970.

Bór-Komorowski, Tadeusz. *The Secret Army*. New York: Macmillan, 1951.

Central Commission for Investigation of German Crimes in Poland. *German Crimes in Poland*. 2 vols. New York: Howard Fertig, 1982.

Ciechanowski, Jan M. *The Warsaw Uprising of 1944*. Cambridge: Cambridge Univ. Press, 1974.

Garliński, Józef. *Poland in the Second World War*. New York: Hippocrene Books, 1985.

Gross, Jan Tomasz. *Polish Society under German Occupation: The General-Gouvernement, 1939-1944*. Princeton: Princeton Univ. Press, 1979.

Gumkowski, Janusz, and Leszczyński, Kazimierz. *Poland under Nazi Occupation*. Warsaw: Polonia Publishing House, 1961.

Hanson, Joanna K. M. *The Civilian Population and the Warsaw Uprising of 1944*. Cambridge: Cambridge Univ. Press, 1982.

Hrabar, Roman, et al. *The Fate of Polish Children during the Last War*. Warsaw: Interpress, 1981.

Iranek-Osmecki, Kazimierz. *He Who Saves One Life*. New York: Crown Publishers, 1971.

Karski, Jan. *Story of a Secret State*. Boston: Houghton Mifflin, 1944.

Korboński, Stefan. *Fighting Warsaw: The Story of the Polish Underground*

State, 1939-1945. Trans. F.B. Czarnomski. N.p.: Minerva Press, 1968.

———. *The Polish Underground State: A Guide to the Underground, 1939-1945*. Trans. Marta Erdman. Boulder, Col.: East European Quarterly, 1978.

———. *The Jews and Poles in World War II*. New York: Hippocrene, 1989.

Lukas, Richard C. *The Forgotten Holocaust: The Poles under German Occupation, 1939-1944*. Lexington: Univ. Press of Kentucky, 1986.

Nowak, Jan. *Courier from Warsaw*. Detroit: Wayne State Univ. Press, 1982.

Polish Ministry of Information. *The Black Book of Poland*. New York: G.P. Putnam's Sons, 1942.

Republic of Poland. *German Occupation of Poland: Extract of Note Addressed to the Allied and Neutral Powers*. New York: Greystone Press, 1942.

Zajączkowski, Wacław. *Martyrs of Charity*. Washington, D.C.: Saint Maximilian Kolbe Foundation, 1987.

Zawodny, J.K. *Nothing But Honour: The Story of the Warsaw Uprising, 1944*. Stanford: Hoover Institution Press, 1978.

INDEX